GEORGE S. KAUFMAN

GEORGE S. KAUFMAN

NEW YORK *Atheneum*

1972

An Intimate Portrait

---

by Howard Teichmann

The author is grateful to Martin Levin for permission to reprint "An Open Letter to Rex Harrison" (from Mr. Levin's column "Phoenix Nest," in the *Saturday Review*), and to *The New Yorker* for permission to reprint "Lines Written After Four Weeks in a Hospital" (Copr. © 1954 The New Yorker Magazine, Inc.) and excerpts from "The Great Kibitzers' Strike of 1926" (Copr. © 1949 The New Yorker Magazine, Inc.), "My Book and I" (Copr. © 1951 The New Yorker Magazine, Inc.), and "Memoire" (Copr. © 1960 The New Yorker Magazine, Inc.). "What is Direction, Anyhow?" is from *Producing the Play*, by John Gassner and Philip Barber (Holt, Rinehart & Winston, Inc.).

THIS BOOK IS FOR

EVELYN,

WHO ALSO LOVED HIM

Author's Note

PLAYWRITING AND SAFE-CRACKING ARE SIMILAR OCCUPATIONS. Both are lonely work, tedious and tense, and, for the most part, not especially rewarding when one considers the time, effort, and risk involved. Furthermore, unless each job comes off to perfection, as George S. Kaufman often said, the newspapers treat both the safe-cracker and the playwright as common criminals.

It is not unusual for playwrights to duck as much playwriting as possible, and when the opportunity comes along to write something else, most of us grab at it for dear life. Such an opportunity came my way ten years ago. Simon Michael Bessie, the president of the publishing house that is bringing out this book, asked me if there was anything worth writing about in the life of George Kaufman. Over a cocktail, through lunch, and deep into the late afternoon, I recalled story after story about Kaufman. It was dark as we left the restaurant, and the publisher had liked what he heard and felt I should get right to work.

The Kaufman I knew was the Great Professional of the Golden Age of the American theatre. The Kaufman I knew was a man who had feet of clay up to his knees. The Kaufman I knew was a great wit, a fine director, a play doctor, but what else?

I saw Kaufman almost daily for the last ten years of his life. If I didn't see him, I spoke with him on the telephone every night he was in this country, and occasionally when he was in England. We wrote regularly. I thought I knew George S. Kaufman reasonably well. That was a mistake. I hardly knew him at all. This I learned when I began to interview his family, his friends, his collaborators, the men and women who worked for him, loved him, were in turn loved by him, and even the people who hated him—some for good reason, others out of envy. I sought out retired newspapermen, playwrights, actors, box office personnel, people with whom he played cards or croquet, doctors, lawyers, producers, society matrons, trollops, publishers. An interview with one person generally led me to five others.

Midway through the tapes, telephone calls, letters, newspaper clippings, magazine articles, plays, and books, a devil of a mystery arose in my mind: who *was* George S. Kaufman? It looked as though it would take a long time to solve that question. Not to solve it seemed cowardly. Also, my own inquisitiveness refused to allow me to stop. As a result, a decade slipped by before all the questions as to who George S. Kaufman actually was were answered. Now I am prepared to tell almost all about George.

Even though time has passed, it is still difficult for me to believe that he is dead. I have been so immersed in reading and researching Kaufman, and he was such a hypochondriac, he took such good care of himself and lived in such fear of death, that I never really believed he *would* die. I rather imagined if Death did work up the courage to approach him, one short stinging

sentence from Kaufman would send the Dark Angel cringing off
to a different victim.

Having done my graduate work at the University of Wisconsin in American history, I am familiar with the shrapnel of
footnotes. The Ibids and the Op. Cits. have not only ruined the
flow of the writing I have read, they have also made my eyes
function very much like the pump-shaft of the old windmill we
had on the farm in Pleasant Prairie: up and down, up and down.
Should any reader miss them in this book, I ask him to turn to
the very end, where I have justified and given credit to every
source within these pages.

In terms of gratitude, I must thank Simon Michael Bessie
for ten years of patience, exhortation, and advice. Additional
thanks must go to Pat Irving for her intensive and devoted
editorial counsel. Further gratitude goes to Judith Steckler for
nine years of valuable and detailed research. To my colleague of
twenty-five years in the English Department of Barnard College, Columbia University, Dr. John Kouwenhoven, I am grateful for scholarly encouragement and stern guidance.

More thanks must go to Arthur Ochs Sulzberger, president
and publisher of the New York *Times*, Nathan William Goldstein, circulation manager, and John Joseph Sheehan, retired
cashier of that newspaper, for generously providing me not only
with their employee records but also with every word about
George Kaufman printed by the *Times* and by the New York
Herald Tribune, the New York *World Telegram*, the New
York *Sun*, the New York *Graphic*, the New York *Mail*, the
Brooklyn *Eagle*, the Brooklyn *Citizen*, the Brooklyn *Standard Union*, the Brooklyn *Times*, and *PM*. My thanks, too, to
Richard E. Berlin, president of the Hearst Corporation, for
graciously making available to me everything carried by the
Hearst Press about George Kaufman. I am indebted to Floyd
Barker, then managing editor of the *Daily News*, and Anthony

Burton of his reportorial staff, for a complete photostat of the *Daily News* morgue file on George Kaufman, as well as permission to examine and record the actual diary sold to the *Daily News* by Mary Astor's former husband, Dr. Franklyn Thorpe. The diary was not burned by court order, as was reported by the wire services, but is locked in "The Managing Editor's Confidential File" in a vault three levels under East 42nd Street in New York City.

Additional thanks go to Arthur and Barbara Gelb for suggestions in coping with the large and ungainly amount of research accumulated during the writing of this book. My gratitude must go to Lewis Bergman, editor of the Sunday *Times* Magazine, for his insistence that this book be written in the shape and style that it is. More thanks go to the Library of Congress for photostats of the editorial pages of the Washington *Times*, 1912–13; to Paul Myers of the Theatre Collection of the Lincoln Center Branch of the New York Public Library; to Mr. Herbert Cahoon of the J. Pierpont Morgan Library; to the Wollman Library of Barnard College; to the Butler Library and to Low Library of Columbia University; to the New York Society Library; to Abel Green, managing editor, and Hobe Morrison, drama editor, of *Variety*, for use of the extensive theatrical records of that publication; to Leslie Fischel and Barbara Kaiser of the Wisconsin Center for Theatre Research, State Historical Society, University of Wisconsin, for copies of the letters in the George S. Kaufman papers, the Moss Hart papers, and the Ruth Goodman Goetz papers; to Kitty Hart and Ruth Goodman Goetz for permission to use those letters; to Leonard Bakrow for use of his sister's letters; to Ruth Friedlich, Ira Gershwin, and Mrs. Herman Mankiewicz for permission to use their letters from Kaufman.

Those contemporaries of George Kaufman who granted me the courtesy of interviews by telephone, through the mail, in person, and on tape may hold me deeply in their debt. They are listed properly and individually in the back of this book. In addition, to George's daughter, Anne Kaufman Schneider, must go my gratefulness for permission to reprint many of the letters written by and to her father, many of the photographs used in this book, plus two invaluable scrapbooks belonging to her mother, as well as her early blessings and later cooperation on the entire project.

Finally, my everlasting gratitude goes to the lady to whom this book is dedicated. Without her creative encouragement, editorial advice, and critical aid none of this would have been possible.

H.T.

Contents

Illustrations

xiii

Edna Ferber
(*United Press International Photo*)

Sam H. Harris, Lorenz Hart, Richard Rodgers, Moss Hart,
Kaufman, George M. Cohan

Mary Astor
(*Wide World Photo*)

Barley Sheaf Farm
(*courtesy of Anne Kaufman Schneider*)

Kaufman, and smoke rings

Moss Hart and Alexander Woollcott
(*courtesy of Richard C. Wood*)

Singing in the New Year: Charles Friedman, Moss Hart,
Bea Kaufman, Frank Sinatra, "Yip" Harburg, Fred Saidy,
Harold Arlen, Ethel Merman
(*courtesy of Margaret Leech Pulitzer*)

Kaufman, with daughter Anne
(*courtesy of Anne Kaufman Schneider*)

Kaufman and Moss Hart at work
(*Wide World Photo*)

Alexander Woollcott and Harpo Marx at play
(*courtesy of Anne Kaufman Schneider*)

Kaufman and Harpo Marx at croquet

Kaufman, with Kitty Carlisle and Moss Hart at the Stork Club
(*Culver Pictures, Inc.*)

Kaufman and Leueen MacGrath
(*Wide World Photo*)

"This Is Show Business": Sam Levinson, Clifton Fadiman,
Jacqueline Susann, Kaufman
(*Columbia Broadcasting System Photo*)

In Hollywood: Nunnally Johnson, Gene Fowler, Jr., Gene
Fowler, Sr., Kaufman, Ella Raines, Peter Lind Hayes
(*Universal Studios*)

Poker game: Rupert Hughes, George Jessel, Kaufman
(*United Press International Photo*)

Kaufman and daughter Anne aboard the *Queen Mary*
(*courtesy of Anne Kaufman Schneider*)

Kaufman, with friend Adam

GEORGE S. KAUFMAN

Poor General Motors

By nature I am a late riser. Eleven o'clock in the morning, eleven-thirty, is just about right for me. So it was something of an oddity to find myself awake at nine o'clock one morning in August 1952.

Having satisfied myself that I could sleep no longer, I arose and stumbled into my workroom. It was hot and stuffy, the air conditioner was not on, and the telephone was ringing. After I picked up what the Bell Company refers to as "the instrument," my entire life changed as simply as if I had turned the lock, opened a door, and stepped from one room into another.

A female voice announced that Max Gordon was calling and would I wait? I had waited for Max Gordon fourteen years. Why shouldn't I wait a little longer?

Fourteen years ago to the month I had come to New York City to become a playwright, but a playwright has to earn a living until his plays start paying, and I had been promised a job as an assistant stage manager for Max Gordon, the celebrated Broadway producer. His next production was to be *Mis-*

1

souri Legend, starring Dorothy Gish and Dean Jagger. By the time I had arrived in New York, however, *Missouri Legend* was out of rehearsal and on the road. And there I was, in Manhattan and out of a job. My timing had been wrong. Max Gordon didn't need me.

But now, here he was on the telephone.

During those fourteen years I had written countless words for radio, television, newspapers, magazines. I also had written an unhappy stack of plays that had been praised, optioned, mimeographed, rewritten, even cast, but never put into rehearsal. And that's what counted. That's what I really wanted. The theatre.

"How would you like to write a play with George Kaufman?" Max Gordon asked me over the telephone. Now, I knew who Max Gordon was. He was Kaufman's producer and partner.

And I knew who Kaufman was. He had collaborated on more plays, more successful plays than anyone anywhere in the twentieth century. He had made more money and more headlines than any living dramatist. He had three kinds of lives: a private life, of which I knew very little; a public life sensationalized in the tabloids, especially during the Thirties as "Public Lover Number One" in Hollywood's Mary Astor diary scandal; and, finally, a professional life as a man whose wit, whose unchallenged gift of satire, whose skill as a director and producer on Broadway made him the undisputed king of theatrical comedy throughout the world. He was the first man after O'Neill to win two Pulitzer Prizes in the theatre. He was quoted in newspaper columns and at dinner parties from New York to Hollywood. He had a wicked tongue, and a sense of timing that was without equal. In recent years, radio and television had made his voice and face familiar in almost every American home. He was a formidable-looking man; tall and lean, he would peer intently or laconically over his glasses, and he spoke infrequently. When he did, he could be devastating. The Gloomy Dean of Broadway was a title well suited to him.

It wasn't just the heat on that stuffy August morning that made my hand wet as it held the telephone. There was something genuine in the way Max Gordon had asked that question, like the ring of a dime on the marble counter of a soda fountain.

I said I would like to write a play with Mr. Kaufman very much.

"Well, he wants to do one with you. He's down in Bucks County. Why don't you call him?" He rattled off a series of numbers.

Without moving from where I stood, I picked up the telephone again and dialed long distance. I remember precisely what words he used.

"Max Gordon says you want to write a play with me." Kaufman's voice was quiet. He came directly to the point. "Do you have an idea?"

"No."

"Neither have I," Kaufman answered. "We're a pretty good pair. Let's get together."

When?

He told me that he intended to stay in the country for the remainder of the summer, but would return to New York on September 30. He asked that I meet him at one o'clock on that day, and gave me his Manhattan address. I thanked him and said good-by.

If the Gallup Poll had shown that I led all other presidential candidates by 97 per cent of the voters, I couldn't have been more excited. I couldn't believe it.

I had to talk. I had to tell someone. I raced back into the bedroom and awakened my wife.

"I'm going to collaborate on a play with George S. Kaufman," I shouted.

3

She looked at me, and nodded her head slowly. "That," she said, "is what I call news to wake up to."

The time was exactly one o'clock on the last day of September.

"What floor does Mr. Kaufman live on?" I asked the doorman at 1035 Park Avenue.

"Penthouse," was the answer.

The elevator door opened and I walked right into the Kaufman apartment. It was light, white, beautiful, and airy.

The butler stood in the middle of the foyer. With a nod of his head he indicated that I was to go to the left.

Walking down a hall, I glanced into a large white and beige bedroom. Filmy silk curtains billowed into it through the open doors of a terrace. The odors of French perfume and bath oils drifted out at me as I walked by. This, I learned later, was Mrs. Kaufman's room. Continuing down the hallway, I came at last to the bedroom in which George Kaufman slept and worked.

Kaufman himself, that first day, looked tall, skinny, dour, with the aged remains of a shock of white hair combed straight up on his head. He was wearing a blue shirt, bow tie, a deep-red smoking jacket, and slippers. He was lying on the narrow bed watching a baseball game on the television set. He stabbed his right index finger into the air as his sole form of greeting. I nodded.

On the television screen the New York Yankees were murdering an unremembered team by a score I shall never recollect. He asked me if I liked baseball. I said I did. I was a Yankee fan. He asked if I was from New York. I told him no. He said that he wasn't either. I asked whom he was rooting for.

"I'm always for the underdog," he said.

Looking back, that was the most significant statement he made all afternoon.

While he watched the game, I glanced about the room. It was

4

small with a narrow Spartan-like bed, a straight-backed chair, a bookcase, and a battered desk that looked as if it might have come from the Salvation Army. And, because Kaufman was concerned with the exactitude of the words he wrote, there was a wastebasket fully two feet wide and four and a half feet high.

Kaufman was supposedly a caustic, bitter, and unfeeling man, but covering the walls of this room were photographs of his father and mother; of Beatrice, the wife he loved, and of Leueen, the wife he adored; and of his daughter Anne. Facing him when he went to sleep at night and when he awoke in the morning were photographs of Alexander Woollcott and George M. Cohan. Next to them was a snapshot of a young dancing class, Pittsburgh, circa 1898; the girls wore ribbons in their pigtails and the boys wore white gloves—even George, but he was only ten then and couldn't put up much of a fight. Above this were the inscribed photographs of Edna Ferber and Lynn Fontanne, and a framed letter from Franklin Roosevelt to Aleck Woollcott jovially alluding to the length of Woollcott's visits to the White House and their similarity to a Kaufman play. Then came the photographs of his two favorite producers, Sam H. Harris and Max Gordon. Next was a framed box office statement signed by the house manager of a London theatre in which a musical he had directed was running; under "Additional Comments" the manager had written, "The Queen Mother, Princess Margaret, and Mr. George S. Kaufman attended this night's performance."

There were many more signs of his deep sentiment, but perhaps the truest was a photograph of a much younger and somewhat plump Moss Hart, his most successful collaborator, who had written on it what words could not express, with gratitude and perception for us all: "To George—without whom . . ."

Dominating all the photographs of his friends and family, bigger than almost all of them put together, and hung in the midst, the very center, of all those who were dear and important

5

to George Kaufman was an etching in henna print on buff paper. Captured within the frame was a likeness of Mark Twain.

Later, he asked me to turn off the television set and we talked of plays and ideas for plays and characters and situations. Nothing came of it. At four-thirty or quarter of five, he arose, got into his shoes, put on a sports jacket, and said that he was going to his bridge club.

I followed him to the elevator. As we rode down, he asked me where I lived and said he would drop me in his cab. As I recall, we rode from 86th Street to 77th Street in silence. There had been no bon mots during the entire afternoon. No repartee, no wit, no devastating lines.

When the cab stopped at 77th Street, I got out and thanked him. It was then that he made the second most significant remark of the day.

"See you tomorrow. One o'clock. Sharp."

I nodded and closed the door; the cab pulled away. From that parting line of his, I slowly began to accept the reality that I was indeed working with George S. Kaufman.

At one o'clock sharp every day I presented myself to Jean, the French butler. He greeted me silently. If he lowered his head to the right, I went into Mr. Kaufman's bedroom. If he nodded to his left, I went into the living room. There, slouched in an easy chair before the fireplace, his slippered feet high on a footstool, sat Mr. Kaufman. I sat across from him on the edge of a hard, chocolate-colored sofa. Between us was a large circular coffee table. As the days grew colder, the fireplace was lit.

We worked six days a week. I took notes, and as they accumulated I spread them out on the coffee table. Slowly, a play began to take shape. It was a comedy about the United Nations; not about the delegates but about the men who sat three and four chairs behind the delegates—the translators, the message

6

coders, the chauffeurs and bodyguards, and their wives and women.

George S. Kaufman sat across from me, and if he said what we were doing was right, it was right. He approved of a few of the things I wrote, or peered over his glasses or looked pained or uttered gentle reprimands such as, "This isn't worthy of you."

On January 22nd (I remember the date simply because it was my birthday) I rode up in the elevator at one o'clock—and when the door opened I knew at once there was trouble. The French butler wasn't there to greet me. George S. Kaufman stood in his place. A gaunt man anyway, that day his figure loomed up like a spectre.

He wouldn't allow me into the living room. Instead, he pointed to a red velvet settee in the foyer, and we both sat down. He didn't have to tell me the bad news. I knew it already.

"Max Gordon likes the play," he intoned. "He thinks it's very amusing. But," and here it came, "he's afraid the United Nations people will picket the theatre and the critics will kill us for it. So we've decided to drop the whole thing."

He mumbled something about how difficult these things were to take, then he arose and rang for the elevator. It arrived almost at once. I got in. The way I felt, it would have been a mercy if the God damn elevator cables had snapped!

The wrath, the sheer disappointment I felt is still impossible for me to describe. I was in such a state of anger and despair, I could speak to no one. I went to the garage where my car was stored, and getting behind the wheel, whirled north away from the city.

I was out on the Taconic Parkway, a set of parallel concrete ribbons separated by grass, trees, bushes. It was clear, cold, and empty, and I was giving George Kaufman and the accelerator the punishment they deserved. My eyes darted to the rear-view mirror, down to the speedometer, and up to the mirror again.

7

I was doing ninety-five miles an hour, and some maniac was coming up behind me as if he were on the Indianapolis Speedway on Memorial Day. I eased over to let him pass. As he did, I glanced to my left. The maniac wore the uniform of a New York state trooper.

I pulled over to the right shoulder of the road. He stopped in front of me. There then followed the entire ritual of the driver's license, the ownership registration, the big black leather book, and the baby-blue ticket.

"Where were you going?" he asked.

"Nowhere."

"Then why were you going so fast? Take it from me, General Motors doesn't build cars to last long at the speed you were going."

My body stiffened. My mind began clicking like an IBM machine.

"I'm sorry I have to give you a ticket," the trooper said.

"That's okay."

"Especially on your birthday."

"Okay, okay." I was barely hearing him.

"You see, I know it's your birthday from your driver's license."

I needed to think. I pointed to a car just passing us. "Get him! He's speeding."

"Damn right he is!"

And with that, one of the most important men in my life dashed for his gray and white patrol car. That state trooper had provided the motivating words: "General Motors."

Ten days before, Kaufman had been at the Regency Whist Club. The stock market was off. A player had complained about the drop in General Motors stock. Another player had sighed, "Poor General Motors."

Kaufman had told me the story the next day. He was intrigued with the title and the notion that anyone could feel sorry for the world's richest corporation. "One day," he had said, "you and I will have to pay a little respect to that company." By then, I knew Kaufman well enough to understand that when he said, "Pay a little respect," he really wanted to beat, pummel, satirize, and laugh the company off the face of the earth.

More than anything else in the world, I wanted to write a play with George S. Kaufman.

Quite deliberately, I made an illegal U-turn, crossed the grass, and headed south for New York. I drove slowly, very slowly, because I was thinking of a story and I wanted it to jell before I got home.

I have a friend whose parents died when he was quite young. That was bad. On the other hand, they left him several million dollars. That was good. His decision was not to work himself to death as his parents had.

At forty, he retired and drove across the United States. Unmarried, childless, bored, he found himself one morning in a small place in Alabama. There was one factory in town. It made hand trucks, the sort of thing used to carry luggage at airports, steamship docks, bus stations. It occurred to him that he owned a small amount of stock in the local corporation, and having nothing better to do, he sauntered over to the plant and entered.

He was met by a middle-aged southern lady who took note of his name, his clothes, and his northern accent. When asked what business he had in mind, he explained that he was a minority stockholder who wished to make the acquaintance of the president of the firm. Picking up the phone, she enlightened the president as to the sort of person who wanted to see him. The president was not in. Could he speak with the vice president? On hearing who was waiting for him, the vice president was not in. Perhaps the secretary? Negative. The treasurer? Never. The general manager? Out.

My friend slammed out of that little factory, dashed back to the hotel, raced into his room, and called his stockbroker in New York.

"What'll it cost me to get 51 per cent of that company?" he demanded.

The broker touted him off the stock. The firm had a poor earning rate and a low dividend payment, but my friend wanted that company and either the broker would get it for him or he'd get a broker who would.

An hour later, my friend banged the screen door shut as he re-entered the factory. Leveling his finger at the middle-aged southern lady, he instructed her to tell the president, the vice president, the secretary, the treasurer, and the general manager that the man who now owned 51 per cent of the stock in the firm was ready to meet them.

Quick as that they were out of their offices and lined up in front of him. Then, with the sweet smile that only revenge can bring, he waved his hand and said, "Gentlemen, you're all fired!"

With that story in mind, I pressed down on the accelerator and sped back to New York and George S. Kaufman. Jean took my coat and nodded to the left. I went into the living room and without preamble launched into the story. By now, of course, I had altered it slightly. Instead of being rich, the man was poor. Instead of being forty, he was old and frail. Instead of a small factory in Alabama, the company was poor General Motors.

Somehow, motivations still to come, the little old man went to a stockholders meeting, and somehow, motivations still to be found, with ten little shares of stock, he took over the company and fired the whole kit and caboodle.

Mr. Kaufman listened patiently. He took off his glasses. He

put on another pair, grimaced, and asked, "Suppose the little old man was a little old lady and the little old lady was Josephine Hull?" He could have mentioned any of the Borgia women, and I would have leapt at the suggestion.

For six days Mr. Kaufman and I worked. Ideas, plots, sub-plots, characterizations, curtains, innovations, insights, everything a play seemed to need poured out. The longer we worked, the more enthusiastic we became. Mr. Kaufman even cut the last two afternoons of bridge so we could get on with the play, which by then had assumed the title *Ten Little Shares*. Around nine o'clock on Friday evening, Mr. Kaufman telephoned me at home. We spoke for four hours. The pile of notes I was making was already thicker than any play should be.

On Saturday I stepped out of the elevator at one o'clock into the pit of disaster. Where the butler always stood there was now a grim-faced nurse in a white uniform. I could hear Mrs. Kaufman sobbing in her bedroom. A man with a stethoscope murmured to the nurse, who fixed me with a professional gaze and said, "Please be seated."

Bewildered, I went to my usual place on the edge of the chocolate-colored sofa. Presently, Mr. Kaufman entered, wearing slippers, robe, and eyeglasses, his long thin legs looking whiter and skinnier than they had any right to look.

"I'm going to have an operation," he said.

I asked when, where, why?

He was too nervous to talk about anything except the play.

When the doctor appeared and beckoned, I wished Mr. Kaufman luck, he wished me luck, and we parted.

The short operation developed into three operations. It was six weeks before they let him out. By then I had sorted the notes into scenes and the scenes into acts.

As soon as he was back home in his own bed, he demanded to see the script. I was amazed that despite his weakness he attacked it with such vigor. Pages flew. Lines were cut, rewritten, thrown out. The very act of working gave him strength. With a new script in his hands his recuperative powers awed us all. Before long he was out of bed, and spring was coming in off the terrace.

One night he sat me down for a talk on financial affairs. Immediately I told him I would accept whatever share he offered me. That seemed to please him. He told me I would receive 75 per cent of the author's royalties and he would receive 25 per cent. I didn't understand. He explained the arrangement to me again. I protested. It did no good.

"This is your play," he said.

I challenged that. It was as much his as mine. He didn't like arguments. I knew that by now, and this was developing into a nasty little scene. I changed the subject.

"Mr. Kaufman," I said, "I've got a new title for the play. I'd be pleased if you'd put your name underneath it."

"What's your title?" he asked.

I told him.

"That'll do fine," he said. "Now as for putting my name on the play . . ." He shook his head and launched into a tale of his failures. He hadn't written a hit, a smash hit in fourteen years. Yes, he'd had them as a director, but as a writer his name meant death to a play. Every critic hated him, deprecated his work, poured vitriol on his style. No, his name on a play was a sure sign of a bomb. He was a failure as a writer and that was that.

"Everyone remembers your hits, Mr. Kaufman. No one remembers your flops."

"I do," he said softly.

Repeatedly, he refused to do what I asked. At length, he said he'd sleep on it.

Next afternoon he showed me the title page. It read:

THE SOLID GOLD CADILLAC
A NEW COMEDY BY
Howard Teichmann and George S. Kaufman

Rehearsals began in the John Golden Theatre on the day after Labor Day. The magic semicircle of chairs on the bare stage was filled with actors. Mr. Kaufman, Mr. Gordon, and I sat behind a small table facing the actors, our backs to the empty, darkened theatre. At a signal from Mr. Kaufman, the actors began reading the script. They read, they laughed, and two hours later had cheered themselves.

"Well," Mr. Gordon observed, "it looks like you have the beginnings of something."

"Maybe," Mr. Kaufman added.

I said nothing. The musty coolness of a theatre at the end of summer was familiar to me. Not until today, however, had any word I had ever written been read aloud by a first-rate professional group of actors readying it for a Broadway opening.

Rehearsals were a breeze. No temperament, no trouble. Three and a half weeks later we opened at the New Parsons Theatre in Hartford, Connecticut. The audience roared. There was curtain call after curtain call. Later we adjourned to Mr. Kaufman's hotel suite.

I had never seen so small a sitting room filled with so much big talent. Three Pulitzer Prize playwrights—Thornton Wilder, Moss Hart, Abe Burrows—plus Max Gordon. Everyone was talking, everyone had different suggestions, everyone had the same suggestions. It was a hit. A big one. A small one. It needed polishing. It didn't. Moss Hart took me into the kitchenette and begged me to get Mr. Kaufman to fire a bit player. Abe Burrows wanted to add a joke. Thornton Wilder spoke brilliantly about the play's universality. I still do not know if he was for it or against it, because the door to Mr. Kaufman's bed-room opened and we all stopped talking.

He wore his slippers, glasses, and a white nightshirt that ended just above his knobby knees. He cut a comical figure, but nobody laughed. Caesar at the height of his power could not have addressed the massed legions on the Rubicon more im-periously or benignly.

"Gentlemen, this play is too long," Mr. Kaufman pronounced. "It will be cut by two men. Thank you for coming, and good night."

The others withdrew silently. Mr. Kaufman got into bed. I pulled up a chair. He changed glasses. Together we cut the script.

In the capital, Mr. Kaufman occupied a large corner suite in the best hotel in town. There when he arrived were a huge arrangement of flowers and an invitation from one of Washing-ton's great society matrons asking him to dine with her that Sunday evening. Mr. Justice Frankfurter would be among the guests, her note read. My wife and I had received a smaller bouquet and a similar invitation.

Mr. Kaufman advised my wife to write her regrets, explaining that we were weary from travel. Instead, we would dine with Mr. Justice Douglas the next evening.

I was nervous the next night, especially as the play was opening in a large sophisticated city. The big round table in the center of the main dining room didn't help. Mr. and Mrs. Max Gordon were present, Mr. Kaufman, my wife and I, and of course Mr. Justice Douglas. Mr. Kaufman made the introduc-tions as easily as he directed the play. At the next table sat John W. Davis, one-time Democratic candidate for the presi-dency of the United States. More introductions. A cocktail. Food. Wine. Conversation. All the while the clock kept running toward curtain time.

At eight-thirty, while we lingered over coffee and dessert, Mr. Kaufman gently suggested, "Max, call the theatre. Have them hold the curtain, please." I marveled at his composure.

At quarter of nine we arrived with high spirits at the National Theatre. The audience, having been kept waiting, was in an angry mood, clapping in rhythm, stamping.

The curtain rose. The scenery failed to work properly. So did the recorded tape of Fred Allen's voice doing the narration between scenes. The actors, unnerved by all this, fell to the occasion and gave their very worst performance. To top it all, a thousand-watt bulb exploded during a blackout and sent a shower of fireworks raining down upon actors and audience alike.

We didn't have to ask anyone how it went. Of *The Solid Gold Cadillac*, the kindest critic in Washington wrote, "Drag this tin lizzie out of town."

Before the papers hit the streets, Mr. Kaufman was on a train back to New York.

Washington, D.C., was where young George Kaufman had begun his professional life. This is where he had been molded and broken. In 1913 he had left feeling precisely as he did in 1953: beaten thoroughly and completely.

1 *The Newspaperman and Sundry Items*

IN 1912, THE WASHINGTON *Times*, A DAILY NEWSPAPER WITH subscribers in the nation's capital and environs, presented to its readers a new humor columnist. His name was George S. Kaufman, and he was as green as new money in the mint.

He had been born in Pittsburgh on November 14, 1889, to a highly neurotic mother and a financially unsuccessful father. Nothing in his social or cultural background hinted that when he reached his early twenties he would have a column of his own on the editorial page of an influential metropolitan newspaper. Truth is, not until he arrived in Washington was he ever paid a cent, honest or otherwise, for anything he had written.

He had been writing, of course, for what seemed to him then many years—jingles, poems, short stories for the high school paper. And when he was fourteen, encouraged by a rabbi in the Reform Temple founded by his Grandfather Kaufman, he had collaborated on a play with another boy.

His teens were peppered with a succession of rejection slips from *Argosy* magazine. *Argosy* had wanted high adventure with dash and sweep and rich florid prose. George reveled in reading such stories but failed miserably in writing them.

When George was eighteen, his father moved the family to Paterson, New Jersey, where he was superintendent of the Columbia Ribbon Mill. George ended up selling ribbons to wholesalers in New York City—but he also hit on the style of writing that he believed he could handle successfully himself.

The pages of the New York *Evening Mail* carried a daily column called "Always in Good Humor" (later retitled "The Conning Tower"). It contained little bits about many things, but each seemed to be a highly polished jewel, each a gem of fashionable prose or poetry. The column was signed F.P.A., and F.P.A. was the genie who granted George the three wishes.

Franklin Pierce Adams was a Chicago boy not unlike George S. Kaufman in appearance, family background, and mental agility. His first job was in 1903 with the Chicago *Journal*, where he wrote a daily weather story. Later he was allowed the luxury of a daily humor column. Although everyone is interested in the weather, Adams' humor column became so successful that he was granted permission to concentrate on it alone. But Adams refused to monopolize the humor column. Instead, he invited contributions from his readers. These poured in like rain in the spring on Lake Michigan. After a year and an increase in salary, Adams was ready for the East.

New York took him and turned him into what New York can do quicker than any other city in the world. It made F.P.A. a celebrity. Now his contributors were Edna St. Vincent Millay, Sinclair Lewis, Dorothy Parker, Ring Lardner, Edna Ferber, Deems Taylor, John Erskine, Alice Duer Miller—in short, the brightest young names in American letters.

It seemed unusual, therefore, that in 1908 witticisms should start coming in from Paterson, New Jersey. Moreover, they were not the usual bumpkin-like banalities. They were good, and

Adams began to run them. The Paterson contributor, taking his cue from Adams' own nom de plume, signed himself G.S.K.

To see his own words in print in a New York newspaper did for George S. Kaufman what the switch does for the electric light bulb. He exploded entire barrages of comments, jokes, puns, witticisms across the river to F.P.A. As a reward, F.P.A. used more and more by G.S.K. Finally, he was invited into New York to dine with the great columnist.

When they met it was as if everything in Adams was exaggerated in Kaufman. Adams was thin, Kaufman was skinny. Adams' complexion was pale, Kaufman's was sallow. Kaufman's nose was bigger than Adams', his eyeglasses were thicker, his hair blacker and bushier. Adams was five feet eight inches in height; Kaufman stood over six feet.

End it right there. Adams was a man. Kaufman was an eighteen-year-old boy. Adams was the most successful humor columnist in America. Kaufman was a ribbon salesman.

Many American boys from eighteen to twenty-two study under professors. Kaufman did his college years under the blue pencil of F.P.A. Although each operated on a distinctly different level—Adams up there, Kaufman down here—they shared similar interests. Both, for example, were drawn to the theatre.

At Adams' suggestion, young Kaufman took a course in acting at the Alveen Drama School. On its completion, George answered an advertisement in a trade paper. A stock company in Troy, New York, was seeking a company manager for the summer season. In place of past experience, one hundred dollars cash would cinch the job. George's salary as a ribbon salesman was painfully small, but he managed to forward the hundred, and arrived in Troy looking ahead to a summer of show business excitement. The theatre, however, was not what he had expected—it was on the second floor of an office building—and at the end of a week George had to wire home for fare back to Paterson.

His telegram to his father read: LAST SUPPER AND ORIGINAL CAST WOULDN'T DRAW IN THIS HOUSE.

Parenthetically, it is worthy of note that George Kaufman developed the craft of telegram sending to its highest degree. During the course of his lifetime, he probably made more and wittier use of Western Union than any other American. In ten words or less he would startle, amuse, dismay, convey, or convulse his kin and others. It is also worthy of speculation that since the death of the great telegram sender in 1961, the Western Union Company has closed office after office and coincidentally curtailed its services somewhat drastically.

Again at the insistence of Frank Adams, George took a course in playwriting at Columbia University on Saturday mornings, but no good seemed to come of it. Not until 1912 did his genie grant George his first wish.

Frank P. Munsey, an East Coast newspaper tycoon, approached Adams with the idea of leaving the *Evening Mail* for the Washington *Times*. To trade what his friend and contributor O. Henry called "Baghdad on the Subway" for a sleepy southern town of a few hundred thousand souls on the Potomac River did not fill Frank Adams with sufficient enthusiasm. But he had a "customer" in Mr. Munsey, and he knew it. So he weighed the prospect judiciously, finally refused it with thanks, and then sold his customer, sight unseen, the brightest, most gifted writer in his entire private preserve: G.S.K. Relying on Adams' personal word, Munsey directed that the new man report to the Washington *Times* immediately.

Carrying a cardboard suitcase, a sheaf of his own clippings from F.P.A.'s column, and a box of chocolate candies, an elated George Kaufman took the train from New York, arrived in the nation's capital, and showed up for work in the city room of the Washington *Times* all on the same day.

He was given a desk, a typewriter, and a column on the editorial page. He slugged it "This & That." At the beginning, it was a replica of F.P.A.'s column in the *Evening Mail*. Kaufman turned out jokes, puns, light verse, poetry, and an appeal for material from his readers.

To Kaufman's immense pleasure, contributions came in at once. He had been and would continue to be all his life a devourer of mail, be it his own or anyone else's. The baskets of incoming letters formed another outlet for his apparently limitless energy. He raced through the mail each day, discarding most of it, but keeping and refining what he considered good.

In the column itself, he slowly began to veer away from simple jokes and poems. In the very best American tradition of protest and dissent, George Kaufman started jabbing at what today is called the Establishment, or what was called then very big people and very formidable institutions.

Bit by biting bit there began appearing in his columns such items as these:

Of the President of the United States: "Mr. Wilson's mind, as has been the custom, will be closed all day Sunday."

Of the United States Senate: "Office hours are from 12 to 1 with an hour off for lunch."

Of the mighty: "Has anybody ever called it the Slandered Oil Company? Because it isn't."

Of the rich: "It is our case-hardened belief, apropos of the Newport gem thefts, that anyone who can afford to own a hundred thousand dollars' worth of jewels can afford to have them stolen. Promptly upon disproof of this we shall turn on the sympathy spigot in full."

On conditions social and political: "A Neat Little Classification (from the *Times*):

"'Two men were killed yesterday in the construction work at Panama. One was an Englishman, the other a laborer.'"

It was in his early days in Washington that Kaufman began to choose those subjects deserving deflation. What he held up to ridicule and derision was worthy of lampoonery, raillery, irony. Looking back more than half a century into the dried and fragile pages of the Washington *Times*, one can see that this was more than timely humor. It was wit that deserves to be placed under the classification of satire.

From the beginning right until the end, George S. Kaufman never saddled himself or anyone else with the stuffiness and conceit known as "the pride of authorship." If he could improve his work, he did so. If it wasn't good enough to suit him, he threw it into the wastebasket without a moment's hesitation.

He generally wrote with startling speed. He would twist his long legs around the legs of his chair, then, unfolding them, retwist them two or three times around themselves. Although he had been taught typing and shorthand at the Pittsburgh Secretarial School, he typed with his index fingers only. He would insert a sheet of copy paper into the typewriter and then bang away mercilessly at the machine until the page was filled, hesitating only to consult his notes. When his work was completed, he would untwist his legs, wrap them anew, and start cutting his own material.

There can be no doubt when it comes to the question of "how" George Kaufman turned out as much work as he did in his long and incredibly prolific lifetime. The answer must be in the sure speed and unerring confidence with which he cut. Rather than get hung up on a word or a phrase, Kaufman would discard pages. The result of this was a constant progression in his work.

The rejection slips from *Argosy* magazine seemed less harsh now. He was building a style of his own. It was short. Staccato. In a day of fat and flowery language, Kaufman kept his writing as thin as himself. He was learning the pressure of a deadline. More than that, he was learning to become a newspaperman.

He was ideally suited for the work he was doing. Newspapers wanted copy that was lean and cut to the bone of meaning. That was a cinch for Kaufman. The smell of printer's ink was getting to him and he loved it. Here, at last, seemed to be his life's work. In work he found his greatest single source of pleasure, and, as writing is a solitary occupation, he didn't mind the absence of family and friends.

Always a shy person, he did not make social contacts easily. But he did suddenly find himself making what was then considered a solid salary for a newspaperman. Thirty dollars a week could go a long way in 1912. Accustomed to living with his family in boarding houses in Pittsburgh and Paterson, he now treated himself to the luxury of a furnished room. What meals he took, he had out.

Of the three daily meals, he preferred breakfast, particularly if it included hot oatmeal. Dinner was a matter of meat and potatoes. Vegetables were out of the question even in childhood.

"They tried to sell me the idea that lima beans were filled with mashed potatoes," he once reflected, "but I was a pretty bright kid. One bean was enough."

Chocolate candy had been and always would be his favorite food. Next came apple pie. But food in general held no special attraction for George Kaufman. Nor did whiskey.

It was a sound he yearned for, the sound of one person speaking to another. This he found in the Washington Press Club.

In the days prior to World War I, that then mildly exclusive institution was located above the drugstore on 15th and F Streets. Long on listening, short on talking, Kaufman quietly allowed himself to be lured by local reporters into a card game called poker. The locals regretted it at once, for the most strenuous regular exercise Kaufman had taken as a boy was pinochle.

His father, a strapping, well-put-together man, had been unhappy in many ways with his unathletic child. The initial rapport between father and son came when Joe Kaufman tried to explain the intricacies of pinochle to George.

For an eight-year-old boy, George proved remarkably adept. When the time arrived that the son was beating his father nightly, they switched to a three-handed bridge game that included George's mother. Right down to the end of her eighty-one years, Nettie Kaufman admitted to an extraordinary sense of cards. Right down to the end of his eighty-three years, Joe Kaufman would confess that he was a bit of a sharp at the card table. But neither of them could beat little Georgie.

Neither could the boys at the Washington Press Club. The stakes were low, but George was generally a winner. And this was important because money itself was important to George Kaufman. His father had suffered a constant lack of success as a businessman, and the progressive downward trend in the family's manner of living made an early impression, which Kaufman was never able to shake.

One of his protégés, the author, editor, and raconteur Alexander King, observed, "Kaufman wore an expression that looked like he was always worried about next week's rent."

He was now nearing his twenty-third birthday, and while many young men away from home for the first time immerse themselves in the traditional wine, women, and song, Kaufman proved that in Washington he could get along without any of them. When he wasn't playing cards, he spent the nights discovering and exploring a world that began to mean a great deal to him.

It was in Washington that George came across the writings of Mark Twain, and devoured them. He began to pattern himself after Sam Clemens. Giving up the idea of trying to control his unruly hair, he allowed it to grow long and combed it upward as Clemens had done. There were other similarities in the two men. Both had fathers who were chronic business failures, both were thought to have been in danger of death as infants, both had delicate hands, each avoided touching others whenever possible. Twain was a newspaperman. So was Kaufman. Twain could dominate an audience, make it laugh and respond to his will. Kaufman at that point was a fair if immature copy. Both were in business, as Justin Kaplan, one of Twain's biographers, wrote, "to excite the laughter of God's creatures."

If Samuel Clemens was a genius, Kaufman was a gifted disciple. Samuel Clemens had died two years earlier in 1910, but for George, who read him at night and quoted him frequently in his column during the day, Mark Twain was very much alive. "To Helen," he wrote on the flyleaf of a book he sent as a gift to his older sister, "Not Twain yet but doing my damnedest."

Happy for the first time in his life, he might have remained in Washington if Frank P. Munsey had not walked into the plant one day and looked at the faces behind the typewriters. When he saw Kaufman's, Munsey, never a pillar of racial tolerance, barked out to an editor, "What is that Jew doing in my city room?"

There was the terrible silence that follows such acts of brutality, a few murmured words, and within minutes George Kaufman was out on the street. Fired.

His new, highly productive world was at an end.

While the outward differences between the George Kaufman who left Washington in disgrace in 1913 and the George Kaufman who fled that same city in 1953 are obvious, one factor remained constant. From the time he became a newspaperman right up until the last few days of his life, George Kaufman found escape from emotion in work. His life-long fear of death, the deep shame of scandal, his bitterness following failure, anger, futility, all could be swept away by writing.

Precisely as an alcoholic or a drug addict can find escape in whiskey or heroin, Kaufman achieved it with notes scribbled onto a slip of paper or hours of pounding away at a typewriter. The vast numbers of plays, musicals, sketches, short stories, poems, letters all prove that in Washington, D.C., Kaufman had become a compulsive writer.

From a town that ran only an occasional streetcar, George returned to the swift tangle of New York. Manhattan at that time boasted fourteen daily newspapers. Of these, only three interested Kaufman, and of the three, only the *Evening Mail* and the *Tribune* carried any immediacy about them. F.P.A. was leaving the *Mail* and joining the *Tribune*. The job for a humor columnist on the *Mail* was open, and George was granted his second wish. Frank Adams recommended him for the post.

Kaufman went to work at once, but he simply could not compete with the established stable of brilliant writers who owed allegiance to Adams. At the end of a year he was dismissed, not as cruelly as in Washington but with equal effectiveness.

The third and final boon granted by Frank Adams was a job for Kaufman as a reporter on the *Tribune*. He began by covering hotels, local political events, and incoming passenger ships.

For George Kaufman to cover passenger vessels arriving from Europe was something of a coincidence, for it was aboard just such a craft that his grandparents had arrived in this country.

No doubt the ship that brought Carl Schurz to America had the same gigantic proportions as the *Mayflower*. Fully as many German-Americans trace their ancestry to the former vessel as earlier settlers claimed kin from the little ship that put its passengers ashore in Massachusetts.

Joe Kaufman's parents came over with Carl Schurz. So did Nettie Meyers'. Fortunately for all concerned, the Kaufmans and the Meyerses both headed for Pittsburgh, where the Meyerses grew rich and the Kaufmans grew enough sons to field a baseball team. The tallest, smartest, rangiest of the nine Kaufman boys was Joe. He was also, depending on which relatives are consulted, the best looking.

In 1876 America experienced one of its frequent financial upheavals. Things being what they were—no jobs, not much money—Joe Kaufman and a second cousin, name of Frank, went out West.

The West, in those days, was like the West today on television. Leadville, Colorado, was a town named by a pessimist. First there was a gold strike, then lead, then they finally found silver. By the time the two young men from Pittsburgh got there, it was a mining camp where men dug for but no longer struck large amounts of ore.

The Frank boy had been graduated from college recently as an engineer and surveyor. For him there was work and money. For Joe Kaufman, there was a short oath, a tin badge, and a hand gun. Being a deputy sheriff and a vigilante, he kept the peace, joined in the regional practice of stringing up claim jumpers, and fought briefly and courageously in an Indian war with the Utes.

Four years on the frontier and he returned to Pittsburgh, broke but the most glamorous young man in the tightly knit German-Jewish community.

Henrietta Meyers was beautiful, tall, an excellent pianist, and she carried herself like an aristocrat. Joe Kaufman courted her and married her in January of 1884.

Toward the end of that year, their first child, Helen, was born. Two years later, their first son appeared. He was named Richard, and he was to live only seven and a half months before dying of what was then called "the summer complaint." Three years later, when George was born, a nurse was immediately engaged.

"He was the kind of baby who was never taken out when

26

it rained or when the wind blew or when the clouds were low or when the sun was hot," his older sister remembered.

The memory of Richard's grave remained ever fresh in Nettie's mind and that memory, unknowingly, was transferred into the mind of young George. When happiness did come to George it was repetitively diluted by unknown and unseen anxieties.

From the beginning of his life, every consideration was taken for George's well-being. The family tried to make him physically perfect in every way. To no avail. At the age of four, he had to have eyeglasses. And, since he was urged to protect himself at all costs, he learned to shun athletics. As his mother told him constantly that he was delicate, he considered himself to be just that all of his life.

On his seventh birthday, George was hoaxed by his parents into believing that the infant girl who had been born in the house that day was a gift for him. While she was growing up, Ruth found it was no bargain having him for a brother. He was chicken, it turned out, a self-admitted physical coward. If he wouldn't use his fists, though, he was learning to jab with words.

"George," his mother said one day, "Aunt Margaretta is coming to visit later. It wouldn't hurt us to be nice, would it?"

"That depends on your threshold of pain," he answered at once.

The next recorded remark out of him came when a lady visited the Kaufman household one afternoon. As a gift, she brought a large box of licorice. George detested licorice.

"Thank you very much," he said as the box was thrust into his hands. "It's nice to know there'll *always* be candy in the house."

However, George wasn't allowed to be the center of attention for long. Shortly after the birth of her third child, Nettie showed signs of developing a first-class neurosis. Within a few years she hit such a nerve-wracking pitch, it had an effect on everyone. The strong learned to avoid it, but George was weak.

All forms of strange maladies struck at all hours of the day and night. Gasps and shrieks and moans were followed by orders for George to run at top speed for the doctor. Breathless and terrified, George would return to be the audience for his mother's infinite variety of brink-of-death scenes.

His father solved these problems by announcing, "Nettie, I'm going out for a walk. I'll be home when you get back to your senses."

Helen, George's older sister, solved it another way. She had a large wedding at the Concordia Club ("German Jews Only") and left town with her husband, Frank Lieberman.

Ruth, George's birthday present, beat it still another way. Hours and hours of piano practicing kept all of mama's moaning from Ruthie's ears.

Only George remained to take it. Nettie's hysteria and fear of death made for scenes that never ended. For George, they were so traumatic that when the time came for him to write true emotion, he quickly hid behind a joke. What insights he might have had as a serious playwright were forbidden to come to the page. He had all the emotionalism he wanted as a boy. What he wanted was an escape. Oddly enough, he found it at Sunday school.

A new rabbi had been hired two years before, an Englishman named J. Leonard Levy. Dr. Levy loved the theatre, and it was from him that George caught the bug. In a community house adjacent to the temple, Dr. Levy indulged in theatricals. George's initial experience on the boards was playing the role of a Scotsman in an opus entitled A *Pair of Spectacles*. Truly impressed with his pupil's ability, Dr. Levy approached Joe Kaufman, strongly suggesting that George should become an actor.

Joe Kaufman looked down on the man of God who was trying to send his only son onto the stage and growled, "I think, Dr. Levy, that maybe *you* should have been an actor."

When George reached his teens, he was an underweight introvert. His father, fed up with his son's finicky eating habits, lack of exercise, and aversion to fresh air, put his foot down. George should go out West. George should learn to ride a horse, get out into the open, work with his hands, sweat, eat whatever was put on the table before him.

An old friend had a ranch in Idaho. There Joe Kaufman—ex-deputy, ex-vigilante, ex-Indian fighter—sent his only son to fill out, toughen up, become a man.

The ranch was as advertised. The hands turned out of the bunkhouse at dawn, drank scalding hot coffee, and mounted up.

George got into a saddle that first morning. He never forgot what the world looked like from atop a horse. It was very high up there, he felt very shaky and insecure, and, finally, the animal was a mean one. Promptly George got off. He never mounted a horse again.

He spent the rest of the summer in a hammock reading *Argosy* magazines. As for eating what was served at the chuck wagon—salt pork, baked beans, and flapjacks—George flatly refused. He subsisted for two months largely on chocolate candy and biscuits, and returned to Pittsburgh skinnier than ever.

———

Back to George Kaufman, ship's reporter for the New York *Tribune*, who soon turned away from the sea and the harbor, and wandered inland as far as 42nd Street and Broadway. Theatre aisles appealed more to him than ship's gangplanks.

Theatre reporters were assured free seats for as many plays as they chose to see. Night after night he would step up to the brass grilles of the box office windows and announce, "I'm Kaufman of the *Tribune*." And sure enough, tickets would be forthcoming.

The next day he would scour the offices of the Empire Theatre building or the New Amsterdam Theatre building, making friends, listening, getting off an amusing line or two, picking up bits of theatrical interest. Before very long he was taken off general news and assigned to the drama desk. There he began to write second- or third-string reviews of plays.

In 1914, Lester Markel, the young marvel of Columbia University, came onto the *Tribune* as a reporter and quickly became assistant managing editor. His nod of approval made Kaufman drama editor.

At last. His contacts with the leading managers, as theatrical producers were called in those days, grew steadily. Familiarity with leading men and leading ladies increased. Energetic news collecting during the day and trenchant drama criticism at night led him to believe there was more in his future at the *Tribune*.

This was not to be. When the first-string drama critic left the paper, George had every reason to expect the job. Instead, "the young editor in the tall tower," Ogden Reid, Sr., chose to elevate to the post an unknown, a "bum" from the *Tribune* sports desk named Heywood Broun. The "bum" proved to be enormously gifted and later became a good friend of Kaufman's.

At the time, however, furious at being passed over, Kaufman went directly to 229 West 43rd Street, spoke with Carr Van Anda, the managing editor, and come out as drama editor of the New York *Times*. The date was September 10, 1917. His salary was thirty-six dollars per week.

The drama department of the *Times* was in a cubbyhole on the third floor of what was then called the *Times* Annex on 43rd Street. Its personnel consisted of the chief drama critic and the drama editor. Because the chief drama critic at that time was in Paris, busily engaged as a sergeant on the staff of the U.S. Army's official newspaper, *Stars and Stripes*, the new drama editor had great freedom. Borrowing Shakespeare's line "What news on the Rialto?" from *The Merchant of Venice*, Kaufman began a Sunday column that was crammed with theatrical gossip and fact, and written with what was then considered rich humor. To this day, the Sunday *Times* carries a vestigial remnant of the original Kaufman column on the front page of its drama section.

But on August 4, 1919, the chief drama critic of the *Times* came home from the wars. Alexander Woollcott, "God's big brother," as the younger men on the paper called him, returned in triumph.

His resumption of that role meant the beginning of an association, professional and social, with George Kaufman that lasted beyond either man's life. Woollcott's flair, his acerbity, was contagious, but no matter how acid his tongue, a few words from Kaufman could curdle Aleck Woollcott's milk—and very often did. Woollcott himself paid tribute to his junior colleague. "I can testify," he said, "that Mr. Kaufman has always been careful to treat me like dirt."

With Woollcott covering the first-string shows and Kaufman reviewing those of secondary importance on the same night, the *Times* drama department appeared to be solidly staffed. But they were as unprepared as the rest of the country for the phenomenon that was the Twenties.

To a nation still largely agrarian and conservative, the Twenties had the effect of an ice-cold, needle-point shower. On midnight of January 16, 1920, the Eighteenth Amendment went into effect. In its wake came Al Capone, Texas Guinan, hip flasks, peepholes, Stutz Bearcats, Mah-Jongg, crossword puzzles, bobbed hair. Skirts were short, busts were flat, the nickelodeon advanced to moving pictures, and an Italian gadget Americans called the radio made its appearance. Sports became everyone's interest, and everyone cheered Jack Dempsey and the million-dollar gate. Red Grange was the Gallopin' Ghost of the Gridiron, the House that Ruth Built became Yankee Stadium, Bill Tilden ruled the tennis courts, Bobby Jones ruled the fairways, Johnny Weissmuller and not Britannia ruled the waves. Harding and Coolidge were the presidents, but who cared? Incandescent bulbs turned Broadway into the Great White Way, and such players as George Arliss, Fanny Brice, Will Rogers, George M. Cohan, Marilyn Miller, Billie Burke, Ina Claire, Pauline Lord, Katharine Cornell, Jeanne Eagels, Al Jolson, Eddie Cantor, the Barrymores, the Astaires, and the Marx Brothers were waiting for new plays and musicals.

No one had to wait long, for with the flagpole sitters, Aimee Semple McPherson, and jazz, came the Golden Age of the American theatre. Eugene O'Neill had just written his first full-length play, *Beyond the Horizon*. Other hits from other playwrights were *The Awful Truth*, *R.V.R.*, *Craig's Wife*, *The Show-Off*, *Lightnin'*, *Blossom Time*, *The Student Prince*, *Liliom*, *A Bill of Divorcement*, *Rain*, *Six Characters in Search of an Author*, *The Adding Machine*, *They Knew What They Wanted*, *Outward Bound*, *The Guardsman*, *What Price Glory?*

As the New York theatre exploded into the Twenties, more hands were hired by the drama desk. On January 12, 1920, a young man fresh out of the navy was engaged at six dollars a week as the copy boy; his name was Sam Zolotow. On December 4, 1922, J. Brooks Atkinson was engaged by the book review department. Almost at once Kaufman dragooned him into covering the third-show opening on any given evening during which Woollcott and Kaufman were already reviewing. Herman Mankiewicz, John Byram, Morrie Ryskind, and a clutch of others began gravitating to the drama desk of the *Times*.

As the drama editor, Kaufman was a wizard, a mystery, but above all a professional newsman of enormous integrity. "He was the boss," Mrs. Herman Mankiewicz remembered. "He was a very hard taskmaster. He wanted the job done and he wanted it done on time."

His integrity demanded that he give no space to any show with which his friends were connected, and finally, to any piece supplied by a press agent. These steadfast decisions by the *Times* drama editor resulted in a series of classic feuds between that gentleman and other members of the theatrical profession. Today, they seem too petty to mention in detail. The important fact is that Kaufman as a newspaperman held his ground over the world about which he wrote and edited: the theatre.

"How do I get our leading lady's name into your newspaper?" a press agent once asked him.

"Shoot her," Kaufman snapped.

This was in line with his predecessors' opinion of what constituted news in the *Times* drama department. Brock Pemberton claimed, "If a man is murdered, the story goes to the city desk. But if the murdered man is found to have a pair of theatre tickets in his vest, the story belongs to the drama desk."

The mystery of Kaufman the drama editor lay in the fact that he was rarely in the office. He was always out, gathering news, lunching and making quotable remarks at the Algonquin Round Table, dining and playing cards at the Thanatopsis and Inside Straight Poker Club, the New York Bridge and Whist Club, the Cavendish Club, the Regency Whist Club, attending dinner parties, costume parties, and supper parties.

In the middle of any of these, Kaufman would abruptly excuse himself by muttering, "Got to go, got to get back to the *Times*." With that he would depart swiftly and turn up at 43rd Street to see the copy just before the paper went to press.

Of Kaufman's quick comings and goings, Brooks Atkinson observed, "He always did his work very scrupulously, but he was so organized that it was almost impossible to know when he was working and when he wasn't working. He would pop into the office at, say, eleven o'clock in the morning, and sit down at his typewriter, and for about half an hour he would work with great intensity. And then he was gone for two or three hours. Then he'd pop in and do another half hour's work, and then he'd give directions to Sam Zolotow to get this picture or that picture or arrange for a piece of copy here or there. And Sam would write down the orders. George would issue these orders quickly and tersely and then leave Sam to execute them."

As the anonymous second-string critic of the New York *Times,* he was a figure in his own right. Mrs. Oscar Bernstein, who worked with him back on the *Tribune,* watched him carefully on many an opening night in the years that followed. "When he sat there," she said, "he looked as if everything he saw and heard was revolting to him. Just to be in the theatre was dreadful. But his reviews were kind and generous, and he knew more about the theatre itself than any other critic who was writing about it."

Another contemporary saw his reviews as "Crisp, curt, and to the point."

As he did in Washington, so he did in New York. He would come in from a play, sit down at his typewriter, twist his legs about his chair, insert the copy paper, and type away at a furious pace. Sam Zolotow, who saw all of the *Times* drama critics from Alexander Woollcott to Clive Barnes, believed that Kaufman was the speediest he ever witnessed in action.

As for his kindliness, it wasn't always in evidence.

"There was laughter in the back of the theatre," one of his reviews began, "leading to the belief that someone was telling jokes back there."

"I saw the play at a disadvantage," he once wrote, "the curtain was up."

Reviewing another play, he wrote, "I was underwhelmed."

In the autumn of 1922, Woollcott resigned. He was followed by John Corbin, and then Stark Young, who, in turn, was succeeded by Brooks Atkinson. That Kaufman, who knew the theatre "in and out," should not have been chosen drama critic astounded Atkinson. Lester Markel, who in 1923 followed Kaufman from the *Tribune* to the *Times* and became its great Sunday editor, firmly believed that Kaufman did not want the job.

An examination of the employees' records of the New York *Times* tends to give strength to Markel's opinion. Atkinson needed only four lines in the records. Kaufman's leaves of absence required two full pages.

For whatever reason, Kaufman never complained that he missed the opportunity. Instead, he remained with the *Times* as drama editor and second-string critic. When play after play appeared on Broadway bearing his name as co-author and director, when success after success came season after season, still he clung to the job on the paper. Some believed it gave him an opportunity to slip away from dull dinners or duller people. Some suspected it gave him an easy excuse for other things. Atkinson was convinced otherwise.

"A curious thing about George's relationship with the *Times*," Atkinson said, "is that I think he always trusted the *Times* more than he trusted the theatre. I think in some curious way he always had it in the back of his mind that he was going to be a flop."

———————

Why? The answer goes back to those days in Pittsburgh and Paterson when George was a boy and Joe Kaufman was something less than an ideal breadwinner.

Kindliness often collided with the truth in opinions concerning George Kaufman's father. Joe Kaufman read philosophy, cared about his fellow man, and won the undying admiration and love of his son. The fact is, he married the richest girl within his social sphere and, despite numerous attempts at financial glory, led her and their children down the road almost to the poorhouse.

Half of the large double house in which George and his family lived had to be rented as a boarding house. Times grew even worse, and the boarding house people were given permission to break through the living room wall and occupy the entire downstairs. The Kaufmans retained a few rooms on the second floor, but necessity forced them to dine with the boarders.

Shabbiness and indignities became their lot. In Pittsburgh as in every other place at every other time, the family with the good name but no money learns with painful bitterness how the poor fail to manage.

When it was time for George to go to college, his father's fortune, or lack of it, decreed that he end up in a local "commercial college," which, having few academic requirements, hurried him on to Blackstone and the somewhat dubious pursuit of the law. Fortunately, this lasted only three months, and then the family doctor decided that George "was weak in the chest," and prescribed a job in the open air. Accordingly, George was apprenticed to a land surveyor.

Picture an eighteen-year-old boy, more than six feet in height and less than 130 pounds in weight, crawling up and down the wooded hills of West Virginia carrying a surveyor's tripod and transit, a lunch pail, the ever-present box of chocolates, and a notepad on which he wrote variations of "I am master of all I survey." He was such an inept surveyor, he swore solemnly once, that the town of McCullom, West Virginia, is actually three feet lower than the site it should be on.

Relieved at last of the outdoor life, he wound up in a Pittsburgh secretarial school. Three months later, he was a stenographer for the Pittsburgh Coal Company.

"Actually, I was the secretary to the comptroller. I didn't know what a comptroller was until I got the job," George liked to reminisce. "Then I found out that a comptroller was a man who began to dictate letters at five-thirty in the afternoon."

In 1908, when he got the job as superintendent of the Columbia Ribbon Mill in Paterson, Joe Kaufman was guaranteed twelve thousand dollars a year. But his debts in Pittsburgh were so large that Joe, Nettie, George, and Ruth were forced to continue living in wretched boarding houses.

Put politely, his father parted company so many times with so many businesses—his father's pantaloon factory, Charles Schwab's Crucible Steel Corporation, his own Vulcan Steel and Foundry Works—and ended up with so little, that George never in his own lifetime felt a sense of financial security.

Brooks Atkinson was unaware of George's background, but from his vantage point, he was able to comment on what he saw. "There was nobody less sure of himself as a theatrical genius, and nobody was less willing to accept failure. I think, in a curious way, he felt that if everything else blew up, he could always come back to the *Times*."

The 1929 stock market crash that triggered the Great Depression did not go unnoticed by Kaufman, a man of deep insecurities and keen sensibilities; it required him to take action. In addition, Fredrick Birchall, acting managing editor of the newspaper between the old days of Carr Van Anda and the new days of Turner Catledge, felt that Kaufman was away from his desk so often that he might not have time for the *Times*. Accordingly, Atkinson went down to Philadelphia, where George was trying out in *Once in a Lifetime*. Diplomatically and

37

delicately, he broached the subject to Kaufman. "He's absolutely right," Kaufman replied, and promptly sat down to write his letter of resignation. It was dated August 16, 1930.

Just a little less than thirteen years had been spent on 43rd Street as a newspaperman. George Kaufman would never forget them. Nor did he forget that from that time on he belonged on 44th Street, the street with the theatres.

From a humor column in Washington to the end of his job on the drama desk of the New York *Times* took eighteen years. He needed every one of them to become George S. Kaufman the successful playwright.

2 *Bea's Fella*

BEFORE HE BECAME A PLAYWRIGHT, GEORGE KAUFMAN BECAME a husband, and one thing, evidently, had a great deal to do with the other.

He was twenty-eight years old, and as far as women were concerned, he was totally inexperienced. When he was fourteen, the young men of his age group in Pittsburgh became excessively vexed with the young men a few years their senior. The older boys not only began dating girls with whom George and his friends had grown up but they also were indulging themselves in the fleshpots of Pittsburgh's red-light district. Infuriated by this, the boys of Kaufman's age determined that men as well as women should remain virtuous until marriage.

Seven of those boys drew up a covenant stating this in writing. There it was in black and white. If you signed it, you pledged your word to live up to it. George Kaufman signed it and carried out his part of the compact faithfully, as did the other six boys. Because it was there in writing, they called themselves the Black and White Club. Later they were known as the Galahads. "The seven of us who kept the pact were

39

Irving Pichel, Clarence Fink, Arthur Katz, Walter Cohen, Milton Jana, and George and I," testified William K. Frank. "It was in 1905 when we founded that club. I know for myself I remained a virgin until I was married, and I have been assured by the others that they did too."

In 1916, during his stint with the *Tribune*, George Kaufman was still gawky, still shy, but by now he was inquisitive to the point of nosiness. He was a wit without confidence, and he was fearful of almost everyone and everything.

Ruth, seven years his junior, was considered the talented member of the family. At four, she was a prodigy at the piano. In her teens, she studied the languages that would be necessary during her projected triumphant tours of Europe. When she grew up, Ruth was the only girl the drama editor of the New York *Tribune* ever dated. They went to the theatre regularly, and if the play ran late, George left to write the review while Ruth remained to see the third act and phone it in to him for inclusion in the story. If he wasn't reviewing a play, he and Ruth went to the theatre because they loved it. When they didn't go to plays, they stayed home and had long, serious talks or made fudge in the kitchen. Imagine, therefore, what an unsettling time it must have been for George when Ruth, at the age of twenty, suddenly married a man in the clothing business named Allan Friedlich. His only importance to this story is that he had family connections in Rochester, New York.

In the early summer of 1916, Rochester was a half rural, half industrial town, largely insulated from the rest of the world except for the telegraph and the railroad. The former brought in stories of a distant war in Europe and a scarcely less distant incident along the Mexican border, while the latter brought in the bridal party of Allan Friedlich and his wife Ruth nee Kaufman.

Her brother George, now a member of the working press in New York, had planned his summer vacation cruising aboard a steamer on the Great Lakes. Such was the fashion of the middle classes in the years prior to World War I. Wishing to avoid the loneliness of traveling by himself, George jumped at the chance to join his kid sister on her honeymoon. Destiny and the New York Central took him to Rochester.

Adler Brothers & Company, Manufacturers of Clothing, Rochester, New York, was a firm founded by Sarah Adler's father and uncle in the days between the German exodus to the United States in 1848, and the American Civil War. They set up shop just in time to turn out some of the cloth and clothes that became known as "Union Blue." Men in these uniforms marched and fought from Shiloh and Fredericksburg, from Chancellorsville to Gettysburg, right down to Atlanta and Appomattox.

When Sarah Adler married, it was to a man from the border state of Kentucky. Jules Bakrow was a traveling man, good looking, with an eye for the ladies, and a smooth line of talk. He was not an especially educated or talented man, but he *did* marry the boss's daughter. They had three children: Julian, Beatrice, and Leonard.

Born on January 20, 1895, in a large house on Oxford Street, Beatrice grew up "really as kind of a pudding. Her hair was a little bit kinky and a little bit frizzy and parted in the middle," Dorothy Michaels, her childhood friend recalled. Looking back, Dorothy considered Bea unchic even for those days, unsophisticated, and as plain as the countless coats cut each day by Adler Brothers. Together, Bea and Dorothy formed the Two Spooner Club, an organization comprised solely of two very young ladies who would buy one soda topped with the richest whipped cream, and consume it with a spoon apiece.

Puberty came and along with it grew desires for knowledge,

41

which was not dispensed very readily in Rochester. What Bea and Dorothy wanted to know, they found in the Bakrow home. "Their library contained a set of Balzac including the 'Droll Stories.' It was in a locked case," Dorothy wrote in later years. "We found the key and read them secretly and omnivorously. We were thirteen and fifteen, and the stories offered a fairly complete sex education. At this age, we must have been in love with each other for we called each other 'Pee Wee' (both the same name) and two years after that wrote to each other as husband and wife. I was the wife. Neither of us was aware of it until we were mature, and nothing of a sexual nature took place between us."

College for Bea was Wellesley, but not for long. For repeatedly staying out after hours, she was bounced from that genteel institution before her freshman year had been completed. Picture Sarah Adler Bakrow standing in the April rain on the platform of the Rochester Railroad Depot waiting for her only daughter to return home in disgrace. Tears coursed down her face as the young woman in question stepped off the Pullman car. "Beatrice," Sarah wept, "you've been thrown out of Wellesley. What kind of man will have you now?"

No one had to wait long to find out. Summer came and with it arrived Allan Friedlich and his bride Ruth. Shortly thereafter came George Kaufman.

At a party given for the newlyweds, Bea and George were introduced. By now, Bea had developed into one of those large, unattractive girls who compensate for their lack of beauty by being bright, warm, ambitious, stylish, and charming. There was enough charm, enough style, enough ambition, enough warmth, and enough brightness within her to keep him at her side for the entire evening. Like her father, Bea had a full, slow, and rather lazy way of speaking. She did all the talking, and, characteristically, George listened—with interest.

42

The next morning, Ruth and Allan Friedlich drove by motor car to Niagara Falls. In the back seat were George and Beatrice. By the time they returned home, Beatrice Bakrow told her family that she was going to marry George Kaufman.

"Who's he?" her father, mother, and brothers demanded. A vehement argument followed, but Bea stood firm and emerged victorious. That night, in her mother's garden, with strings of Japanese lanterns gently bobbing in the soft summer breeze, Bea herself made the formal announcement of her engagement. Her friends in Rochester were astounded. Not only who was George Kaufman but who were his family, what were they, where did they come from, what business were they in, what did he do for a living, and, of course, the ultimate question: how did his future prospects look?

Beatrice Bakrow had a great talent: she was a people picker. Throughout her adult life she could intuitively spot a "comer." Bennett Cerf, Oscar Levant, Clifford Odets, Moss Hart, Fiorello La Guardia, William Saroyan, the list is too long to be counted. But the best pick she ever made was George S. Kaufman.

"Keep the middle of next March open, will you, Frank?" Kaufman asked F.P.A. "I've found a kid upstate who's a peach."

"Are you telling me you're getting married?" Adams gasped.

"Unless it's declared unconstitutional, I am," Kaufman replied.

It was during this courtship period that he got his nickname. Such words as "spoon" and "snuggle" were much in use then, and when Bea learned that George had no middle name, that he'd been born plain George Kaufman, and that to contribute to F.P.A.'s column he'd arbitrarily chosen to sign his pieces G.S.K., she began calling him by her own pet name, "Sniggy." She was, of course, the only person who dared address him by that unsuitable sobriquet, but it stuck. Throughout their marriage, she called him Sniggy, and he not only responded to it but frequently used it himself. It was years later, when J. P. McEvoy, a humorist of the day, wrote that the "S" in George S. Kaufman stood for "Swank," that George chose the name Simon, after his maternal grandfather.

Pet names, weekend parties, spooning, and snuggling made a happy winter pass quickly.

In the early spring of the following year, they were married in high style at the Rochester Country Club. George's best man was Franklin P. Adams. Rochester had never been exposed to the great world of New York newspaperdom. All the Adlers and Michaelses and Sterns and Rosenbergs, all the "Our Crowd" contingent of Rochester turned out and sent handsome gifts. It was March 15, 1917. Glancing at the newspapers as they boarded the train that chugged them back to New York, George said, "Well, it took the Russian Revolution to keep us off the front page!"

There was no honeymoon. In the *New Yorker* magazine profile, Alexander Woollcott credited Kaufman with having gone to his wedding with two railroad tickets and seventy-five dollars pinned to his underwear. According to Woollcott, on Kaufman's return the money was still hidden there.

George took his bride to what he considered a lavish suite in the old Majestic Hotel in Manhattan. Her childhood friend, Dorothy Michaels, who recently had become the wife of Robert Nathan the novelist, found the Majestic to be a damp, musty, fourth-rate hotel. She had gone there because Bea had telephoned her as soon as she reached town. "You must come up. You must meet George," Bea had said. Dorothy found Bea looking big and puffy and conventional in a somewhat lackluster setting. And then George came in from the outside.

He had a derby atop his head; after taking it off, he kept trying to hide it under the pile of newspapers on a table. He was self-conscious and timid as a bride, and Bea talked for all three. To another friend in later years, Bea confided, "We were terribly innocent. We were both virgins, which shouldn't happen to anybody."

Despite a sex life that was far from satisfying for either of them, Bea found herself pregnant during the first year of their marriage. Well after the normal period of gestation, an infant boy was "taken" from her. The issue of that union was deformed and stillborn.

Beatrice was as crushed as any woman would be, but George's reaction was totally unexpected and heartbreaking to both of them. Following their misfortune, George found himself physically unable to have sexual intercourse with Bea. His psychiatrist, Dr. Ruth Conkey, heard him speak of this problem many years later. After her pregnancy, Bea became a mother figure to George, and a mother figure represented purity in his mind. Dr. Conkey felt he had difficulty in synthesizing a woman and a wife. As a result, he knew even before Bea that he no longer thought of her as a woman to take to bed. There were embarrassed conversations followed by empty promises. First came twin beds, then separate bedrooms, and although George remained Bea's husband, he never again was her lover.

To Alexander King, Beatrice was "one of those great daring women who knows that her husband is having extramarital relations and knows that everybody else knows it, and knows that this can be borne either by throwing fits in lobbies or by being Wife Number One. And she was Wife Number One." To Jed Harris, theatrical producer, "Beatrice wasn't in love with him." To Morrie Ryskind, "It was a great love affair." To Dorothy Michaels Nathan, her friend from childhood, "Beatrice started seeing men even before George started with women."

This much is clear: it was "an arrangement." This much is also clear: if Bea was not his wife in bed, she would have to be his wife in many other ways.

The ambition that began stirring within her in Rochester grew to big-city size in New York. George, who had been toying

45

with plays since childhood, needed encouragement, drive, time, peace, advice, harmony, contacts. These were what his wife provided. He was content to be the drama editor of the *Times*, but Bea lit a fire under him that burned for the rest of his life.

When she married him he was making a pinched thirty-six dollars per week from the *Times*. Although she continued to receive a clothing allowance from her family of one hundred dollars each month, Bea went out and made a job for herself. Beginning as a press agent for the Talmadge sisters, when those two were stars in silent films, she then became a play reader for the Broadway managers Morris Gest and Al Woods. From there, she went into the literary world. She started as a typist for Horace Liveright the publisher. Before long she became a manuscript reader, and then quickly charmed and wisdomed her way into an editor's chair.

She and George began married life in a bedroom and sitting room. New York hotels then, as now, were expensive, so Bea moved them rather quickly to a three-room apartment on upper Riverside Drive. Later, with the money she made at the publishing house, she moved them down to West End Avenue in the Eighties.

Even before his first hit opened in 1920, the Kaufmans had moved to 200 West 58th Street, where they paid a rent of five hundred dollars each month. It should be noted that, as she had before and as she would continue to do in the future, Bea found the apartment, rented it, furnished it. George simply moved in.

Within three years, Beatrice Bakrow, the ugly girl from upstate New York, made herself into Bea Kaufman, in whose home the high-born, the wealthy in talent as well as riches, the proud and the promising could be and were found at all hours of the day and night. To visit the Kaufman home was a gay and exciting experience. To be visited by the Kaufmans was an honor.

George, still withdrawn and inhibited, had to have an audience for his dry but hilarious sayings. No matter how good a line is, it will get no response without people to react to it. So Bea provided constant and select audiences for her husband. And she moved both the audiences and the homes with regularity and dispatch. If the new apartment or new town house was not quite ready, George merely moved into the St. Regis while Bea cajoled the painters, plumbers, and furniture haulers. When the new home was ready, the master moved into it.

From the apartment on 58th Street, they took possession of a town house on East 94th Street. And from there to another town house on East 63rd Street. Back to an apartment again on Park Avenue in the fashionable Fifties. Salted and peppered among these varied locales were camps in the Adirondacks and Maine as well as estates on Long Island and in Bucks County, Pennsylvania. Bea wasn't a gypsy; she was a woman who, with her husband, was on her way up.

Not all of this was accomplished without a given amount of resistance from George. Mrs. Ogden Reid, wife of the publisher of the New York *Herald Tribune*, was once in Bea's bedroom when George came home complaining about some of Bea's plans.

"Why is it that I feel I'm on the road even though I'm living in New York?" George blasted.

"Oh, George," Beatrice said, trying to quiet him.

"I'll tell you why. It's because we're always moving. And moving costs a helluva lot of money, Bea. I know because I sign the checks for it."

"Change is wonderful, George. It's good for you."

"If you're a newspaper boy, change is wonderful. *Then* it's income," he carried on.

"You never like anything new. If you were the first baby, we'd all still be crawling," Bea said. Then, trying to soothe him, "Now cheer up. I'll get the cook to fix you a hot chocolate."

"And that's another thing! All those servants!"

47

Bea lowered her voice. "George, Helen Reid is in the bedroom." With that, Mrs. Reid appeared in the door of the library.

"Hello, Helen," George said. "I hope you got an earful. You're rich. Why don't *you* pay for all this?"

It was so quick and so on target that all three burst into laughter.

The servants were managed skillfully by Beatrice, as were the food, the furnishings, and the transportation. There were three separate telephones in the Kaufman household—one listed in the New York directory, an unlisted phone for George, and a second unlisted one for Bea. And, of course, separate bedrooms; but that arrangement not withstanding, home was where Bea made it for George.

In 1925 they adopted a baby girl. It was Bea's idea, and George had no objection. He practiced up on his funny faces to amuse the baby, and was disappointed when they frightened her and made her cry. Bea told everyone that now she felt fulfilled as a woman. Her social calendar, however, showed little time for motherhood. She appeared to be as friendly with the Vanderbilts and the Swopeses and the Pulitzers and the Harrimans and Harpo Marx and Aleck Woollcott as she was with her daughter. Politics, charity, literature, theatre, and a social life left some room, but not too much, for the role of mother.

The playwright Ruth Goetz described Bea and her relationship with George best. "They really lived high. Beatrice liked all the goodies of life. She was a great, robustious, fat, yummy woman, bouncy as hell. She loved people and drinking and eating. And she proposed to live that way. She was driven to work by her chauffeur, in her limousine, with a lap robe across her knees. She liked funny people and she liked fellows and she liked women. She was wonderfully hospitable and dear. She wanted a good time, and George was a man who never wanted a good time in his life. I think he *had* many good times, but they came to him by accident. She had to fill in many a long, dreary spell, which she did. She filled it with thousands of friends and a household that she ran extremely lavishly. Beatrice and George, in a curious way, they made it with that marriage, they really did. It was totally unsuited. The things she liked, he didn't. But he would have had no friends without her. She served her end of the marriage and he his. The marriage was on the surface, although one knew that the core was out of it and had been for many years. Still she really loved him. And so it worked. If one person goes on loving, it can be managed."

"The wonderful Beatrice was the great influence in George's life," said Edna Ferber, the novelist and Kaufman collaborator. "Sustaining, warm, perceptive, enormously companionable, she could go out to the corner to mail a letter and make the errand sound more adventurous and amusing than Don Quixote's journeyings."

Perhaps with one exception. The incomparable pianist and wag Oscar Levant recollected, "I once took Beatrice to Carnegie Hall to hear Stokowski conduct Bach's B Minor Mass. (Like George, Beatrice hated even good music.) We were late. 'In heaven's name, let's hurry,' said Beatrice, 'or we'll miss the intermission.'"

"Beatrice was like putting your hands in front of a warm stove. She was so appreciative and humorous," said Mrs. Franklin P. Adams, wife of the man who gave George that necessary start.

"Beatrice was admired for her good looks and brightness," noted Thornton Wilder, the novelist and playwright.

"She was a very unattractive woman," observed Richard Rodgers the composer.

Beauty was not the word for Bea. In her prime she stood five feet six inches and was inclined to heaviness. A hirsute condition about the face had been corrected by electrolysis, which left her complexion somewhat pockmarked. But Bea was "handsome." The head of a lioness, the carriage of a queen, she became one of those very few chic women who set the styles. She was one of the first women in New York to bob her hair. Before Freud was popular in America, Bea was on a couch being psychoanalyzed. Before Marlene Dietrich ever dreamed of leaving the Fatherland, Beatrice was wearing slacks. She chain-smoked cigarettes from a very long holder, refused to wear hats, and when the Women's Millinery Association of America threatened to pull all advertisements out of *Harper's Bazaar*, of which she had become the fiction editor under Carmel Snow, she told them what they could do. And they didn't. She was the first woman I ever saw in my life who wore blue hair.

When George lacked confidence—and beneath the aloof exterior he was beginning to present to the world, Kaufman was constantly lacking it—Bea supplied that confidence. As for her own confidence, it soared with each passing year.

Both Bea and George had separate profiles in the *New Yorker* magazine. Bea's appeared first. It was written by Ring Lardner and ran on July 7, 1928, while George's by Alexander Woollcott was not printed until May 18, 1929.

"George listened to Bea very carefully and took her advice very deeply," stated Lillian Hellman the playwright.

Arthur Kober, the short-story writer and dramatist, said, "I think until the very last, George valued her opinion probably more than anyone else's."

"He couldn't run a peanut stand. She ran the house, she did everything. She attended to his business, she was his counsellor, he couldn't make a move without her," asserted Max Gordon, Kaufman's friend and producer. "He read everything to her, and talked to her. Of course, Beatrice was a theatrical woman in her own right and knew a great deal about theatre."

Annie Laurie Williams, John Steinbeck's agent, sent the galleys of *Of Mice and Men* to Beatrice. She read them and turned them over to her husband. George got hold of Steinbeck and taught him how to make a play of a novel. After a few weeks Steinbeck sheepishly reported to Kaufman that although the first draft of the play had been completed, Steinbeck's dog, left unattended for a few hours, had eaten every scrap of the manuscript. "What an editor," Steinbeck acknowledged.

"I wish I'd had a few dogs like that for a few dogs of my own," Kaufman retorted.

Steinbeck rewrote the draft. *Of Mice and Men* won the Critics' Circle Award for the best play of 1937.

Bea herself wrote plays, but, unlike her husband's, her collaborations did not succeed. *Divided By Three*, which she wrote with Margaret Leech Pulitzer, was about a woman who was emotionally trisected by her husband, her lover, and her son. Directed by Guthrie McClintic, it ran thirty-one performances. *The White Haired Boy*, which she wrote with Charles Martin, was produced by George Abbott. There is no record of its opening on Broadway.

When there were differences of opinion between her husband and his many collaborators, it was Beatrice who patched up matters if they needed patching, or ended them if that was what was required.

"She would never permit a criticism of George," said Oscar Levant, "however she had a host of friends, and she was ever ready to tell all about them."

But they and everyone else were getting ready to talk about Bea, an event for which she was not prepared.

What had been open knowledge to a handful of New Yorkers suddenly became the juiciest scandal in the world in 1934.

A Hollywood actress had been seeing George Kaufman. No harm. No news. But when that Hollywood actress sued in California to regain custody of her child, and when her husband entered in evidence her imprudent, handwritten diary that named times and places with George Kaufman, the gossipy little secret sprang out of proportion completely.

Mary Astor had the face of an auburn-haired madonna. Her profile was a study in classic beauty. She was easily one of the most beautiful women in Hollywood. She had a zest for living and an appetite for romance that proved boundless.

Four-column headlines appeared on the top of the front page of the New York *Times*. Day after day tabloids throughout this country and Europe turned the great wit into the great lover. This was in the middle-Thirties when the Japanese were raping Manchuria, when the Great Depression was still great. And the hottest story for weeks was about Bea's fella and another woman.

One newspaper publisher offered ten thousand dollars for a photo of George in trunks or bathing suit. But what he got and ran was a picture of George Oppenheimer, writer, editor, drama critic, and close friend of both Kaufmans. A witch of a Hollywood gossip columnist wrote that Oppenheimer "was going around as proud as a peacock."

When the story broke, Bea was in Paris with Edna Ferber. The actress Helen Hayes, and her husband Charles MacArthur the playwright, were also there. Imagining the torment Mrs. Kaufman was going through, Miss Hayes sent her husband to spend a consoling day with Bea. Charlie returned in a daze. Bea was sick at heart, not at George or at what he had done but at the very idea of the lady in question writing it all down in such precise detail in her diary. "Charlie came back starry-eyed from the day he spent with Bea in Paris," Miss Hayes said. "He thought it was the most elegant behavior he'd ever seen."

Bea left Paris for Holland, hoping to find seclusion in that country. Reporters found her in Amsterdam, and the questions began again. She left the Dutch press expecting to find a more civil behavior among the British. She was mistaken. London was filled with dailies being hawked by men and boys carrying

what the English call content bills but what are known to
Americans as sandwich boards. The headlines read MARY AS-
TOR'S DIARY and MARY ASTOR AND FAMOUS AMER-
ICAN PLAYWRIGHT.

Margaret Leech Pulitzer joined her at the Grosvenor Hotel.
"She was terribly upset and embarrassed," Mrs. Pulitzer recalled.
"Newsmen were standing around waiting for her, and she
couldn't even go out to a restaurant without being mobbed by
them."

Another friend, Raoul Fleischmann, publisher of the *New
Yorker*, found Bea in her hotel, red-eyed from crying. "I'm so
sorry," Bea told him. "I'm so horribly upset that this should
happen to George. I can't stand the thought of how badly he
feels."

Together, Mrs. Kaufman and Miss Ferber, along with the
Irving Berlins, crossed the Atlantic. Edna Ferber later remembered that there were at least forty reporters at the pier in New
York City waiting for Beatrice and that Beatrice was more than
ready for them.

"I am not going to divorce Mr. Kaufman." She spoke with
her chin just a little higher than usual. "Young actresses are
an occupational hazard for any man working in the theatre."
And with that she swept past the reporters and through customs.

Style, Beatrice Kaufman's style, at its zenith.

There is a corollary to this, of course. At one of the larger
parties that she and George gave so regularly, Beatrice spotted
an attractive young man. There were several bedrooms in the
Kaufman apartment, but none seemed appropriate. Stepping out,
she and the young man went to the Plaza Hotel, where he
signed the register. The room clerk looked over this unlikely
couple with no baggage and a single intention. He muttered to
the young man, who returned to Beatrice.

"Man says there are no rooms available," he is supposed to have told her.

Beatrice descended on the room clerk.

"See here," she announced in terms of no nonsense, "*I am Mrs. George S. Kaufman!*" And she got the room.

The diary scandal didn't finish Bea. Far from it. What she needed and what her husband needed too was a refuge, a retreat from the reporters and photographers, from the understanding smiles of their friends and the prying questions of their acquaintances. As always, Bea was a woman who worked with sureness and dispatch. Her childhood friend Dorothy Michaels had remarried and was now Dorothy Pratt, living in Bucks County, Pennsylvania. The country showplace, owned by Mrs. Juliana Force, director of the Whitney Museum in New York City, was up for sale, and Bea lost no time in driving down to see it. One look at Barley Sheaf Farm was all she needed.

She telephoned George from Dorothy Pratt's home. George was so disgruntled that his voice carried clear across the room. "But, Bea, I don't *want* to own a house in the country," he told her.

"You'll love it, George," Bea assured him. "There'll be no one here. No social life. Only quiet country people who mind their own business and will let us mind ours."

"Every time you get me out into the country I want to come back."

"George," she said, "this is different. It's an isolated farm. Away from everybody. It's near a darling little town called New Hope."

"You invented that name just now, didn't you?" he said accusingly.

"No, really I didn't. Now you just take the two-ten out of Penn Station tomorrow. It's the same train that goes to Philadelphia. Pretend you're going to a try-out, but get off earlier."

To his own surprise, to say nothing of everyone else's, George took one look at the place and said, "It's yours if you want it, Bea."

The farm was an estate complete with authentic early American antiques, a modern American swimming pool, and enough grounds to employ two full-time gardeners. There were fifty-seven acres, for which the Kaufmans paid forty-five thousand dollars, and then spent another hundred thousand dollars for improvements. Bea staffed the place on a year-round basis.

George took to Barley Sheaf Farm quickly. He liked the informality of Bucks County life. He liked dropping in to visit his friends, or having them drop in to visit him. As for its isolation, within a few years Bucks County would have homes owned or rented by Oscar and Dorothy Hammerstein, Gus and Ruth Goetz, Jerry and Rhea Chodorov, Moss Hart, John Hess, Budd Schulberg, Joe Schrank, Dorothy Parker and Alan Campbell, Theron Bamberger, St. John Terrell, Artie Shaw, Tom Ewell, Louis Calhern, and a host of other New York theatrical and literary folk. The drawing power of Bea Kaufman as a hostess or as a confidante was not to be underestimated.

Unlike George, Bea was very much a political creature. She was an ardent pro-Roosevelt Democrat, a friend of Mr. Justice Frankfurter, and the author of a pair of speeches and one article for the new vice president, Harry S. Truman, whom she admired very much. During the war years, when George was collaborating with John P. Marquand, the Boston novelist, in adapting his book *The Late George Apley* for the stage, Bea exerted her prerogative as a hostess and a Democrat.

Mr. and Mrs. Marquand were guests of the Kaufmans at the Bucks County farm. While Kaufman and Marquand were writing, it was fine. But when Mrs. Marquand took to telephoning Mrs. Charles Lindbergh, wife of the champion of the right-wing "America First" organization, Mrs. Kaufman asked Mrs. Marquand to stop. Mrs. Marquand countered by suggesting that

Mrs. Kaufman invite Colonel and Mrs. Lindbergh to Barley Sheaf Farm and be educated. This was more than Bea would accept. She telephoned for a taxi. On its arrival, Mrs. Kaufman asked Mr. and Mrs. Marquand to leave her home immediately. When the Marquands questioned the seriousness of Mrs. Kaufman's intention, Bea threw open the front door and invited them out. After that, no one doubted the depths of Bea's political opinions.

When George heard of the episode, he thought Beatrice had ruined an entire month's work for him, but Marquand called the next day. Each man apologized for his wife's behavior. They agreed to meet in New York and continue work on the play. The rest of the afternoon George spent on the telephone telling his Bucks County neighbors about Bea. "Can you imagine?" he asked Ruth Goetz. "That's what analysis must do. *I'd* never have the nerve."

Bea had no qualms about behaving arrogantly. Albert Hirschfeld, the brilliant caricature artist whose work frequently decorates the front page of the Sunday *Times* drama section, made a foe of Beatrice by including her in a drawing he sketched of some fifty persons who attended the opening night of the Bucks County Playhouse. Among them were Harpo Marx, Aleck Woollcott, George and Beatrice Kaufman. Mrs. Kaufman took exception to her likeness—strong exception. By the time Monday rolled around, she went into New York, arrived at the fourteenth floor of the *Times*, and spewed out such outrage at her friend Arthur Hayes Sulzberger, publisher of that newspaper, that Mr. Hirschfeld was immediately sacked. It took quite a while before he was re-engaged and even longer before Bea finally forgave him for drawing her as he saw her. So she *did* have influence, and she was not beyond using it.

George felt chagrined when he learned of the incident, but not Bea. Continuing her own career, she served for a few years as Samuel Goldwyn's eastern story editor. After Aleck Woollcott's death, Bea and Joe Hennessey, one of Woollcott's companions, edited the collected letters of Alexander Woollcott. Later, she became one of the editors of Marshall Field's New York newspaper experiment, *PM*. She also continued to hold her head high, to laugh that throaty, irrepressible laugh, and to reign as the wife of George S. Kaufman.

With all that, she remained a most dutiful daughter. Bea wrote her family in Rochester daily all of her life. She wrote rapidly on a typewriter, a small one that was usually in her bedroom. Her mother wanted to know what she did, where she went, whom she saw. And she got just that.

In the summer of 1935, Bea wrote from Hollywood:

Dearest Folks:

It's warm as toast; like a lovely summer day, and I am wishing that I had brought more lightweight clothes. It seems to be very changeable out here and a rather difficult climate to dress properly for.

It's like old home week; the Swopes arrived yesterday, and Oscar [Levant] is coming on Wednesday. I really could close my eyes and think that I was back in New York with my buddies around me, which is both pleasant and unpleasant, according to how you look at it.

The party at the [Donald Ogden] Stewarts was great fun the other night and my evening was made for me when Mr. Chaplin sat down beside me and stayed for hours. Or did I write you that: I can't remember. He is very amusing and intelligent and I enjoyed talking to him a great deal. Pauline [sic] Goddert [sic] was there too—very beautiful; everyone says they are married. Joan Bennett, Clark Gable, the Fredric Marches, Dotty Parker, Mankiewiczes, etc. A delicious buffet dinner, with talk and bridge afterwards. Their house is lovely. Saturday night's party which Kay Francis gave was swell, too. She took over the

entire Vendôme restaurant and had it made over like a ship
—a swell job. I seemed to know almost everyone there—
there were over a hundred people. A sprinkling of movie
stars—James Cagney, the Marches again, June Walker, etc.
I arrived home at a quarter to five completely exhausted,
having danced and drunk a good deal. Before it, we went
to Pasadena to have dinner at the Alvin Kingsbachers—
you remember them. Mrs. K asked particularly to be remembered to you, Mother. Said she thought you were so
beautiful. They had an assortment of people to meet us—
not much fun really. And last night we went to dinner at
Zeppo's [Marx] and later to small party at the [Samuel]
Goldwyns' where I played bridge. The Goldwyns are off
for England in a few days. And today I am lunching with
Ruth Gordon and Maggie [Swope], having my hair done
afterwards, dining with Mr. K and going to the opening
of *Merrily We Roll Along*. And so it goes. I am dated up
all week, but I am thinking of going to the desert instead.
There is difficulty getting a room, however. It's a little too
much like New York for me here and rather exhausting.
One could have luncheon dates, tea dates, and dinner dates
every night here indefinitely, I suppose. . . . Got your letter,
Mother dear. I suggest that you send them air mail. It's
so much quicker.

All my love, and take care of yourselves.

B.

From Bucks County in 1944, she wrote:

Dearest Kids [her brother Leonard and his wife]:

Well, all plans are made and I am leaving here Sunday
night, the twentieth, and will come right to Canandaigua,
getting there in the morning. The train leaves Grand Central at 11:35 P.M. I have a lower with priority on the drawing room unless a wounded soldier wants it. I think it is

much better to come right there rather than go to Rochester and then go to the lake. I am looking forward to the trip for every reason; I am anxious to see you both, see the house, get a change and I love lake life. So that's that.

George and I went to town Monday taking Marquand and Charlie Friedman with us, and had a busy day and a half before we returned here late last night. We had dinner with the Bill Paleys Monday night; Bill has a terrific job which is one of great power and importance and secret, but he is on Eisenhower's staff, and although he is working very hard, he is mad for it. He is leaving again for England the end of the week. . . . He refused to talk about the robot bombs except to say they are terrifying. . . .

I sent you a couple of boxes of candy from out here; we were suddenly avalanched with much more than we could possibly handle, and I also sent you a few books that I thought you might enjoy.

I have just done two baskets of eggs and now I must go to Doylestown, after which we are playing croquet with Moss and Raymond, so you can see how very busy we are. My love to you, and I'll be seeing you soon now.

B.

Once again from Bucks County, this time in the summer of 1945.

Dearest Kids:

God, is it hot! It's only noon and already the temperature is ninety. That dreadful white heat. I sit inside with the electric fan and barely move; even the trip to the pool is too much as the water is so warm that a shower in the tub is really better. I was going into town tomorrow to have a permanent wave, but I shall wait for a cooler day.

Letters from both of you; I, too, am looking forward to my trip and to spending some time with you. . . . Well,

we will have a lot of ground to cover and the lovely view
of those hills across the lake to look at. . . . George got
my reservation for the sixteenth so I am all set to arrive
at any rate. I shall try to get you some little bits of food—
I have someone on the trail of a ham for me but I'm not
sure yet.

Mossie just phoned; his house is full of strange theatrical
people and we have not been over. He has a new pair of
servants, and at the moment, there are six eating in the
kitchen and seven in the dining room—quite a lot of people
to handle in this weather.

Hollywood Pinafore has curled up in this hot weather;
they will have to close very soon. It's too bad but I think
George is reconciled now. I hate to think what it must
have done these past few broiling days.

Not a very newsy letter but I've seen no one. Oh, yes,
our cow had a heifer and Oscar Levant has another daughter
. . . and your cousin Julia called up and we had a chat.

Much love to you both.

B.

By the time she had reached fifty years of age, she had moved
into a fashionable section of Manhattan: 410 Park Avenue.
For that important birthday, in addition to other gifts, her
husband gave her a joke of her very own.

"Well," he said, "you've reached the fifties. But remember, at
least it's the East Fifties."

What finished Bea was neither high drama nor high comedy.
High blood pressure did it.

Her physician, Dr. Edward Greenspan, one day early in 1945
told George she didn't have much time to live. Emotionally
shattered by this news, George became especially attentive to
her. This was guilt on his part for his past behavior and also
a genuine attempt to make her last months more pleasurable.

He spent many more hours with her than he normally did.

When she died, it was in her own bed, with her husband sitting beside her. The time was six o'clock in the evening on October 5, 1945. Five minutes later, when Moss Hart entered the apartment, he found George literally beating his head against the wall.

In death as in life, Beatrice managed everything. A letter stated that she was to be buried from the Frank E. Campbell Funeral Home, that no one was to look at her after she was gone, that the lid of the casket was to be sealed.

Moss Hart spoke the eulogy. George was as white as the paper he wrote on. All of their friends were afraid he wouldn't live through the funeral. Later, he said to his friend Russel Crouse, "I'm finished. Through. I'll never write again."

He did, of course, but the fact that George Kaufman doubted his own ability to write again was something more than a tribute to a girl whose mother, meeting her in the Rochester railroad station after she'd been bounced from Wellesley, asked, "What kind of man will want you now?"

As for Wellesley College for Women, although they threw her out before her freshman year was ended, among the names of the most successful alumnae twenty-five years later was: Beatrice Bakrow, Mrs. George S. Kaufman.

3 59 West 44th Street

IT WAS IN THE DINING ROOM OF AN INCONSPICUOUS HOTEL AT the above address that George Kaufman learned how to deliver the verbal coup de grâce. It was here that he trained and perfected the timing that would in future years mark him as the fastest wit in the East.

New York in 1919 had a population of slightly under five and a half million persons. The island of Manhattan was home to two million souls. The city itself had nineteen daily newspapers. Times Square was just beginning to wrestle the theatre district away from Herald Square. Broadway and 42nd Street was becoming the new area for playhouses; Broadway and 34th Street was fast becoming the old.

Dominated on the south by what was called The New York Times Tower, a moderately high edifice shaped like a pie wedge, Times Square and its kissing cousin just to the north, Longacre Square, proved to be an ideal location for theatres. Land was relatively inexpensive, and all forms of surface and subsurface transportation converged there. It is true that the Shubert theatrical dynasty had already erected a few houses in the neighborhood. So had David Belasco and Daniel Frohman, two of the leading impresarios of the day. But the great theatrical construction boom was just beginning along West 44th, 45th, and 46th Streets. Eventually, the legitimate theatres in the area would number seventy-six, and the number of annual productions would be three or four times that. Add to this the fact that a successful Broadway show would cast and rehearse anywhere from four to eight touring companies, and it begins to be apparent what a busy place Times Square was. Furthermore, almost all vaudeville in the United States was booked from offices in the district.

Optimism, excitement, confidence are the words to use in describing the time and the place. One other factor remained: appetites. All of those actors, authors, directors, producers, designers, choreographers, composers, lyricists, musicians, dancers, and singers had to eat. So did the reporters, columnists, editors, publishers, and proofreaders of the many newspapers that ringed Times Square.

An elite group of the aforementioned, including the ubiquitous George Kaufman, were gently steered to the Algonquin Hotel's dining room. Although he was not present for the first couple of gatherings, Bea urged her husband to accept later invitations. George only toyed with his food; it was the conversation that brought him back.

At first the group that began meeting there for lunch called itself "Luigi's Board." That was because their favorite waiter was named Luigi and everyone was fond of him—well, not everyone. George Kaufman didn't dislike Luigi as much as he disliked most waiters, but after a while the truth surfaced: Kaufman simply had an antipathy toward *all* waiters. They irritated him, they interrupted him when he was speaking, they failed the test of promptness over and over, they shoveled food under his nose when he wasn't ready for it, they were late in clearing the table, and finally, when at length they condescended to bring the tab for the meal, Kaufman, who was quite a man with numbers, frequently found that waiters added the bills incorrectly—in *their* favor. "I know I shouldn't treat them this badly," he admitted. "I know they're overworked and underpaid and I shouldn't behave this way toward them. But they're stupid, stupid, stupid; I hate them all." Even Luigi. So they stopped calling it "Luigi's Board" and began referring to it as the Algonquin Round Table.

"The Algonquin Round Table came to the Algonquin Hotel the way lightning strikes a tree, by accident and mutual attraction," wrote Margaret Case Harriman, daughter of the owner of the inn.

That's one way of explaining it, but something less than microscopic examination shows that it was in fact the creation of press agents of that period. John Peter Toohey, flack for George C. Tyler, the Broadway producer, wanted a story out of Aleck Woollcott. Fresh back from World War I, and with a well-known sweet tooth, Woollcott was lured by Toohey into the Algonquin and seduced by an angel-cake dessert. That signaled the beginning. Other press agents soon involved in the Round Table included Murdock Pemberton, (house tub-thumper for the Hippodrome, in its day a minor-league Madison Square Garden), Ruth Hale, Herman Mankiewicz, and David Wallace.

That the Algonquin should have been brought to such prominence by press agents was no more surprising than the fact that Broadway was beginning to make more and more use of those ever-ready friends of the Fourth Estate. Actually, the Algonquin was the first of many restaurants to gain postwar attention through the efforts of press agents. A later generation of them would establish Vincent Sardi's restaurant as the foremost gathering place for theatre folk, society p.a.'s would make the Colony the lunching and dining spot for the Social Register group, the space grabbers for sports would make Toots Shor's the joint for the athletic crowd. Hollywood public relations people would convert "21" into *the* place for visiting movie stars, and another old speakeasy would be turned into the famous Stork Club, not by a press agent but by the most influential and powerful columnist of his era, Walter Winchell.

Columnists were a very important ingredient of the Round Table: F.P.A., Heywood Broun, Robert Benchley. Editors included Harold Ross of the *New Yorker*, Frank Crowninshield of *Vanity Fair*, Art Samuels of *Harper's Bazaar*. Music critics: Deems Taylor and Bill Murray. Drama critics and editors: Kaufman, Woollcott, Robert E. Sherwood, and Dorothy Parker, plus assorted reporters or ex-reporters such as Ring Lardner, Laurence Stallings, Jane Grant, Ben Hecht, Charles MacArthur, and Marc Connelly. Completing the cast were actors Alfred Lunt, Lynn Fontanne, Peggy Wood, Harpo Marx, Margalo Gillmore, Noel Coward, and Tallulah Bankhead. Irregulars were Bea Kaufman, Edna Ferber, Margaret Leech Pulitzer, and Neysa McMein.

"We all lived rather excitedly and passionately," Marc Connelly recalled. "In those days, everything was of vast importance or only worthy of quick dismissal. We accepted each other—the whole crowd of us. I suppose there was a corps of about twenty or so who were intimate. We all ate our meals together, and lived in a very happy microcosm."

From time to time, other folks dropped in, but only on invitation and always at their own peril, for the Round Table was more than a circular luncheon board. It was a place where the liveliest young men and women of the New York literary and theatrical scene traded shop talk and fast-flowing wit.

This wit was quoted regularly in the press due to the fact that what was said was quotable and those who heard it had the newspaper space in which to print it. Not since the days of Artemus Ward, William Cullen Bryant, and Walt Whitman had Manhattan seen such a merry group of writers lunching together and making talk that those outside the semi-magic circle imitated, told, retold, and committed to print.

Their host, Frank Case, quickly recognized them as an attraction to his restaurant and hotel. He moved them from the Pergola Room to what became known as the Rose Room, and within a year customers were pushing into the restaurant to eat, to see, to be near, possibly to hear what they had to say.

At the beginning, they were almost all young, aspiring, and relatively poor. By the time they gave up the Round Table, all of them had made it. Big.

When John Peter Toohey took Woollcott to lunch that first day, it was the beginning of the fall theatrical season in 1919. From then on the Round Table grew, and lasted for eleven years before it faded into memories and stolen quotations. What is remarkable is that during the period in which the American people voted to legally deprive themselves of all alcoholic beverages—when drinking therefore became a national sport, when gangsters and bootleggers sprang into existence, when cabarets changed their names to speakeasies—only four members of the Round Table became hard drinkers. The remainder existed on an elixir of their own conversation.

Sample a few sips, but remember, most of it is fifty years old—and humor, unlike cognac, does not always improve with age.

Franklin P. Adams, the senior member of the Round Table, was all of thirty-eight years old when it began. As Elder Statesman and Columnist Without Peer, it is only fitting to lead off with a few of his lines.

F.P.A. entered the Algonquin one day with an incredible story. He had just seen Harold Ross, the founder of the *New Yorker*, tobogganing.

"For God's sake! Ross tobogganing?" Kaufman asked as he set him up. "Did he look funny?"

"Well," Adams answered, "you know how he looks when he's *not* tobogganing."

He listened patiently as a friend told a story that never seemed to end. At length, the fellow drew near the finish.

"Well," said the friend, "to make a long story short . . ."

"Too late!" Adams cried.

Preening himself as he was autographing copies of his latest book, Alexander Woollcott asked, "What is so rare as a Woollcott first edition?"

"A Woollcott *second* edition," Adams answered.

"Guess whose birthday it is today?" F.P.A. asked Bea Kaufman.

"Yours?" she inquired.

"No," he told her, "but you're getting close. It's Shakespeare's."

•

Robert Benchley was a drama critic for twenty years, but no one held that against him. He was also a columnist, a short-story writer, and, as the Fates would decree, he took the easy way out and became an actor. Nothing prevented him, however, from always remaining a deliciously amusing man.

It was Benchley, and not Woollcott, who said, "Let's get out of these wet clothes and into a dry martini."

"In America, there are two classes of travel: first class and with children."

Benchley and Dorothy Parker shared a small office.
"One cubic foot less of space," Benchley said, "and it would have been considered adultery."

•

Woollcott called Mrs. Parker a combination of Little Nell and Lady Macbeth. She was much more than that. Compared to the other members of the Round Table, she didn't write much, but what she wrote she wrote beautifully. Mrs. Parker wielded as wicked a butter knife as the Algonquin provided. It was she who unreasonably damned a Katharine Hepburn performance: "She ran the gamut of emotions from A to B."

"That woman speaks eighteen languages and can't say 'No' in any of them."

When she was asked if she had enjoyed a cocktail party, Mrs. Parker answered, "Enjoyed it! One more drink and I'd have been under the host."

"I-can-give-you-a-sentence" was a favorite game played during lunch at the Round Table. One of the best examples was given one afternoon by Mrs. Parker. "You may lead a horticulture, but you can't make her think."

•

Puns were popular in those days. Peggy Wood, the star of such operettas as *Bitter Sweet* and *Maytime*, got off a pretty good one as she returned to rehearsal from lunch at the Algonquin. "Oh, well," she said, "back to the mimes."

•

Woollcott the Cruel or Woollcott the Lovable, depending on what he said to you last, had the sagacity to criticize himself before his friends did.

"All the things I really like to do," he said, "are either immoral, illegal, or fattening."

He also is credited with a telling line about the stock market. "A broker is a man who runs your fortune into a shoestring."

Reviewing a volume of inferior poetry entitled *And I Shall Make Music*, he addressed himself directly to the woman who wrote it. "Not on my carpet, lady."

On the Kaufmans' fifth wedding anniversary, they received the following telegram from Woollcott:

I HAVE BEEN LOOKING AROUND FOR AN APPROPRIATE WOODEN GIFT AND AM PLEASED HEREBY TO PRESENT YOU WITH ELSIE FERGUSON'S PERFORMANCE IN HER NEW PLAY.

•

Heywood Broun was such a large and constantly unkempt man that during World War I when he was being reviewed by his commanding officer, General John Pershing, the general stopped in front of him and asked incredulously, "What happened? Did you fall down?"

Broun was a softhearted, immensely gifted man with a deep interest in humanity and a keen sense of observation.

"The only real argument for marriage," he said, "is that it's still the best method of getting acquainted."

"The ability to make love frivolously is the chief characteristic which distinguishes human beings from beasts."

There was so much of it around the Round Table that Broun said, "Repartee is what you wish you'd said."

•

Like Broun, Ring Lardner began as a sports writer. From there he became a columnist and short-story writer whose bitterly humorous and satirical sketches of twentieth-century American life earned him a high place in the literature of his day.

Lardner was the man who said, "Frenchmen drink wine just like we used to drink water before prohibition."

He was sitting in a speakeasy in Times Square when an actor-type creature with long hair and a flowing bow tie came up to him. "How do you look," Lardner asked, "when I'm sober?"

•

Marc Connelly, a reporter on the *Morning Telegraph*, became Kaufman's first successful collaborator and his lifelong friend. Connelly, a round, winning, Puckish fellow, had few inhibitions.

As he was sitting at the Round Table, an acquaintance walked by and ran a hand over Connelly's bald head.

"That feels just as smooth and as nice as my wife's behind," the fellow said.

"So it does," Connelly answered.

•

At the Round Table, Kaufman appeared daily, pretended to eat his food, looked morose, and listened very carefully. He would keep his silence minute after minute until the right one arrived. Then, and only then, would he speak.

Asked to describe his colleague Woollcott in a single word, Kaufman thought carefully.

"Improbable," he said.

He returned to the Algonquin following a visit to his physician.

"Fool told me I'm going to live to be a hundred," he said gloomily. "Well, I won't."

"How do you know, George?" Edna Ferber asked.

"I'll kill myself at eighty," he told her. The table grew quiet.

"How?" Miss Ferber demanded.

"With kindness," he announced.

Referring to a belligerent writer, he once said, "He's in the chips now, but most of them seem to have stayed on his shoulders."

During the depression he feigned pity for his friend Harold Vanderbilt. "Poor Harold," he commented. "He can live on his income all right, but he no longer can live on the income from his income."

Woollcott brought a titled European as his guest at lunch one day. Not realizing the company he was in, the guest made the mistake of bragging about his lineage. "I can trace my family back to the Crusades," the gentleman bragged. But not for long. George measured him and then let go.

"I had an ancestor, Sir Roderick Kaufman. He went on a Crusade, too—as a spy, of course."

Speaking of his own name, he said, "Kaufman is a very popular name. In fact, Lee is Kaufman in Chinese."

Kaufman returned to the Round Table after a session at Jed Harris's hotel room. The producer sat naked throughout their meeting. When it was over, Kaufman stopped at the door and delivered the now classic line: "Jed," he said, "your fly is open."

71

In the beginning, George attended these luncheons be-
grudgingly, but after a while he found that sitting in a dining
room could be fun. Bea frequently ate in the same restaurant at
a different table with business associates, but after she met
Woollcott, he was so charmed by her that he insisted whenever
she was in the neighborhood she join them.

George had only one real complaint about the set-up of the
Round Table. In front of Marc Connelly he once grumbled,
"Bea, it's so damn conspicuous. Everyone stares."

Bea answered with her usual far-sighted answer. "You'll get
used to it, George."

Connelly noted years later that not only did George get used
to it but on the road with plays—especially if things were
going well—there would be a quick whisper to a head waiter,
and George and his fellow workers would be seated at a table
in the center of the room.

"Just like home," he would say with satisfaction.

By 1924 the Kaufman home in New York had become the
second gathering place for the "Vicious Circle," as Woollcott
called the group. Frank Case said the Kaufmans fed more of
them at dinner than the Algonquin did at lunch. Of the
Round Table set, Kaufman did not go along with Woollcott's
vituperative adjective "vicious." Kaufman preferred to have his
cronies and himself called by the name created for them by the
novelist Gertrude Atherton. It was she who watched the Algonquin crowd and introduced them into literature in *Black Oxen*.
Miss Atherton called them the Sophisticates, and that was the
pose Kaufman assumed during those years.

Cool, worldly, unapproachable, the façade he presented to
the world then was the very essence of the Round Table.

While he was enjoying the reputation of a sophisticate, Kaufman in reality was a maze of contradictions. He was a shy, inhibited man who was on occasion a "show off." He was a calloused cynic who wrote schmaltzy poems to his mother-in-law. He was the wastrel who saved uncanceled stamps and reglued them onto out-going envelopes. He was thrifty with dimes but generous with dollars.

Secret generosity was a Kaufman trademark. One of the many things he really couldn't bear was being thanked. When the 1929 stock market crash hit Broadway, almost everyone was wiped out. Except Kaufman. To him, the Great Depression was merely something about which he could write. For those less fortunate than himself, he had a trick that no one ever saw through. He'd lend $500 to this friend, $1,000 to that friend, $1,500 to a third, but always with the cash went the same story. "I'm only doing this for you," he would mumble to each one, "only you. And don't tell a soul. If word of this ever leaks out, I'll never give you another cent!"

Dozens of people have told the same story. Each received help; each believed he was the only one.

Years later, when an actor pleaded poverty, Kaufman turned to his last stage manager, Joe Olney, and said, "Here. Give him a hundred dollars. Tell him it came from David Merrick."

So much writing talent sat at the Round Table each day and so many good lines were spoken it was only natural that the authors' palates should become whetted by the taste of ham. Sure enough, it happened.

A Russian revue with a French title came to New York in 1922 and turned into a hit. *Chauve Souris* was stylish and different and ran up a total of 544 performances. The Round Tablers wrote their own revue and called it *No Siree!* They played it one Sunday night only at the same theatre that the *Chauve Souris* played, the 49th Street.

73

The great leading lady Laurette Taylor was given Woollcott's space in the New York *Times* to review the evening's work. "I think the two who will come out of it the best now," wrote Miss Taylor, "will be the ones that would have no nonsense but came downstage and sang 'I'm Kaufman and that's Connelly.'" Not a bad notice considering that Robert Benchley, Aleck Woollcott, Robert Sherwood, Tallulah Bankhead, Lenore Ulric, Helen Hayes, Frank Adams, Alice Duer Miller, Heywood Broun, and Harold Ross were among those on stage. Jascha Heifetz played the offstage music. Of the very least interest to the one-shot *Times* drama critic was an almost unnoticed monologue by Robert Benchley called "The Treasurer's Report." Although Miss Taylor dismissed it, Benchley and "The Treasurer's Report" turned up in the third *Music Box Revue* and later in motion pictures. Still, the big hit of the night was "Kaufman and Connelly from the West." It was not only successful during the performance but throughout the supper party given for the cast by Mr. and Mrs. Herbert Bayard Swope.

A final bit of gratuitous advice offered by Miss Taylor was that all of the writers in *No Siree!* stick to newspapers and leave the stage to professional actors and playwrights. Fortunately for two generations of theatre-goers, this advice, as almost all advice in the theatre, was not followed.

George was also the inventor of the never-to-be-done show called *The Poor Taste Revue*; when people used offensive language or other words that outraged his sensibilities, he would snap, "*That* belongs in *The Poor Taste Revue*."

On the other hand, his favorite joke concerned an actress who was born in Philadelphia, went to New York, made a big hit, and returned home in triumph. Kaufman claimed he gave her a curtain speech indicating that though she now worked in Manhattan, her heart was still in Philadelphia. However, he would say, the actress improved on the platitude and said, "Folks, I've got one foot in Philadelphia and one foot in New

York." Whereupon an oaf in the balcony called out, "Oh, you Trenton!" Originally, the line was attributed to Lillian Russell, the beauteous singer of the Gay Nineties, but Kaufman told the story so often, he began to believe it was one of his actresses and that he had participated in the joke.

Assuredly, this was not the sort of story that would have scored big at the Round Table. But then, Kaufman was careful not to tell it there. At the Round Table, shop talk, humor, and a variety of causes were the mainstreams of conversation. Almost all the members were passionately committed to one issue or another. Adams was a practicing perfectionist on the correct usage of the English language. Woollcott was devoted to murders and wrote extensively about them. Heywood Broun and Dorothy Parker became deeply immersed in politics and spoke and preached political dogma constantly.

The women at the Round Table had all fought to bring about female suffrage. Many of them, including Beatrice, belonged to the Lucy Stone League, a predecessor of the Woman's Liberation Movement. At least two of them, Ruth Hale (Mrs. Heywood Broun) and Jane Grant (Mrs. Harold Ross) refused to be called by their married names. None of them expected doors to be opened for them or chairs to be held while they sat down at the Table. The result, of course, was that whenever they approached the Round Table, the men never arose.

Kaufman, who satirized politics, social behavior, manners and mores, curiously said little. He was a political creature only in a critical sense. When he saw inequities in the political system, he attacked them in his work. Rather than crusade on behalf of "the poor people," he concerned himself with "the poor person." "I keep thinking about those bonuses for the office boys and wish they could have been larger," he wrote to Max Gordon one Christmas. "Any chance of giving them something extra?"

He wasn't much of a joiner. For short periods of time, he

belonged to the Lambs and the Players, two New York theatrical clubs. He was never a member of any social movement.

The one organization he did join was the Dramatists Guild,
a loose but effective group of playwrights who banded together
to put an end to the inequities—humiliation and financial deg-
radation—forced on them by the Managers Protective Organization, today reorganized under the name of the League of New
York Theatres. Before the Dramatists Guild came into existence, it was quite ordinary for producers who lived in town
houses and were chauffeured about in Pierce Arrows and Deusen-
bergs to employ "house writers." These unhappy fellows received between twenty-five and thirty-five dollars a week *when*
the plays they had written were running. When they closed,
the dramatists raced back to their desks to grind out other
plays as quickly as possible, because all income for them had
ceased. If a picture sale was made or a foreign production
mounted, all royalties went to the owners of the "grand rights,"
the producers. Royalties from stock productions and amateur
versions were kept by the owners of the "grand rights." Moreover, under the old system, the dramatist had absolutely no
control over what he had written. Management could rewrite
the entire play, change its meaning and message; the dramatist
had no recourse. Nor did he have even a word to say about
who directed his play or who the actors would be who delivered
his lines.

It was to correct these matters that thirty-two dramatists met
secretly on December 7, 1925, and agreed to withhold their
plays from producers until those producers signed the first Minimum Basic Agreement guaranteeing the playwrights just royalties and participation in subsidiary rights to the plays. Each
dramatist who signed the agreement agreed to forfeit to the
group one thousand dollars as "liquidated damages" in event of
any personal breach. No breach occurred, and other dramatists

were quickly recruited. By January 7, 1926, a month later, 121 dramatists had pledged themselves to concerted action. Not every important playwright went along, but there were enough so that a committee could be formed to draw up the Minimum Basic Agreement. The committee included George Middleton as chairman, Eugene O'Neill, George Kelly, Otto Harbach, Channing Pollock, and George S. Kaufman. For three weeks they met daily at the home of Rachel Crothers. The agreement they pounded out was accepted by the Dramatists and backed up by their pledge to withdraw all plays, submit no new ones, and to contract with no producer until he had signed the Guild's proposed agreement.

The Shuberts, who controlled the bulk of the theatres in New York and on the road, balked. Failure for them to sign the Minimum Basic Agreement could mean death for the Dramatists Guild. It was then that George Kaufman the dramatist, who felt more deeply about this cause than most others, was aided by George Kaufman the drama editor of the New York *Times*. Sam Zolotow, who by then was a full-fledged *Times* drama reporter, telephoned Lee Shubert. Were Mr. Lee and Mr. J. J. going to sign or were they not? Lee Shubert did not feel it necessary to answer the question even for the New York *Times*.

It was at that point that Kaufman loped into the city room. "George, I've got Lee Shubert on the wire and he won't talk," Zolotow told Kaufman. "You know the ins and outs of this Dramatists Guild story. Here, you talk to him." With that, he handed the telephone to Kaufman. Kaufman paused. "Hello," he spoke into the telephone. "How are you, Mr. Shubert?" Lee Shubert paused even longer. If he didn't want to talk to the man from the *Times*, he certainly wasn't sure if he wanted to refuse to speak to the most successful writer of comedies in New York. Jack Morris, Mr. Lee's secretary, sat on an open phone listening to both conversations.

"Are you calling as a playwright or the fellow from the New York *Times?*" Lee Shubert asked.

"Both," Kaufman replied. "In 1917, you said you'd rather close your theatres than recognize the Dramatists Guild. Do you still feel that way?"

"To tell you the truth, we've got a lot more theatres today than we did ten, eleven years ago," Mr. Lee answered. "I'd like to keep them open."

"Now about the Dramatists Guild . . ." Kaufman persisted.

"You just keep writing those plays. I can't speak for my brother, but as far as I'm concerned, I'm not going to rock the boat," Mr. Lee concluded.

"Thanks for the statement," Kaufman said in closing. Not only did he have the story for the *Times* but within twenty-four hours the Shuberts had signed with the Dramatists Guild. It meant much to George because the Guild was the only public battle he willingly allowed himself to be drawn into. And as so much in his character shows, when he fought it was to win. Moreover, his telephone conversation with Lee Shubert made for lively conversation at the Round Table.

Kaufman never belonged to any political party.

Just when his friends were convinced he was part of the liberal left, he turned and wrote a devastating musical about Franklin D. Roosevelt. *I'd Rather Be Right* was a smash hit, and his left-leaning friends asked him how he could commit such an anti-administration act.

"There's nothing funny about a dead elephant," he told them.

At the time the elephant was almost dead, the Round Table was itself expiring. Benchley, Sherwood, Mrs. Parker, Hecht and MacArthur, Mankiewicz, and the Marx Brothers had gone to Hollywood. Woollcott and F.P.A. gave up newspaper work for lecturing and radio, the first as "The Town Crier," the second as a regular on "Information Please." Deems Taylor gave up musical criticism for work in the same medium; Bill Murray gave up music criticism for work as a talent agent at William Morris. And before anyone knew it, that shining Camelot of 44th Street had vanished as if Merlin himself had cast a spell.

4 *The Playwright*

THE GREAT COLLABORATOR OF THE AMERICAN THEATRE WROTE his first play in Pittsburgh, Pennsylvania, in 1903. He was fourteen years old and his partner was a boy named Irving Pichel. Pichel later became a fine Hollywood actor-director and a leading light in the Pasadena Playhouse. Some of his fame, however, may rest in the fact that he was the first of a long line of people who were privileged to have written with George Kaufman.

In one way it was symbolic that Kaufman's first play was entitled *The Failure*. Throughout his life, no matter how often he had a hit, Kaufman always said to himself and to those who were close to him, "I was lucky with this one. It was easy. But I'll never have another big one again."

So, in 1903, with Kaufman and Pichel acting as well as writing, *The Failure* was produced at the Rodeph Sholom Community House. It was a melodramatic story of a father who sacrificed all for his son, who, as the title indicates, did not quite make it.

For years thereafter there was no further theatrical activity for George Kaufman. Then in the early days of the First World War, he met the great actor George Arliss. Arliss became Kaufman's second collaborator, although the play they wrote never saw light from the inside of a theatre.

In 1917 a gentleman named Henry Stern formed an organization that, for a slight percentage of the royalties, would assist young playwrights. So to the Henry Stern Music Company George S. Kaufman submitted a farce entitled *Going Up*. He actually wrote thirty-five drafts of this one play, but no good ever came of it. What it did do, though, was attract the attention of John Peter Toohey. Toohey was not a theatrical producer, but for Kaufman's purpose he was the next best thing: he was the press agent of a theatrical producer.

Introduced by Toohey to George C. Tyler, Kaufman finally got a job in the theatre. In 1918 Tyler was one of the most important impresarios in America. When he offered Kaufman the job of rewriting a play by Larry Evans and Walter Percival, George reached for a typewriter.

Although he dropped all mention of it in his later biographical material, the first work Kaufman did in the professional theatre was on that comedy, *Among Those Present*. It had opened in 1918 in Philadelphia; almost at once it was evident it needed work. Tyler summoned Kaufman, and by the time *Among Those Present* opened in Chicago, the billing read: by Larry Evans, Walter Percival, and George S. Kaufman. There, for the first time, his name was on the program of a legitimate play! There too it ended, for Tyler closed it in Chicago.

No one except the actors was upset, however. Evans and Percival had another play that required Kaufman's ministrations. In the autumn of 1918, *Someone in the House*, by Evans, Percival, and Kaufman, arrived in New York. Even though it was something less than a hit, it deserves mention, because the first authentic Kaufman witticism appeared as a result of it. Reviews for the play were not good, business at the box office was worse, the flu epidemic caused even further havoc, and the result was that George C. Tyler asked Kaufman to write an ad for the play. Kaufman did:

BEWARE OF FLU

Avoid Crowds

See

SOMEONE IN THE HOUSE

Despite the advertising copy, the play failed.

Next year, he tried an adaptation, *Jacques Duval*. A play by the Danish dramatist Hans Müller, it had been translated into German and French, and was a hit in Berlin and Paris. As Kaufman had picked up a working knowledge of German from his grandparents, and as the play's subject matter was right up Kaufman's hypochondriacal alley—a doctor is researching a cure for tuberculosis, his wife takes a lover, the lover contracts tuberculosis, should the doctor save the lover?—Kaufman plunged into an English translation. Even with George Arliss playing the title role, this too failed.

It seemed that nothing Kaufman wrote was acceptable. On a larger scale, this was remindful of the rejection slips that had flowed back to him from *Argosy* magazine not too many years before. Obviously he was writing in a style that did not suit him.

But George C. Tyler, reputed for his good taste, continued to have faith in George S. Kaufman. He was also one of those theatrical managers quick enough to give the public what it wanted. He had a young actress who was just about ready for stardom. He had a young director who he felt could be trusted to bring a radiance out of that star-to-be.

What he needed was a script . . .

Marcus Cook Connelly was born in McKeesport, Pennsylvania, in 1890. Although McKeesport was "just across the river from Pittsburgh," and although Connelly worked on the newspapers in Pittsburgh, it wasn't until each man was a member of the working press in New York City that they met. Both were covering theatre, Connelly as a reporter for the *Morning Telegraph*, a popular sheet devoted to sporting and theatrical events.

Finding a common interest, Kaufman and Connelly took a liking to each other and decided to collaborate on a play for which Kaufman had an idea. It was based on a character who appeared frequently in F.P.A.'s column. Her name was Dulcinea and she was the very stuff of pure Kaufman. Although he involved himself in every style of play known to his generation of playwrights, he returned over and over again to the bumbler, the little person, the innocent who, through his or her own misadventures, outwits the slick, the sly, the smooth, the sharp fellows, and ends up with love, power, and, above all, money. Pure Kaufman: rooting for the underdog and allowing him to triumph at the conclusion of the play.

As a dramatist, he employed other characters and other plots, some tragic, some sophisticated, but none with more effectiveness and success. What was revolutionary about *Dulcy* was that it blew up a balloon labeled Business, held it up for the audience to laugh at, and then stuck the sharp pin of satire into the balloon—and when it burst the audience laughed even harder.

Lynn Fontanne as Dulcy opened in Indianapolis, where Booth Tarkington and George Ade, both great friends of George C. Tyler's, were on hand to lend wisdom and support.

On the opening night, George Kaufman did something unheard of in the theatre. He actually paced up and down the center aisle of the orchestra floor. Not the back aisle but the center aisle, from the rear of the house right down to the footlights. He was so thoroughly racked by nervousness and fear that he literally didn't know what he was doing. "Who is that drunk in the audience?" Tyler is reported to have asked an associate.

George was cured of walking through the audience, but the pacing and the acute anxiety remained with him as long as he had opening nights in the theatre.

Dulcy managed to get through Indianapolis and move on to Chicago. When it opened there at the Cort Theatre on February 20, 1921, H. B. Warner, at that time a leading man of the legitimate stage, drew Kaufman's sister Ruth into the lobby and sternly admonished, "I hope, young lady, that this will put a stop to any further ideas your brother may have for writing for the theatre."

H. B. Warner was destined for the salt mines of Hollywood.

Howard Lindsay, the young director into whose hands Tyler entrusted his play and star, and who also acted in the production along with Elliott Nugent, handled the cast superbly.

On August 13, 1921, George C. Tyler and H. H. Frazee presented Lynn Fontanne in *Dulcy*, a comedy in three acts by George S. Kaufman and Marc Connelly, at the Frazee Theatre in New York City.

The temperature and the humidity were as high as befits Manhattan at that time of year. The New York theatre had not even advanced to the stage where giant fans blew across one-hundred-pound blocks of ice to provide comfort for the audience. As a result, Lynn Fontanne was awash in perspiration and her costumes were soaked through and through.

But no matter. On August 14 *Dulcy* was a hit, Miss Fontanne was indeed a star, and a new style of comedy laughed its way into the American theatre.

Having done it once, Kaufman and Connelly decided they could do it again. They would meet at George's apartment on 58th Street, Marc's place in the Algonquin Hotel, or late at night in the city room of the New York *Times*. They would first talk out the structure for a play, then go their separate

84

ways. Marc would write one scene, George another. Then they would meet and compare them. They both argued and fought for their own points, examined the scenes, discussed the lines, and sometimes rewrote together.

Other times, Kaufman wrote alone. During most of his life he was an insomniac. Rather than turn miserably in bed waiting for sleep to come, he would get up, take whatever script he was working on, and go to his typewriter. He had a theory that proved so effective, he allowed it to become a habit. He would begin retyping the play at the start of any scene. As he typed, he cut, eliminating more and more extraneous words. The tightness, the terseness, the economy of the Kaufman style was almost as much a result of sleeplessness as talent.

Kaufman and Connelly did very well. As collaborating playwrights, Connelly was a whimsical optimist and Kaufman was the cynical pessimist.

A perfect example of their teamwork was an incident in New Haven in 1922, following the opening of their fourth play, *Merton of the Movies*. At the first reading in New York, the actors had sat in the chillness of an unheated theatre, their chairs placed on the stage so that they faced the authors, the producer, the director, and the darkened footlights. The murkiness of the empty theatre, scarcely lit by a single work light, brightened noticeably when Glenn Hunter read a line that seemed so hilarious the entire cast broke up with laughter. During every rehearsal, the company fell apart, the stage manager dropped his prompt book; it was *the* laugh line of the play. But in New Haven, with an audience out front, Glenn Hunter uncorked the line and there was silence.

Later in the hotel, Kaufman began, "Now about that line, Marc."

"It's the best line in the show," Connelly said.

"Yes," said Kaufman, "the only thing is that it doesn't go."

"Now let me tell you why it's funny, George." And Connelly

launched into the comedic situation preceding the line. "She knows the fellow when he comes in. So when he says his line, she knows he's lying and the audience knows it, and when she says her line, his line has to work."

Kaufman listened patiently, "Then, what is your conclusion, Marc?"

"I think it's a very funny line."

So they tried it the next night. Nothing. At the matinee, still nothing. Following each performance, Connelly would explain why it was a great line.

After listening to six explanations, Kaufman finally said, "Well, Marc, there's only one thing we can do."

"What's that?"

"We've got to call the audience in tomorrow morning for a ten o'clock rehearsal."

The collaboration with Connelly produced four more plays, and then abruptly, in 1924, it was finished.

"When each of us decided to do a play on his own," said Connelly, "the decision ended only our constant professional association. We never ended our friendship."

Confidentially, Kaufman told me that Connelly was constantly late for work, often missing entire sessions. "But he always had an excuse," Kaufman said. "Margalo Gillmore always had a dead cat to bury, or someone was always arriving and had to be met. Or someone was always sailing and a bon voyage party was being held aboard ship. Finally, I told him, 'Marc, someday New York harbor will freeze over and you'll write the best damn play anyone's ever seen.' It didn't, but he did." *The Green Pastures* by Marc Connelly *was* the best play of the 1929–30 theatrical season, as the Pulitzer Prize Committee for Drama duly agreed.

It wasn't so much ending the collaboration with Connelly as it was starting to write with someone in addition to Connelly.

Throughout his professional life, Kaufman had the astonishing ability to write with two, three, even four persons on four different plays at once. His energy and his drive to write continued throughout his life and scarcely ever slackened.

In 1924, while he was writing the last two plays with Connelly, he started writing with Edna Ferber.

In her first autobiography, A *Peculiar Treasure*, Miss Ferber conveyed her impression of Kaufman: "Ah, here comes the Duke now!" A duke at the very least is what Edna Ferber thought George Kaufman really was, although in conversation she said of him, "He was like a dry cracker. Brittle."

In many ways she was very much like Kaufman: middle-western birthplace, same German-Jewish background, same training as a newspaper reporter, same discipline toward work.

In other ways she was the direct opposite of Kaufman. She was small in physical stature, and a great believer in exercise. She had great personal courage, an overwhelming desire to travel, to seek new people, new places, new ideas. She did not have Kaufman's wit, but she did have the ability to write rich, deep love scenes.

Edna Ferber was already a well-known short-story writer (the Emma McChesney stories) and novelist (*Dawn O'Hara* and *So Big*). It was Beatrice who brought them together. Bea had bought a volume containing "Old Man Minick," one of Miss Ferber's better short stories, and had recommended it to George to read. He did. When he was convinced it could be made into a play, she urged him to write the author.

Miss Ferber and Mr. Kaufman met at the Kaufman apartment. Once they decided to collaborate on the play, they followed a new Kaufman theory: get away from the telephone, friends, family, everyone and everything, and concentrate on playwriting.

In a White Plains hotel, George and Edna sequestered themselves. At a concentrated but still astounding pace, they wrote *Minick* in three or four days. "Anything to escape from that awful hotel," Kaufman liked to say in later years.

Minick was a hit.

The Royal Family (1927), the next Kaufman-Ferber play, took time more in keeping with Kaufman's "ten minutes a day" line. Kaufman liked to tell people it took two years to write a play with Miss Ferber. "That is," Kaufman said, "because Edna works from nine A.M. to three-ten P.M., and I work from three P.M. to nine P.M., which gives us ten minutes a day in which to collaborate."

Having decided to do a play about a theatrical family—not similar enough to the Barrymores, whom they both knew quite well, but also different enough from the Barrymores to gain approval from their respective lawyers—Kaufman and Ferber spent eight entire months writing it.

Each morning, promptly at the stroke of eleven, George would arrive at Edna's apartment on Central Park West. As she was a lady and had the choice of sitting or standing, Edna chose the chair in front of the typewriter. This freed George to pace constantly, tie and untie his shoe laces, stretch out on the couches, indulge in small idiosyncrasies such as making faces at Edna, gossiping, twirling curtain cords, and the like.

"My God," he once complained to her, "everyone has telephoned you this morning except Queen Mary!"

Lunch was served in the Ferber household at one-thirty: sandwiches and coffee, which George wasn't wild about, and pastry and chocolate candy, which he savored.

Work would stop when George felt it was time for him to appear at his bridge club. But even a six-hour day, month in and month out, was not time enough to lick *The Royal Family*. To do that, they had to fall back on the Kaufman theory: isolation.

Edna had chosen the hotel for *Minick*. George was given the choice for *The Royal Family*.

Brooklyn. The St. George Hotel. Adjoining rooms.

Edna never quite understood why he chose Brooklyn, but she went along. All she insisted on was that when they finished work for the night, George retire to his room to get enough rest for the next day's work.

And he did retire. Until he was certain Edna was asleep. Then he would quietly let himself out and take the subway into Manhattan, where he was having an affair with a very demanding young woman. Early in the morning, he would return to the St. George Hotel, catch a few hours' sleep, and be ready for work with Edna at eleven.

Although they finished the play, although it was a hit, although Edna said she'd rather work with George than anyone else, she never wanted to go back to Brooklyn. She said it didn't agree with George; he never looked rested those days.

Later in their collaboration Miss Ferber acquired a country house, and for a while they worked there. Frequently, however, an impatient buzzer would sound; Edna would excuse herself and leave the room. A few minutes later, she'd return, work would resume, and then the buzzer would sound again.

Infuriated by these interruptions, George demanded an explanation. "Well, here in the country, help is so hard to get that I don't ring for the servants," she said. "When they want something, they send for me."

"They're acting like actors, Edna," he bristled. "Pretty soon they'll want their names above the title of this play."

It was years before she gave up her country house. Nevertheless, between 1924 and 1948, they wrote six plays. Among his co-authors, Edna Ferber was an exception. With Miss Ferber, Kaufman plays always had a larger variety of plot and a broader spectrum of color and characterization. Their plays darted back

and forth between drama and comedy. Although he wrote an occasional drama with Connelly or Hart, Ferber made him dig
deeper into what he called "the rich, red meat of playwrighting."
Even so, he enjoyed himself much more while working with
all of his other collaborators.

"Edna," he once said, "reminds me of a Confederate general.
And I'm from Pittsburgh."

Miss Edna Ferber, a spinster, tolerated his quips, his eccen-
tricities, his other women—even his wife. Miss Edna Ferber was,
in the opinion of many of their close mutual friends, in love with
George Kaufman from the time of their first play. Edna had the
insight to know what George thought of her. Edna was, in fact,
one of those strong, courageous, dynamic women about whom
she wrote in her own novels. She lacked only one quality:
beauty. And it was *that* that a woman had to have for George
to be attracted to her. He respected Edna's intelligence and
talent, but for Edna herself, alas, he could offer only the com-
panionship of the typewriter.

Although Miss Ferber never revealed it to him, she was always afraid of Kaufman. "When he needled you, it was like a
cold knife that he stuck into your ribs," she said. "And he did
it so fast, so quickly, you didn't even see it go in. You only
felt the pain." And although he never showed it, he lived in
mortal fear of Miss Ferber. Her temper, her love of quarrels, her
threats and bombast were all contrary to Kaufman's personality.
From the time he was a young man he lived in fear that a
Grade-A argument would bring about a Grade-A seizure. Soft-
spoken, gentle, economical when it came to explosive emotion,
he detested the good-fight-to-clear-the-air that Edna was always
ready for. While they were enjoying hits, he forced himself to
put up with her. After two flops, he found her guilty of being a
shrew and a scold.

Toward the end of his life he wrote to her, "I am an old man and not well. I have had two or three strokes already and I cannot afford another argument with you to finish my life. So I simply wish to end our friendship."

Miss Ferber waited a sensible amount of time, then telephoned him, and they made up, but not to the extent that they could ever write another play together.

Kaufman made it his business to meet funny men so it was inevitable that he would hit on the Marx Brothers.

His first look at them in action filled him with horror. Personally, he thought they were wildly amusing, but their outrageous antics and ad libs on the stage caused him to say to his producer Sam Harris, "The Marx Brothers? I'd rather write for the Barbary Apes!" But the quantity of laughter they generated from audiences caused him to reconsider. He decided they were best suited for a musical.

By its very name, a musical must possess music and lyrics. Accordingly, George turned to a friendly composer (if Kaufman ever considered such persons friendly) and asked, "How would you like to do a show for the Marx Brothers, Irving?"

And Mr. Berlin answered, "I'd like to."

So Kaufman and Irving Berlin set to work on their individual, soon-to-be-merged efforts.

In time George corralled the Marx Brothers onto the stage of the Lyric Theatre in New York City and read aloud the script of *The Cocoanuts*. The Marx Brothers loved it. More importantly, they loved George Kaufman.

On December 8, 1925, *The Cocoanuts* opened to smash-hit reviews, and the Marx Brothers, George Kaufman, and Irving Berlin had a monumental success.

Mr. Berlin has a crystalline memory of Kaufman walking out of the theatre whenever the music began. That Berlin walked out when Kaufman returned for the dialogue was a sharp memory of Kaufman's. "George hated music so much," Mr. Berlin volunteered, "that if I'd written 'Rock of Ages' he'd have thrown it out."*

The Marx Brothers made separate but indelible impressions on Kaufman. He adored the silent Harpo, was fascinated by clever Groucho, and disliked Chico because Chico always fell asleep at rehearsals. Even when Chico *was* awake, he could never remember the lines Kaufman had written for him.

On the other hand, Kaufman made his own impression on the Marx Brothers.

"He had great integrity, George did. You never had to watch him when he was dealing." So said Harpo, the speechless Marx Brother.

"Kaufman molded me," Groucho said. "Kaufman gave me the walk and the talk."

This was a very generous admission from Groucho, but no more generous than the fact that Kaufman allowed Groucho to ad lib on stage, the only actor he ever permitted that luxury. Of course, when the ad libs failed, Kaufman was quick to criticize.

"Remember, George, they laughed at Fulton and his steamboat," Groucho apologized one afternoon.

"Not at matinees, they didn't," Kaufman snapped.

Even a retort as scorching as that wouldn't stop the Marx Brothers from clowning on stage. Kaufman and Heywood Broun stood backstage watching the Marx Brothers romp through *The Cocoanuts.* Broun was talking, when Kaufman interrupted him and walked closer to the stage and listened. After a moment, he returned.

"Now what were you saying?" Kaufman asked.

---

* Included in the score of the musical was a song that Irving Berlin rather fancied but that George Kaufman thought was terrible. Rather than quibble, Berlin cut "Always," but made a mental note to use it at a later date.

Broun was annoyed. "Why did you stop me in the middle of a story?" he wanted to know.

"Well, I had to," Kaufman said. "I thought I heard one of the original lines of the show."

That same year he wrote *The Butter and Egg Man*, his only straight play without a collaborator. This too was a huge success. The Kaufman gift for satire was employed to the fullest: a simple country boy comes to New York, gets into the producing end of the theatre, and turns a failure into a hit. Critics and public alike cheered, and Kaufman was satisfied that he could write without a partner.

Yet only two more times did he try to work alone in the theatre: once in 1927, with a revue entitled *Strike Up the Band**; and again in 1945 with *Hollywood Pinafore*. These attempts proved that Kaufman could not do his best work alone.

He had an overwhelming craving for instant response, whether it be to a line, a scene, or an entire idea for a play. Kaufman would bounce a line off a collaborator. If it worked, keep it. If it didn't, Kaufman was the most ruthless of editors. He would throw away two dozen lines in an attempt to come up with what he thought was the right one. Remember that wastebasket in his bedroom? He kept it filled.

As a good tennis player may volley, Kaufman would slam the lines back to his partner almost endlessly, hoping to trim, change, sharpen, and achieve the economy of words so necessary to what became known as the Kaufman style of playwriting.

When a playwright who had just sliced twelve minutes out of his script asked Kaufman how he could break such news to

---

* Although Kaufman claimed sole credit for *Strike Up the Band* (1928), Ira Gershwin, who did the words for his brother's music, later wrote in his book, *Lyrics on Several Occasions*, that Morrie Ryskind was called in to rework the second act.

the cast, Kaufman said, "Tell them that the author giveth and the author taketh away."

To the collaborative process Kaufman brought the theme, or asked that his collaborator bring a theme acceptable to him. In return Kaufman would bring dramatic discipline. From his collaborators he would expect a rather large amount of characterization. Such behavior was typical of Kaufman, for if there was a single quality to his professional habits it was that he would not allow a single day to pass without working on a play. There were no moments of gratified relaxation after a triumph; no pauses for depression after a failure. In Kaufman's mind, writing was the major answer to the emptiness he felt between plays. "After an opening night there was a void," as Thornton Wilder said, "that must have been written into the very nervous structure of his whole being. Victory or defeat, there he was: cliff-hanging by his fingernails onto existence itself."

If there had to be a love scene, he could barely participate. Harry Ruby and Bert Kalmar wrote the score for the Kaufman-Connelly production of *Helen of Troy, N.Y.* During a production meeting, Ruby reminisced, Kalmar asked Kaufman to do something about the love interest in the show.

Kaufman arose, wrapped his arms about his body, and hugged his rib cage. "When you talk about love interest to me," he said, "you're up against a stone wall."

More than once he told his various partners, "Count me out. I'll walk around the block while you do the love scene."

Throughout his life, Kaufman was asked, "Which lines were yours?" Because he wished to keep his collaborators, he always denied knowledge of who came up with the line, the scene, or the idea for the play itself. In most cases, it was true, because usually the scene, the play itself had been tossed back and forth so often that Kaufman's modest "We both thought of it" held firm.

When questioned about his great desire to collaborate, he

invariably made light of it by saying, "It's nice to have company when you come face to face with a blank page."

Another time he wrote to George Middleton, founder of the Dramatists Guild, "The reason I collaborate is that I have been so fortunate, in the course of the years, as to find an assortment of gifted dramatic writers who were willing to collaborate with me. In those circumstances I would have been pretty foolish not to collaborate, and pretty hungry if I hadn't."

The brilliant Herman Mankiewicz, whom Kaufman hired as a reporter on the New York *Times*, also became a collaborator in 1926. It was on him that Kaufman first used the oft-repeated threat, "If this play fails, I'll never speak to you again."

The Good Fellow by George S. Kaufman and H. J. Mankiewicz did fail, but George talked with Herman long into their lives. Kaufman thought he was one of the funniest men he'd ever met.

Morrie Ryskind, fresh out of Columbia University and dazzlingly bright, was tapped by Kaufman for the *Times* drama desk. Before long, he too was writing with the boss. The first musical Kaufman and Ryskind wrote officially was for the Marx Brothers in 1928. They called it *Animal Crackers*. *Cocoanuts* had been about a group of confidence men operating in Florida and *Animal Crackers* utilized the same brand of swindlers. In this case, however, Chico played a musician, Harpo was a professor, and Groucho was given his most memorable character, Captain Geoffrey Spaulding, the African explorer. "Africa is God's country," Captain Spaulding said, "and he's welcome to it. . . . You know what a moose is, that's big game. The first day I shot two bucks. That was the biggest game we had. . . . One morning, I shot an elephant in my pajamas. How he got into my pajamas, I don't know."

Harry Ruby, the *Animal Crackers* composer, gave an idea of

Kaufman's music appreciation. "He had a funny attitude about songs," Ruby said. "He just didn't seem to care about music. Once, when I played him a concerted number from the show that ran about ten minutes, all he said was: 'Peppy!'"

The summer in New York that year was a brute, so Kaufman and Ryskind did most of the writing at night. Because George was still Ryskind's boss, they worked from his house and on his typewriter. Every now and then, George would stand up to stretch or walk around, and Ryskind would slip behind the machine.

"Let me alone for a minute," he'd say. Then his fingers would clatter along the keyboard.

Kaufman would return, take one look at the spacing, and say "Morrie, let me type it, will you? You know this preciseness I have. I feel better when I do it."

While Kaufman was worrying about Ryskind's spacing, Ryskind was worrying about Kaufman's refusal to make a carbon copy of what they were writing. "I always had a nightmare that we would leave the one copy in a taxicab," said Ryskind.

Finally, they completed their precious document and took it to the typists. Within a few days, they received six or eight copies. They read them over.

"What do you think?" Kaufman asked.

"George, I think it's pretty good."

"So do I." Then Kaufman took the slightest of pauses. "What're you going to do tomorrow?"

"Tomorrow is when the Pittsburgh-New York series starts, and that's where I'm going."

"All right. Fine," Kaufman said irritably. "Then what're you going to do Thursday?"

He never wanted to stop work.

By now, the corrupting but delicious sounds of the cash registers of Hollywood reached New York, filling the ears of the Marx Brothers, Kaufman, Ryskind, et al. Only for the Marx

Brothers would Kaufman write for movies. But since *Animal Crackers* was running on Broadway, he and Morrie Ryskind wrote and the Marx Brothers shot *Cocoanuts* in New York. It was an hilarious film for its day. Then fame, fortune, and swimming pools were offered to all, and all were glad to accept California cash and sunshine.

All except Kaufman. He remained loyal to the New York theatre, where he had, in turn, a failure with an old friend, Alexander Woollcott, and a hit with a new collaborator, Moss Hart.

To help Woollcott, who had become a devoted friend of Bea's, satisfy his craving for authorship in the theatre, George agreed, in 1929, to collaborate on de Maupassant's fine novelette *Boule de Suif*, another tale of a harlot with a heart of gold. The basic property was not Kaufman's "cup of tea," but rather than refuse Woollcott the chance to do a play, he plunged into it. They called it *The Channel Road*. The critics called it several other names.

"We got mixed notices," Kaufman said. "They were good and rotten."

George's reward for doing a favor for an old friend was a tall, handsome, bright young man who admired him and respected him, even called him "Mr. Kaufman." Kaufman called him "Er."

"Er" was Moss Hart, and Moss Hart was to become his most successful collaborator.

"As soon as I met him," Kaufman said, "I knew on which side my bread was buttered."

That was the line George used at the time. As their relationship went on, Moss became closer to George than anyone—even closer than family. The older man smiled on the antics of the talented youth he had made out of a boy on the borscht circuit.

When that young man flowered into a charming, extroverted dandy, George was delighted by him, amused, and ultimately as proud as if Moss had been his own son. He recognized his talent, sensed his warmth, and envied his easy gregariousness.

By the time he started collaborating with Hart, George's skill as a playwright had increased side by side with his idiosyncrasies. He would now stretch out on the floor, and pick pieces of lint, visible or not, from the carpet. He washed his hands compulsively. He grew particularly concerned with the sharpness of the points on his pencils.

It wasn't that he'd become difficult. So many people who had only a nodding acquaintance with Kaufman thought his great success had turned him from a shy and retiring young man into an irascible middle-aged character. Not so. Kaufman's sensitivity, his inhibitions, remained with him always.

When he began his collaboration with Hart, Moss delighted in smoking cigars, the bigger, the blacker, the more smoke they gave off the better. They were generally closeted in fairly small rooms while working, and the blue clouds of pollution would thicken, but not once did Kaufman demand or even hint gently for Moss to stop, although he found cigar smoke particularly revolting. It was only when Moss realized that George was standing in front of open windows on ice-cold days, breathing in air as rapidly as he could without making a display of himself, that cigars ceased to come between them.

Once in a Lifetime (1930) was the first of eight plays written by Kaufman and Hart. It was also a smash.

"When a comedy is a tremendous hit," Kaufman said, "the audience comes in after the first few weeks and starts laughing at the program."

In 1929, when there was a lot to talk about, Kaufman and Ryskind began discussing a new idea for a musical that was about as far away from the stock market crash and the musicals of the day as they could get. On and off for over a year they would speak of it. They didn't see each other very often, but when they met they would talk about their musical.

Finally, when they had a fairly coherent idea, Kaufman sat down and knocked out a five-thousand-word synopsis, which he sent to his partner and producer Sam H. Harris, who was vacationing in Palm Springs. Harris called Kaufman and said, "George, go to it. We'll open it in December." Ryskind came East and they wrote the show in twelve days.

Leaving precise instructions as to where the songs were to go and what type of songs they were to be, they mailed the script to George and Ira Gershwin on the Coast. The Gershwins did what was asked of them—brilliantly—and in the autumn of 1931, Kaufman put the musical into rehearsal.

The only argument was that Kaufman emphatically did not want the word "baby" employed anywhere in the title song of the musical *Of Thee I Sing*. He lost the argument but won the Pulitzer Prize.

Opening on December 26, 1931, at the Music Box Theatre in New York, *Of Thee I Sing* introduced a new form of musical comedy to the American theatre. For the first time a musical had a book with a truly comedic base.

The season in which *Of Thee I Sing* opened was rich with hits. Eugene O'Neill had *Mourning Becomes Electra*. Philip Barry had *The Animal Kingdom*. Paul Green wrote *The House of Connelly*. Maxwell Anderson did *Night over Taos*. S. N. Behrman, *Brief Moment*. Robert E. Sherwood, *Reunion in Vienna*. Elmer Rice, *Counsellor-at-Law*.

"Yet not one of these American dramas was as devastatingly complete a revelation of the American scene as *Of Thee I Sing*," wrote the anthologists Burns Mantle and John Gassner. "Nor is any other play of the time so neatly expressive of that native sense of humor which Americans are quick to acclaim and frequently slow to justify. Statesmen of high standing were so shocked by the exposures of the native politician in this Kauf-man-Ryskind satire that they left the theatre riding high in dudgeon. The plain citizen, however, was happy in its performance and loud in his endorsement."

In the spring of 1932, it became the first musical to win the prize established by Joseph Pulitzer. Theatrical pundits were astounded by the choice, but the Pulitzer Prize drama committee defended its action: "This award may seem unusual, but the play is unusual," the committee spokesman said. "Not only is it coherent and well-knit enough to class as a play, aside from the music, but it is a biting and true satire on American politics and the public attitude toward them. . . . Its effect on the stage promises to be very considerable, because musical plays are always popular, and by injecting genuine satire and point into them a very large public is reached."

By some mysterious fate, George Gershwin was excluded from this honor because the Committee did not agree that music should be included in the award. So the $1,000 laurel that accompanied the prize was divided this way: Ira Gershwin, $333.33; Ryskind, $333.33; Kaufman, $333.34.

"I got the extra penny," Kaufman said, "because I was the eldest."

Five years later, writing *You Can't Take It With You* with Moss Hart, Kaufman became the second playwright to win two Pulitzer Prizes. *You Can't Take It With You* was the high-water mark of Kaufman's tilting against the windmills of money, power, and the prevailing political system. The Sycamore family, dead broke as a result of the depression, are able to enjoy themselves more through hobbies such as ballet dancing, playwriting, and fireworks-making, than the family that has as its single goal the pursuit of the almighty American dollar.

The Kaufman pattern was now set. Anyone who was high,

anything that was mighty, was fair game for him. "He swept romance out of American letters," Brooks Atkinson said. "Kaufman and Theodore Dreiser between them" got rid of the teacups and colonels of the British and the bedroom farces of the French. Taxes, the Congress, the Presidency, the Supreme Court, Big Business, Hollywood—he never took on anything that was not big enough to remain standing after he had chipped away at it from 8:40 to 11 P.M.

The Kaufman style was composed of gusto and flair. It attempted to destroy the logic and sobriety of the Western world. "He was master of the destructive jest and made the wisecrack a part of our language."

In *June Moon*, which he wrote with Ring Lardner, there is a perfect example of what he did with the cynical observation that became known as the wisecrack.

FRED

Thanks. I guess I'm a little late. I got off at the wrong subway station and here was an old woman selling papers, and I stopped to talk to her because I knew she must be somebody's mother.

MAXIE

A fresh slant.

FRED

I was right, too, because she told me she has six sons. I feel sorry for old women who have to earn a living.

LUCILLE

What do the boys do, rent her the stand?

The way he used words in his plays was refreshing and explosive. As society caught up with him, he discarded the wisecrack, and turned to the unexpected and incisive observation. The subtle comedy scenes that had members of the audience nudging each other with a kind of glee, the scenes where he pointed out the frailties of lowly individuals all the way up to the Establishment, these were his favorites.

In a day when the vice presidency of the United States was a position to which few citizens gave any thought, Kaufman and Ryskind satirized it completely in *Of Thee I Sing*. The loveable pixie, Victor Moore, played the vice president, Throttlebottom, in the scene that follows.

(Guide enters with a sightseeing party.)

GUIDE

Right this way, please—follow me. This, ladies and gentlemen, is the executive office. You will probably find this the most interesting room in your entire tour of the White House. It is in this room that the President signs the many laws that govern your everyday life, and from which he controls the various departmental activities.

(One of the sightseers emerges a bit from the crowd, eagerly taking in the scene. He turns out to be, of all people, Alexander Throttlebottom)

Here come the various heads of government for daily consultation with the Executive, and to receive from him the benefit of his wide experience. It is in this room—

(To Throttlebottom, who has strayed a little too far from the group)

I beg your pardon, sir, but would you please stay over there with the others? You see, we're personally responsible in case anything is stolen.

THROTTLEBOTTOM
(*Meekly rejoining the group*)

Yes, sir.

GUIDE

(*Opens door*)

Thank you. (*Resuming his formal tone*) Now, are there any questions?

A SIGHTSEER

Does the President live here all year round?

GUIDE

All year round. Except when Congress is in session.

SIGHTSEER

Where does the Vice-President live?

GUIDE

Who?

SIGHTSEER

The Vice-President. Where does he live?

GUIDE

(*Taking a little red book out of his pocket*)

Just one moment, please. Vice regent, viceroy, vice societies —I'm sorry, but he doesn't seem to be in here.

THROTTLEBOTTOM

(*So mildly*)

I can tell you about that.

GUIDE

What?

THROTTLEBOTTOM

I know where the Vice-President lives.

GUIDE

Where?

THROTTLEBOTTOM

He lives at 1448 Z Street.

GUIDE

Well, that's very interesting. He has a house there, has he?

THROTTLEBOTTOM

Well, he lives there.

GUIDE

All by himself?

THROTTLEBOTTOM

No, with the other boarders. It's an awfully good place. Mrs. Spiegelbaum's. It's a great place, if you like kosher cooking.

GUIDE

Think of your knowing all that! Are you a Washingtonian?

THROTTLEBOTTOM

Well, I've been here since March 4. I came down for the inauguration, but I lost my ticket.

GUIDE

You don't say? Well! First time you've been to the White House?

THROTTLEBOTTOM
(Nods)
I didn't know people were allowed in.

GUIDE

You seem to know the Vice-President pretty well. What kind of fellow is he?

THROTTLEBOTTOM

He's all right. He's a very nice fellow when you get to know him, but nobody wants to know him.

GUIDE

What's the matter with him?

THROTTLEBOTTOM

There's nothing the matter with him. Just Vice-President.

GUIDE

Well, what does he do all the time?

THROTTLEBOTTOM

He sits around in the parks, and feeds the pigeons, and takes walks, and goes to the movies. The other day he was going to join the library, but he had to have two references, so he couldn't get in.

The battle and ensuing triumph of the small man against big government was an endless source of enjoyment to Kaufman, his collaborators, and his audiences. No example is more telling than the exchange between Grandpa Vanderhof and the income-tax collector in Kaufman and Hart's *You Can't Take It With You.*

HENDERSON

Now, Mr. Vanderhof, you know there's quite a penalty for not filing an income-tax return.

PENNY

Penalty?

GRANDPA

Look, Mr. Henderson, let me ask you something.

HENDERSON

Well?

GRANDPA

Suppose I pay you this money—mind you, I don't say I'm going to do it—but just for the sake of argument—what's the Government going to do with it?

HENDERSON

How do you mean?

GRANDPA

Well, what do I get for my money? If I go into Macy's and buy something, there it is—I see it. What's the Government give me?

HENDERSON

Why, the Government gives you everything. It protects you.

GRANDPA

What from?

HENDERSON

Well—invasion. Foreigners that might come over here and take everything you've got.

GRANDPA

Oh, I don't think they're going to do that.

HENDERSON

If you didn't pay an income tax they would. How do you think the Government keeps up the Army and Navy? All those battleships . . .

GRANDPA

Last time we used battleships was in the Spanish-American War, and what did we get out of it? Cuba—and we gave that back. I wouldn't mind paying if it were something sensible.

HENDERSON
(*Beginning to get annoyed*)
Well, what about Congress, and the Supreme Court, and the President? We've got to pay them, don't we?

GRANDPA
(*Ever so calmly*)
Not with my money—no, sir.

Kaufman did not think much of himself as a Writer, as a Playwright of Stature. Kaufman thought of himself best as a newspaperman who had been sidetracked into the theatre and who would be exposed and denounced at any moment and sent back to where he belonged, the city room. He did not believe that what he was writing had any permanence. It was his fear of his own incapabilities and his own mistrust of his talent that made him the Great Collaborator of the American theatre.

"How many persons," he asked, "even among your best friends, really hope for your success on an opening night? A failure is somehow so much more satisfying all around."

For those dire moments on the road, when the play wasn't receiving from the audience the responses expected of it, it was always better, he felt, to have another writer along who was emotionally and creatively committed to the project.

"Almost every play is rewritten during its tryout tour. This is predictable. In the first place, there is no play in the world that cannot be improved by additional work," Kaufman wrote. "And in the second and even bigger place, it is well known that plays have a way of fooling you. No matter how careful are your labors, there is an unpredictable factor. Somewhere in the transition from typewriter to stage there is an almost chemical element that intrudes itself between the play and the audience. Sometimes this works to the playwright's advantage, and a simple scene of which little had been expected suddenly throws the audience into stitches or moves it to tears, as the case may be. This is a good deal like having your bank account gone over and finding that you have two hundred dollars more than you had figured. But more frequently, of course, it goes the other way."

He would grow wild with indignation when amateurs proposed that only good plays be produced. The suggestion that reading the play might spare all concerned from the bother of doing a failure nettled him. "Is it their opinion," he once demanded, "that I sit down at the typewriter with the express intention of creating a flop?"

He was as conversant with failures as he was with success. "In Boston, the test of a play is simple," he said. "If the play is bad, the pigeons snarl at you as you walk across the Common."

Another time, when things weren't going too well with *Strike Up the Band,* Ira Gershwin saw two elegant Edwardian-looking gentlemen buying tickets at the box office.

"That must be Gilbert and Sullivan coming to fix the show," Gershwin quipped.

"Why don't you put jokes like that in your lyrics?" Kaufman countered.

His comedy was unexpected, and so was his subject matter. In 1939, anticipating World War II, Kaufman and Hart wrote a highly uncritical, exceptionally patriotic extravaganza. *The American Way* was extremely unlike anything Kaufman had ever done. It was not a satire, it was not a comedy, and it filled the very large stage of the Center Theatre with no less than 222 actors. Starring Fredric March and Florence Eldridge, this extraordinary production had seven stage managers, an extravagant amount of scenery, and special music composed and arranged by Oscar Levant.

Later that year, Kaufman and Hart wrote a classic American comedy, *The Man Who Came to Dinner*. This was more like the old Kaufman and Hart. It was a wild thrust at the social manners of Kaufman's old boss and close crony Aleck Woollcott. Thinly disguised, too, were Harpo Marx, Noel Coward, and a goodly sprinkling of their friends.

With *The American Way* and *The Man Who Came to Dinner* both running in the same year, *Time* magazine honored the Great Collaborator on his fiftieth birthday: on the November 20, 1939, cover of the magazine was a drawing of George S. Kaufman.

Critically, not every Kaufman comedy was considered a gem, but enough of them were embraced by the drama critics of the day for him to be considered without peer. And reflect on who was writing comedy during those years: George Abbott, Philip Barry, S. N. Behrman, Robert Benchley, Clare Boothe, Ben Hecht and Charles MacArthur, George Kelly, Ring Lardner, Howard Lindsay and Russel Crouse, Robert E. Sherwood, James Thurber, John Van Druten.

Critically, more than enough long runs made Kaufman the leader in the field of comedy in the American theatre. What do critics have to say of Kaufman's contributions in retrospect?

Brooks Atkinson: "Kaufman was one of the great writers of satirical comedy. He was certainly a great constructionist and he was a remarkable director, but I wouldn't take anything away from him as a writer of satirical comedy. When he started his particular kind of comedy, the theatre was very mushy and mawkish and artificial, and being the honest kind of person he was, I think he could not stand this kind of sentimentality. When he came into the theatre, it became very stimulating because he destroyed nonsense."

Walter Kerr: "He had essentially an analytical mind. The person who collaborates tends to be a craftsman, constructionist, analyst, critic, what have you. It seems to me that he did extraordinarily well, that he was a beautiful craftsman, that his greatest strength as a playwright was his wit."

George Oppenheimer: "He was responsible for marrying very high farce and very high comedy, and with his wit, it came out satire."

Howard Taubman: "Kaufman was a hell of a writer. There is a sense of professionalism in every play in which he was involved. His satire was sharp, keen edged. It wasn't bloody. His whole cast of mind was saturnine and sardonic, and directed that way, it did wonderful things in the theatre."

Richard Watts: "Kaufman's greatest assets as a playwright were a great technical skill, a lively, keen, creative mind, and a real love for the theatre. He brought to the theatre a tremendous vitality and inspired a brightness in other people."

As for the numbers, they line up this way—the greatest track record in the American theatre:

1918 *Among Those Present,* with Larry Evans and Walter Percival
Someone in the House, with Larry Evans and Walter Percival
1919 *Jacques Duval* (adaptation)
1921 *Dulcy,* with Marc Connelly
1922 *To the Ladies,* with Marc Connelly
The 49ers, with Marc Connelly
Merton of the Movies, with Marc Connelly

1923 *Helen of Troy, N.Y.,** with Marc Connelly
The Deep Tangled Wildwood, with Marc Connelly

1924 *Beggar on Horseback*, with Marc Connelly
Be Yourself, with Marc Connelly
Minick, with Edna Ferber

1925 *The Butter and Egg Man*
*The Cocoanuts**

1926 *The Good Fellow*, with Herman J. Mankiewicz

1927 *The Royal Family*, with Edna Ferber
*Strike Up the Band**

1928 *Animal Crackers,** with Morrie Ryskind

1929 *June Moon*, with Ring Lardner
The Channel Road, with Alexander Woollcott

1930 *Once in a Lifetime*, with Moss Hart

1931 *The Band Wagon,** with Howard Dietz
*Of Thee I Sing,** with Morrie Ryskind

1932 *Dinner at Eight*, with Edna Ferber

1933 *Let 'Em Eat Cake,** with Morrie Ryskind
The Dark Tower, with Alexander Woollcott

1934 *Merrily We Roll Along*, with Moss Hart
*Bring On the Girls,** with Morrie Ryskind

1935 *First Lady*, with Katharine Dayton

1936 *Stage Door*, with Edna Ferber
You Can't Take It With You, with Moss Hart

1937 *I'd Rather Be Right,** with Moss Hart

1938 *The Fabulous Invalid*, with Moss Hart

1939 *The American Way*, with Moss Hart
The Man Who Came to Dinner, with Moss Hart

1940 *George Washington Slept Here*, with Moss Hart

1941 *The Land Is Bright*, with Edna Ferber

1944 *The Late George Apley*, with John P. Marquand

1945 *Hollywood Pinafore** (rewrite of Gilbert and
Sullivan's operetta *Pinafore*)

* Musical.

1946 *Park Avenue,** with Nunnally Johnson
1948 *Bravo!,* with Edna Ferber
1951 *The Small Hours,* with Leueen MacGrath
1952 *Fancy Meeting You Again,* with Leueen MacGrath
1953 *The Solid Gold Cadillac,* with Howard Teichmann
1955 *Silk Stockings,** with Leueen MacGrath and Abe Burrows

Forty-five productions in thirty-seven years! Of these, twenty-seven were hits, eighteen were failures.

And this does not include the one-act plays, the published short stories and poetry, and the best sketches ever written in the history of the American revue theatre. Sketches for *The Little Show, Flying Colors, The Music Box Revues* are classics to this day. *The Still Alarm, The Pride of the Claghorns, The Great Warburton Mystery* were all written by George alone.

It is safe to state that Kaufman turned out at least four times as many plays as were produced. Some closed on the road, some closed in rehearsal, and many were thrown into the fire never to be read by more than two or three persons whose critical judgment Kaufman accepted.

It is equally safe to state that he aided and abetted more plays and playwrights than anyone can possibly estimate. Although he shunned the words "play doctor," Kaufman shuttled between New York, New Haven, Boston, Philadelphia, Atlantic City, and Washington, D.C., with such frequency he might have been a railroad conductor. In truth, as Norman Nadel, the drama critic, wrote, "Probably the most successful play doctor in modern times was George S. Kaufman." As a director or as a friend, the amount of time he spent working on shows out of town can be estimated, but not with any degree of accuracy.

That George was of enormous help to friends on the road cannot be questioned. Let Garson Kanin, one of his good friends and most illustrious followers, tell it in his own words:

* Musical.

He came down to Philadelphia where *Born Yesterday* was tried out, and he was at me to shore up a couple of weak places. I was getting very tired and George kept saying, "There's that one joke I don't like."

"I think it's all right, George," I said. "It doesn't absolutely rock them, but it's all right, it's just a piece of punctuation."

"Oh, it's not punctuation, it's just a cheap gag," George answered.

Under duress I finally said, "All right." So I cut it out. And the next afternoon we met.

"Well, what's so clever about that?" he said.

I said, "Well, you didn't like it, George. I cut it out."

He said, "That doesn't achieve anything, you need a joke there. You just need a better joke than what you had."

Now George certainly contributed some great jokes to that play, and I hoped that he would come up with one for this spot, but he didn't. He just said, "Why don't you think of something?" And just sat there and squinted and squinted and looked bilious and finally shook his head and looked out the window.

Finally, I had an idea, and I went to the mantelpiece and I wrote it out and I said, "How would this be? What if she says to him when he pays her the compliment, what if she looks at him and she says, 'Lemme ask you, are you one of these talkers, or would you be interested in a little action?'"

George squinted and he made that terrible face again and he looked a little sick and looked out of the window. So I took the paper and I was about to tear it up when he turned around and said, "That may be one of the funniest lines I've ever heard."

He didn't smile, he didn't laugh, he just appreciated it from a professional point of view.

"Do you really think we should try it, George?" I said.
"You don't have to try it," George told me. "It will work."

Those of us who worked with George would agree that there were many times when he would simply hand you a line, usually great, or an idea for a curtain or a very funny piece of business or an excellent cut. But what he did more frequently and with great regularity was to somehow dig out the best, even beyond the best, of the people with whom he was working.

When this biography was conceived, it was my firm belief that all of Kaufman's plays were dead. The years, however, have done something to shake this opinion.

Slowly, from the time of his death, Kaufman's plays have been revived, and generally with acceptance. By its very nature, comedy is much more perishable than drama. Still, with the towering exception of Eugene O'Neill, more plays by George Kaufman are revived to this day than the works of any other dramatist of his period. During the last few years, *You Can't Take It With You, Dinner at Eight*, and the musical *Sherry*, adapted from *The Man Who Came to Dinner*, have been done on Broadway. Off Broadway has brought back *The Butter and Egg Man, Beggar on Horseback, The Royal Family*, and *Of Thee I Sing*. The Arena Theatre in Washington, D.C., has done *Once in a Lifetime*. Summer and winter stock continually use Kaufman. So do amateur companies. Kaufman is being revived regularly in Stockholm, Edinburgh, London.

As Tom Prideaux wrote in *Life* magazine, "George Kaufman is now on his way to becoming a permanent treasure of our stage."

Purely American, thoroughly incisive, Kaufman used his plays to hold up a mirror to the life-styles of his generation. Whether any of these plays will continue to be performed in the future will be decided by fashion. And fashion in the theatre continually changes.

Fifty years from now Kaufman may be out of vogue. If he is, perhaps one line will be remembered that I alone am privileged to know George Kaufman wrote with absolutely nobody else. He had a darling, old character-actress complain, "The trouble with Shakespeare is that you never get to sit down unless you're a king."

Kaufman was not a king. He was a playwright, and as such, he earned enough laurels to sit back and rest on them. How long those laurels will remain fresh does not matter at present, for as the critic John Mason Brown has said of Kaufman's work, "I'd rather see a play I can laugh at tonight than one which I might possibly read fifty years from now."

5 *The Wit*

FEW AMERICANS IN THIS CENTURY ARE QUOTED AS FREQUENTLY
as George S. Kaufman. This does not mean only American
playwrights; this means Americans of every station: playwrights,
poets, plumbers, presidents, sages, scientists, supreme court jus-
tices, clergymen, comedians, characters of every cut of cloth.

Kaufman's wit has stood the test of time so well that it has
appeared and reappeared in everything from the floors of Congress and the *Congressional Record* to anthologies of quotations,
from the chatter of the columns of Broadway and Hollywood
to the correspondence of presidents of the United States, from
a hard-cover journal devoted solely to American history to the
Virginia Law Review.

His voice was softer than people expected. His accent was
more mid-western than eastern. The latter was a matter of
birth while the former was a matter of personality and choice.
People assumed that his wit would be delivered in a rasping
tone, loud enough for everyone to hear. They were pleasantly
surprised to find that he generally spoke slowly and in a voice
that was low in tone and volume. It was a voice filled with

assurance and authority—and yet a suggestion from a young man fresh out of the Yale Drama School once sent him hurrying down the aisle to change a scene that had been rehearsed for three weeks and set permanently.

His wit wasn't necessarily barbed. Often it was a mere observation or even a crack against himself. But always it was short and unerringly to the point. Garson Kanin has stated, "George S. Kaufman ranks without a peer as the wit of the American twentieth century. George's comment, George's cool-off, George's swiftness to pick up the answer was breath-taking. . . . He was taciturn. He didn't say much, but what he did say was stringent, always to the point, cutting, acid, true or true enough. Which was his great trick. His trick of wit and his trick of criticism wasn't that he found what was true, but he would find what was *true enough*."

As we have seen, Kaufman as a child could fight back only one way. Fists were out of the question. Words had to do the job for him. As he grew older, words not only earned his livelihood, they also were weapons with which he fought his way to the championship.

When he grew up, Kaufman had an extraordinary need of such defenses. He could not bear to have other people touch him, he would refuse whenever possible to shake hands, kiss good-by, touch door knobs, and he had a variety of other complexes. The result was that he left himself wide open to cutting remarks that he could either accept servilely or respond to in a manner that would leave him holding the field triumphantly.

So much of what Kaufman said was picked up by others, it is not surprising that here and there a line that in truth was not his would turn up attributed to him. A perfect example concerns the failing musical *Allah Be Praised*, which was produced by the department store heir Alfred Bloomingdale. It was in Boston, Philadelphia, some say it was in Wilmington, that George Kaufman was called in to look at the show. A look was all that was needed. "If I were you," he is claimed to have told the producer, "I'd close the show and keep the store open nights."

Good line? Indeed. Four persons told me that Kaufman said it. I am in possession of a letter from the press agent of the show who advised me as to the time and place Kaufman spoke the bon mot (11:30 to 11:45 P.M. in the bar on the first floor of the Ritz Hotel in Boston.) But the truth is that Cy Howard, a film writer and director, gave that advice to Mr. Bloomingdale in Philadelphia.

How many lines were coined by others and given to Kaufman is as difficult to guess as how many of Kaufman's lines were credited to friends and strangers.

As far as it is possible to know, the witticisms that follow in this chapter are George Kaufman's and only George Kaufman's. Still, there is that single doubt that one of them may have been uttered originally by Aristophanes, a playwright unprotected by the Dramatists Guild.

———————

In his youth, puns were still considered wit, and Kaufman made good use of them. Some are quotable and employed with regularity.

Assistant professors of history still get laughs out of unsuspecting classes by droning into their lectures one of Kaufman's greatest puns: "One man's Mede is another man's Persian."

•

Going back, as it were, to the scene of the crime, F.P.A.'s humor column "The Conning Tower"—specifically to that section labeled "The Diary of Our Own Samuel Pepys"—on Sunday, June 3, 1923, Adams wrote, ". . . so home, and Beatrice Kaufman comes to dinner, and tells me that George hath made a sentence with the word punctilious, thus: A man had two daughters, Lizzie and Tillie, and Lizzie is all right, but you have no idea how punctilious."

•

Not everything Kaufman had to say in "Pepys" was a pun. Word play was now his business, and Adams capitalized on it.

"Saturday, December 1, 1923. To an inn for luncheon, and saw G. Kaufman and I asked him when Beatrice was coming home, and he said he had a letter from her that she would be back bright and early Monday morning, but he, being conservative, would wager only that she would be early."

•

More from "Pepys."

"Tuesday, July 29, 1924. . . . to G. Kaufman's for dinner, and H. Ross says he was lying out in an orchard this afternoon and an apple hit him on the head, and the idea came to him to discover the law of gravitation, and then people would no longer have to walk upstairs as it would lead to the invention of the elevator. But George said he was lying in an orchard, too, only it was a fig orchard, and a fig hit him on the head, and that made him think of gravitation, and from thence it was only a step to the invention of Fig Newtons, an idea he is going to try to sell to some biscuit concern or other."

•

To Howard Dietz, about his new play *Between the Devil*, Kaufman said, "I understand your new play is full of single entendre."

•

Once he was asked to write the introduction to a book. It was sent to him in manuscript form, and he found it peppered with glaring mistakes in spelling.

"I'm not very good at it myself," he wrote the author, "but the first rule about spelling used to be that there is only one *z* in *is*."

•

"I don't see why you people carry on so about the income tax," a millionaire said in George's company. "I managed very well in spite of it," he continued. He then enumerated his corporate holdings in Cuba, Switzerland, and Canada. Kaufman listened long enough.

"Well, Gilbert," Kaufman observed, "you have just one advantage over the rest of us. You're a goddamn crook!"

•

"What're you doing for dinner tonight?" the publisher Herbert Bayard Swope asked George over the phone around eight-thirty one evening.

"Digesting it," Kaufman answered promptly.

•

Harpo Marx and Kaufman were lunching at the Colony restaurant. Harpo looked over the menu and was shocked at the prices: "What the hell can you get here for fifty cents?"

George told him. "A quarter."

•

Ruth Gordon described a new play to him.

"There's no scenery at all. In the first scene, I'm on the left side of the stage and the audience has to imagine I'm in a crowded restaurant. In Scene Two, I run over to the right side of the stage and the audience has to imagine I'm home in my own drawing room."

"And the second night," Kaufman said, "you'll have to imagine there's an audience out front."

•

A backer spotted him in the lobby at *Strike Up the Band* and mistook him for the composer.

"Mr. Gershwin," the backer howled, "how could you let a thing like this happen?"

"My score is perfect," George answered promptly. "The whole trouble is with Kaufman's book!"

•

In the mid-Thirties, the Averell Harrimans gave annual Thanksgiving dinners in their huge country home atop the mountain they owned. The dining room seemed to be miles from the bedrooms. One evening everyone was seated and the feast had begun when it was noticed that George was missing. A Kaufman note for the hostess arrived with the butler: "Sorry to have missed the bus for the first course. Expect to arrive in time for soup."

•

Toward the end of the Thirties, a publisher discovered the hitherto unpublished *Life of Our Lord* by Charles Dickens. Scripps-Howard bought the serial rights and ran it daily in the *World-Telegram*. For three years before this, Marc Connelly had been telling Kaufman about his alleged progress on his new play. With the appearance of the new Dickens book, Kaufman said, "Charles Dickens, dead, writes more than Marc Connelly alive."

•

When Oscar and June Levant's daughter Marcia was born on October 12, it was not only Columbus Day but also Yom Kippur that year. Kaufman wired, CALL THE BABY CHRISTOPHER KIPPER.

•

Unlikely as it may appear, he was taken one evening to Leon & Eddie's, then a nightclub on 52nd Street, where a particularly obnoxious drunk was slipped a mickey finn. As he raced for the men's room, the drunk staggered into the table at which Kaufman was sitting. Somehow, he pulled himself up and muttered, "So sorry. I must leave you here. Will you excuse me?"

"Of course," Kaufman said. "The alternative is too dreadful to contemplate."

•

At dinner one evening a self-made millionaire bragged, "I was born into this world without a single penny."

"When I was born, I owed twelve dollars," Kaufman told him.

•

At costume parties, Kaufman very much favored Abe Lincoln. A beard, a high hat, and a shawl were enough. He bore a striking resemblance to the rail-splitter.

And then actor Raymond Massey scored success after success playing Lincoln. It was with a trace of envy and a touch of pettiness that Kaufman said, "Massey won't be satisfied until he's assassinated."

•

The day the Nazis invaded Russia, the Kaufmans were luncheon guests of the Oscar Hammersteins in Bucks County.

Oscar's wife Dorothy met them at the door and, referring to the invasion, asked, "What do you think? What do you make of all this, George?"

"I think," Kaufman said, "from now on they're shooting without a script."

•

Being a professional, he disliked advice from amateurs. During a rehearsal one day, he was badgered by someone who had been brought into the theatre. Kaufman brushed the pest and his idea aside.

"Possibly you don't realize who I am," the fellow said.

"That's only half of it," Kaufman assured him.

•

Kaufman could be brusque; more proof is hardly needed here. However, he employed his wit to disentangle himself from situations or emotions he felt he could not handle. He could behave engagingly or charmingly by using just a few words. Or he could point to his own weaknesses and fears, and, if he was quick to turn a phrase at the expense of others, he never failed to include himself as a subject.

The first time Abe Burrows met Kaufman was in an Army station wagon. Mike Todd was putting on a show for the troops at Camp Shanks, and Kaufman and Burrows were being driven out there.

Kaufman was terrified of automobiles. Not only was he unable to drive but when possible preferred not to ride in one.

Burrows recollected the time as winter, the weather sleety, the West Side Highway covered with ice. Not a word was exchanged. Suddenly the George Washington Bridge loomed up ahead. The slick approaches to the towering bridge were being taken by the Army chauffeur at a more than goodly speed.

Unable to contain himself any longer, Kaufman tapped the soldier on the arm.

"Sergeant," he admonished, "don't cross that bridge till we come to it."

•

Toward the end of the war, when people were asking what would happen to the women war workers when the troops returned, he offered a solution.

"Keep the women on the job and let the men stay home and have the babies," he suggested. "All that is necessary is a certain amount of retooling."

•

"I have an idea for bipartisan legislation," he said. "It would reconcile every element of the American political scene. It's simply this. It would be called the Sexual Security Act, the point being, every time you did it the government would put one away for you until you were sixty-five. Then you could really use them."

•

Still on a political tack, he foresaw an answer to New York's traffic problem.

"Turn all the lights red," he advised, "and leave 'em that way."

•

When asked his opinion of the play *Skylark*, which starred Gertrude Lawrence, he said, "A bad play saved by a bad performance."

•

Kaufman's hypochondria was fair game even for Kaufman. An old friend recommended a physician whose knowledge of the theatre was remarkable.

"The kind of doctor I want," Kaufman said, "is one who, when he's not examining me, is home studying medicine."

•

He was on the road with a musical that should have been awarded the Purple Heart and Oak Leaf Clusters. George was ill-tempered but trying to be polite, when the leading lady swung out of the stage door after giving a wretched performance.

"How'd it go?" he asked.

"Fantastic!" the exuberant Leonora Corbett said as she swept past him. Kaufman looked at his co-author, Nunnally Johnson.

"You've heard of people living in a fool's paradise?" Kaufman inquired. "Well, Leonora has a duplex there."

•

Kaufman's timing was always perfect. Groucho speaks of it, Jack Benny speaks of it, as do others.

Leonora Corbett was the subject of a classic Kaufman line. The first time he saw her, following the end of a romantic interlude between them, an elevator door opened, and Miss Corbett emerged followed by her latest suitor. Before her stood Kaufman waiting to enter the elevator.

Without batting an artificial eyelash, she introduced the two gentlemen, adding, "Mr. So-and-So is in cotton."

Kaufman peered over the rims of his glasses at the gentleman who was in cotton, then turned his attention to Miss Corbett saying, "And them that plants it is soon forgotten."

The elevator door was still inviting. Kaufman stepped into the car, the door closed, and so did Miss Corbett's open mouth.

•

He invented the joke about the diner who at long last attracted the waiter's attention.

"What time is it, please?" the patron asked.

"I am sorry, sir," the waiter replied, "but this is not my station."

•

He also wrote, "Epitaph for a waiter: God caught his eye."

•

During the Philadelphia tryout of a musical in which he was interested, Kaufman was pessimistic about the dress rehearsal on which he worked all night. At 3:00 A.M., he entered a diner and studied the menu. He told the waiter, "I want something that will keep me awake thinking it was the food I ate and not the show I saw."

•

After a serious illness, Kaufman surprised his friends by turning up at a supper party. Harvey Breit, for many years a columnist for the New York *Times* Sunday Book Review, and recently the author of a very well accepted play, was delighted to see Kaufman.

"George, you're looking positively marvelous," Breit told him.

"I see, Harvey, that you have given up the literary world and joined the theatre," Kaufman said, "and that you now deal entirely in superlatives."

•

Moss Hart's delight in spending money never went unnoticed by Kaufman. When his collaborator bought an estate near the Kaufman place in Bucks County, rebuilt it, put in a swimming pool, and surrounded it with hundreds of freshly transplanted trees, Kaufman took note.

"This is what God could have done if He'd had money," he said.

•

"I like to be near you, Moss," he once said. "It comes under the heading of *gelt* by association."

•

While walking along Fifth Avenue with Nunnally Johnson, Kaufman saw his friend stop in front of the specialty shop of Mark Cross. Johnson looked at the wares in the window. Kaufman shook his head.

"Pay no attention to this," he said. "Moss can take you to Cartier's and get you the same thing for three times the money."

•

When Hart was considering turning the Laura Z. Hobson novel *Gentlemen's Agreement* into a film, he asked Kaufman what he thought of the book.

"I don't have to pay three fifty to find out what it feels like to be a Jew," was his answer.

•

When questioned about his flamboyant but favorite collaborator, Kaufman was asked, "Does Moss always tell the truth?"

"He does," Kaufman replied, "but I don't think he can stand a withering cross examination."

•

In fifty years as a newpaperman and a playwright, Kaufman was exposed to, and scrutinized, every form of fakery. His favorite was the confidence man who promised him that a quick investment in a gold mine would bring him untold wealth.

"You don't even have to dig for the gold," he was told. "It's just lying around."

"Hold on," Kaufman demanded. "Do you mean I'd have to stoop over and pick it up?"

———

The journalist Earl Wilson seemed to sum it up in a pair of sentences. "Kaufman," he wrote, "in a way is a policeman for America, somewhat as Will Rogers used to be. He has been blasting away at somebody or something most of his life."

The blasting, of course, was done merely with words. Words, words, words, words. They were the chisels with which George S. Kaufman carved his reputation into the granite of Manhattan and whatever makes up the rest of the world.

Oddly enough, despite all he wrote and said, he was not a talker. He was, if anything, an intense listener. What was unique about Kaufman as a wit were his great stretches of silence.

Generally, comics are compulsive. Once they get the floor, they fight furiously before giving it up. Kaufman was the direct opposite of this. He would sit and listen to those about him for half an hour or even longer. Then, when the right moment came, he would drop in a single line that would sound like a bell note in the clatter of random chatter. Or, if he did speak, it would be only a few words, just enough to set up the talk as a target. Then he would draw, aim, and fire. He would sit through an entire evening and say five sentences. Yet people would go away vowing that he was the funniest man alive.

Columnists, comedians, hosts on late-night talk shows still employ Kaufman's quips without even knowing their source.

So much of what he said has become part of the humor of America that it is innocently accepted as part of the language. The Kaufman line quoted most frequently is one that he himself disproved. He did it by writing more incisive, funnier plays than anyone in his day. Still, anthologists and high school drama coaches love to quip, "Satire is what closes on Saturday night."

6 *The Director*

By NO SMALL COINCIDENCE, IT WAS HIS WORST ENEMY WHO made George Kaufman into a stage director.

Vienna, 1900. Meyer and Esther Horowitz were blessed with a son. At the age of two, the boy emigrated with his parents to the United States. Later he did time at Yale University as a student. Finished with that, he arrived in New York City, where, in a flashing series of steps, he leaped from theatrical reporter to editor to press agent to producer, and, between his twenty-sixth and his twenty-eighth years, became known as "the boy wonder of Broadway." And that was not a phrase tagged onto him by a public relations man. In less than two years he had produced *Broadway, Coquette, The Royal Family,* and *The Front Page.* In the days when a hit was reckoned at one hundred performances, these four productions ran a total of 1,593 times.

Of course by then his name was not Horowitz but Jed Harris, and he was not Kaufman's enemy but Kaufman's friend, producer, admirer, and mentor. The animosity between the two did not come about until 1929.

In 1927 Harris presented the Kaufman-Ferber triumph *The Royal Family*. The authors were enchanted by the handsome, well-spoken producer. The brilliant and unerring selectivity of his vocabulary, the hypnotic timbre of his voice, his knowledge and easy grasp of the classics, and his positively incisive perception of current theatrical works made Jed Harris irresistible. That he was a genius among producers was never questioned. "He could do no wrong" was a phrase applied to him and completely accepted by him.

Sometime during the rehearsals and the try-outs of *The Royal Family*, Harris took an option on a play written by two Chicago newspapermen *about* two Chicago newspapermen. Ben Hecht and Charles MacArthur had come up with *The Front Page*. It was good, but in the unchallenged opinion of Harris it needed cutting and rewriting. Of equal importance was the fact that no matter how many times the play was rewritten, gangsters invariably turned up in the third act.

The best cutter and the fastest rewriter in the theatre was George Kaufman. He took care of the gangsters. Futhermore, Hecht and MacArthur were newspapermen and so was Kaufman; the three of them spoke a common language. He finally joked and cajoled them into writing a better, tighter, funnier script.

Harris then convinced him, as only Harris could, to take on the directorial assignment. According to Harris' general manager at that time, Herman Shumlin, who later became one of the theatre's most accomplished producer-directors, Kaufman had already done a few jobs of directing, but never with his name on the program. *The Front Page* was his first time out officially.

Stories of the wonderful wildness of Hecht and MacArthur persist in theatrical circles to this day. Kaufman, with his built-in sense of discipline, almost left the show. When he found them in a speakeasy, they would offer him a drink. Kaufman who took whiskey as though it were medicine managed to go through a lifetime of cocktail parties by quietly pouring his drinks into convenient receptacles. "I happen to know," he once told Ben Hecht, "that rubber plant over there has been drunk four times this week on my drinks alone."

Casting a play is one of the director's most important tasks. Kaufman the newspaperman made it his business to see almost every play that opened on Broadway. Kaufman the playwright was keenly knowledgeable as to the exact talent of almost every available actor. Kaufman the director, therefore, cast *The Front Page* almost perfectly. Osgood Perkins and Lee Tracy headed the players. They were supported by actors whose names or faces became nationally and internationally known or recognized via stage and film for thirty years: Allen Jenkins, William Foran, Tammany Young, Joseph Spurin-Calleia, Walter Baldwin, Eduardo Cianelli, Frances Fuller, George Barbier.

As the play went into rehearsal, it soon became apparent that Kaufman's casting was found lacking in a single role. George S. Kaufman had been unable to pick a good prostitute. At the end of five days, the actress, whoever she was, was fired. For a replacement he got Dorothy Stickney. Miss Stickney, who had been married just under a year to Kaufman's friend and first director, Howard Lindsay, created the role of Molly Malloy, the Clark Street tart. Her entrance line on bursting into a roomful of drinking, smoking, and classically cursing reporters was, "I've been looking for you bastards!"

Born in Dickinson, North Dakota, educated at St. Catherine's College, and married to a man who at one time had seriously considered becoming an ordained minister, Miss Stickney at first found that line definitely objectionable. After some hassling, Kaufman took the basically timid, gentle, very ladylike lady aside and explained that "I've been looking for you bastards!" was a line inserted solely for the purpose of arousing sympathy from the audience for the character she was playing. After that, he had no trouble with her.

At the beginning of his career as a stage director, one of his character traits dogged him: shyness showed all over. When he wanted to correct an actor or advise him on a piece of stage business, he was so timid that he actually handed the actor a note. He was mildly surprised to see that the actor would read the piece of paper carefully, nod his head in appreciation, and then do precisely what Kaufman had suggested.

Eventually he gave up writing notes to the cast, but for the rest of his directing days he preferred not to humiliate an actor by calling him down in front of his peers. The Kaufman technique required words whispered into the ear of the actor. What those words were remained a private matter between the player and the director.

An idea of what he might say comes from an actress who worked for him, Jean Dixon. Extremely attractive, and highly talented, Miss Dixon's sense of timing and comedy was almost equal to Kaufman's. She excelled at playing dry, wry humor; in addition she had the ability to throw away lines and take pauses in her dialogue that evoked much more laughter from the audience than anyone had a right to expect. During a rehearsal of *June Moon* she took one such pause, and Kaufman hurried up onto the stage and whispered to her, "If you were Duse, maybe you could get as far as the table with that pause, but I don't think Jean Dixon can." With that, he left the stage and continued directing from the rear of the house, where he paced endlessly, listening to words and tempo.

There were no scenes of hysteria in a Kaufman rehearsal. He was a pragmatic director. He would not leap onto the stage to show the company how the parts should be played. He would throw no tantrums, nor would he try to dig into the characterization of a role by holding forth at great length. He was a kind director, a quiet director, considerate, tactful, prompt, and one who, if he had to fire an actor, never did it in front of the company. A handwritten letter would be placed by Kaufman in the unfortunate one's mailbox backstage.

A young actress, fresh out of the American Academy of Dramatic Arts and filled with Stanislavsky's creative acting suggestions, was given a bit part in *Dinner at Eight*. As rehearsal progressed, she became increasingly involved with character interpretation and motivational responses and reactions until she was shaking with neurotic anxiety. Finally, she appealed to Kaufman. He straightened her out.

"My dear young woman, you are playing the part of a maid," he said. "You have very little dialogue. You come on in two beats, you stand for four beats, and you exit on five."

Enter on two, stand for four, exit on five. She did precisely as Kaufman had suggested, got a pair of kindly one-line mentions from two of the eight kindly drama critics in New York, and played the entire run of the show doing two, four, and exit on five.

Directing a great actress of that day, Jane Cowl, in the play *First Lady*, Kaufman allowed her to rehearse with hat, gloves, all the necessary hand props in the play. During one scene, she had a very long speech, after which she put on her hat, gloves, picked up her purse, took some props from the table, put them into the purse, and then made a grand exit.

"Miss Cowl," Kaufman asked, "wouldn't it be better if instead of saying that speech and *then* doing all that, if you did all the stage business while you were delivering the speech?"

"Oh, but that's impossible," Miss Cowl snapped.

"Why is it impossible?" Kaufman asked softly.

"It just can't be done!" the actress called out.

"Why not?" he persisted, lowering his voice as she raised hers.

"Do you want me to begin," she demanded, "and say . . ." and she started the speech, put on her hat, her gloves, picked up her purse, crossed to the table, snatched up the props, opened the purse, threw the props into it, snapped it shut, and walked off, her cheeks blazing with indignation.

She had done precisely what he had asked.

When she came onto the stage again, Kaufman just looked at her and murmured, "My mistake."

During the run of the play Miss Cowl was the recipient of a Kaufman telegram. After an absence of several weeks, he returned one night and found that Jane Cowl, a playwright herself, had added scores of new lines for her own role. Off shot the telegram: DEAR MISS COWL. YOUR PERFORMANCE IS BETTER THAN EVER. DELIGHTED I CANNOT SAY AS MUCH FOR YOUR LINES.

At this writing, Walter Matthau is one of the most successful leading men in Hollywood. Kaufman was the first to recognize his brilliant ability to play comedy. Prior to his being hired by Kaufman, Matthau appeared as a candle bearer, a fourth Venetian guard, and was an understudy as a foreign correspondent. In 1952 when Kaufman engaged him, he taught him a lesson of no small importance to an actor of comedy.

During a rehearsal one afternoon, Matthau began to experiment with a gesture or two. Kaufman said nothing at the end of the day, so the next morning, Matthau enlarged and developed his series of elaborate gestures. After six days, he was quite satisfied with himself and what he had created. Approaching the director, he proudly asked, "Mr. Kaufman, what do you think of the business I worked out for myself?"

"Mr. Matthau," said Kaufman, quietly but firmly, "not much."

Matthau dropped every gesture the next morning. Kaufman had taught him an essential of comedy: it is better to underplay than overplay.

He sought out actors who could play comedy, actors who were funny even before they read a line; those few who could get laughs without lines he cherished and used whenever he could.

The other side of Kaufman the director showed a man who was impatient with inexperienced actors, with actors whose vanities outweighed their talents. He never called members of the cast by their first names during rehearsals. No matter how well he knew them, it was always Miss, Mrs., or Mr. And he expected the same from them. In short, Kaufman as a director was the absolute essence of a civilized taskmaster.

Edna Ferber's niece Janet Fox had the rule against inexperienced actors bent in her favor by her aunt. After a week, Kaufman called her over to the side and mumbled, "You know, you're pretty good for a niece."

In directing *My Sister Eileen*, Kaufman proved that he knew how to handle both gifted professional and rank amateur. For the role of Ruth, co-author Jerome Chodorov recommended Shirley Booth. His collaborator, Joseph Fields, looked at him askance when Miss Booth walked onto the stage. Picking up the script, Miss Booth read two lines, and Kaufman turned to the authors and asserted, "That's it." He never gave her any direction, he never talked about it because *he* knew that *she* knew her business. Her instinct for a line was perfect. And his instinct wisely was not to interfere.

On the other hand, Jo Ann Sayers, who was cast as Eileen, had never acted on a stage before except at Washington State College. She was lovely but, like most novices, she didn't know what to do with herself physically on a stage.

"That's where George came in," Chodorov stated. "He started to give her props. He had this girl so busy, by the end of a two-hour performance she had more work than a general housekeeper could have done in a week. He had her opening ironing boards, taking out the iron, ironing clothes, lifting things, carrying things, cooking, cleaning; she was so damn busy all night long, and she never realized what it was. That was a marvelous way of making an amateur look professional. She had all the personal qualities for the part, a wonderful, fresh innocence, but she really didn't know what to do with her hands or her body. George was the one who solved it."

Saint Subber, who today is the most successful producer of comedies in the United States, recalled, "I used to watch George direct with his back to the audience, and his great thing was timing. He would keep clicking his fingers. Pace, tempo, were the important things. He could choreograph direction with the best of them, but this did not interest him as much as the way the lines were read. Actors adored working with George. He never gave readings. He was quick. He knew what he wanted. He was disciplined. There was a relaxed blue-room quality about his rehearsals: all right, ladies and gentlemen, now it's time for work. And they would work. Now it's time for play, and there would be laughs, lots of laughs."

While Kaufman the director admittedly pumped for laughter, he was the first to condemn what he considered weakness or staleness.

"These people are paying six-sixty," he said to one writer. "At least give them a new joke."

•

A stage doorman, evidently new to the legitimate theatre, failed to recognize Kaufman as he walked into the semidarkness of a rehearsal theatre.

"I beg your pardon, sir," he asked, "are you with the show?"

"Let's put it this way," Kaufman said, "I'm not against it."

•

In Boston, he was directing a musical that wasn't going to make it. Word was out on it and, to make matters worse, there was a heat wave. Approaching the box office, he asked how much advance the show had.

"Nothing, Mr. Kaufman," the treasurer told him. "About eighty dollars."

Kaufman looked at Max Gordon's nephew, Cliff Heyman.

"Kid," he reflected, "I've been in this business for thirty years and this is the first time the temperature has been higher than the advance."

Craftsmanship, high polish, and a preference for sparseness were the hallmarks of Kaufman's directorial technique. If an actor could cross the stage in four steps instead of fourteen, Kaufman would insist on the smaller number. If a laugh could be landed by the flick of a finger rather than a somersault, Kaufman's direction would demand the flicking finger.

There are three exceptions to this and their names are the Marx Brothers. With those zanies, Kaufman was never really in command as a director. At their first meal together, Harpo ordered chicken pie. When it was served, Harpo touched it with his fork and it flew into the air, across the table, and landed on Kaufman's new blue serge trousers. It was an accident, of course, but nothing could convince Kaufman thereafter that the Marx Brothers were manageable. His attitude toward them, to say the very least, was friendly but apprehensive.

Kaufman, the director-as-artist, worked swiftly, quietly, politely, and with a minimum of fuss. First things first. His casts would memorize their lines, he would block out their scenes, his stage managers would indicate with chalk or tape on the floor where the entrances and exits would be in the acts and where the furniture and other props would be, and then would come the real work of honing the play to its finest edge.

With Kaufman it was never the deep psychoanalytic motivational adjustment of the actor as propounded by the Russian school. Rather, it was the Shakespearean concept of the play as the prime factor in the theatre. And what made the play? The dialogue as it reached the ears of the audience.

In this day of the Freud-Stanislavsky-Actors Studio axis, it borders on heresy to write that frames of reference, personality accommodations, character diagnoses had no place in his technique. His criteria was less oblique, less mystical, less penetrating, perhaps, but certainly more exacting. Does a scene play or doesn't it? If it doesn't, cut it. If it does, improve on it.

To an actor who had received specific instructions during rehearsal and kept coming to him for more, Kaufman finally said, "That will do until the audience tells you different."

In *Once in a Lifetime,* the first of the Moss Hart collaborations, Kaufman wore more hats than anyone since George M. Cohan. He was co-author, co-producer, director, and an actor in the play. The energy he displayed dazzled Hart.

Following the Philadelphia opening, Hart recollected, "We never saw the dawn. Nor the day, nor the night, either. For in the next six days, I never left my room at the hotel. Mr. Kaufman had to leave because he was acting in a play, but his schedule—and I still cannot realize how he managed to do it—ran something like this: He returned from the theatre at eleven-thirty. We worked steadily through the night until ten o'clock the next morning. He would then leave to put the new stuff into rehearsal and rehearse until two. Then, while the actors learned the new lines for the evening's performance, he would return to my room at the hotel and work until eight-thirty; then, back to the theatre for the performance; then, back to my room again to work all night until ten o'clock the next morning . . . I may add, resentfully, that he seemed to blossom through all this; that his eyes sparkled with an unwonted brightness; that his hand holding a pencil was like a surgeon's holding a scalpel."

Arthur Schwartz, the composer, recalled one of the few instances when Kaufman lost his temper. During a rehearsal of *The Bandwagon,* Fred Astaire danced and accompanied himself on an accordion in one number. At the end of the number, the orchestra came up with a strong finish. "George was wild with rage because he couldn't hear the words," Schwartz said. All present hustled George out of the theatre, the orchestra stayed as it was, so did the number, and so did Fred Astaire. After that, they simply didn't rehearse the orchestra when George was around.

When he and Ryskind finished *Of Thee I Sing,* Kaufman declared, "Morrie, you lose the tone of the show if you don't direct it."

His casting of Victor Moore as the helpless, bumbling, con-stantly-at-a-loss-for-words-and-ideas vice president of the United States was considered the height of casting perfection. Kaufman's weakness was that he was never able to judge sex appeal in men. However, he was aware of this and he knew how to compensate for it. He always employed the instincts of women. Casting for the president, he asked Ryskind's wife if she would be kind enough to go over to the Palace Theatre. She did, and she found William Gaxton most appealing. As a result, Gaxton won the nomination and the job.

It was during the run of that musical that Kaufman sent his famous telegram to a "scenery-chewing" Gaxton: I AM WATCH-ING YOUR PERFORMANCE FROM THE REAR OF THE HOUSE. WISH YOU WERE HERE.

The composer of *Of Thee I Sing,* George Gershwin, was fond of sneaking friends galore into rehearsals. Kaufman hated having people watch him direct. At the end of one session, Kaufman announced, "This show is going to be a terrible flop."

"How can you say that?" Gershwin asked.

"The balcony was only half filled today."

This was the same George Gershwin who loved going to parties and playing the entire score of his musical for the guests.

"If you play that score one more time before we open," Kaufman warned, "people are going to think we're doing a revival."

Kaufman was the man who perfected the laugh line at the act curtain. He advanced this theory of arranging the script so that whenever a scene ended, it ended with a laugh. From there it was a natural step to have each actor exit on a laugh. He would work for days preparing actors to get off with entertaining lines.

The Doughgirls was a comedy that Joe Fields wrote and Kaufman directed. From the time he accepted the play, through-out the rewriting period, and on into rehearsals, Kaufman be-deviled Fields.

"These exits have got to be brighter, Joe," he said. "You've got to be funnier, better."

Fields did his best, but Kaufman kept after him.

"Those actors have got to get off with bigger laughs, Joe."

One day, during a break in rehearsals, an old, bedraggled Shubert cleaning woman, her mop in one hand, her pail in the other, somehow got onto the set and slowly crossed from one side of the stage to the other, disappearing quietly into the wings.

"Jesus, George," Joe Fields whispered, "she got off without a laugh."

George didn't bring up the subject of exits again. At least, not *that* day.

As the interpretive artist functioning between the author and the actor, he was not at all interested in explaining the play. He felt there was a certain way the play should go. Specifically, it should go by the words the author wrote. The actors should be moved in a way that looked simple but wouldn't knock each other over.

He used phrases such as, "I would do that a little more lightly." Or, "I would hit that a bit harder."

Some actors understood him, some didn't.

He would say, "Look, I don't run an acting school," im-plying, "I'm a director, I did my job; the actor's an actor, let him do his job."

In the midst of a rehearsal, an actress once called out to him, "How can I do this with all these interruptions?"

"Don't you know what those interruptions are?" Kaufman asked. "Other actors reading their lines!"

As a director, George was one of Broadway's fiercest monitors, and he always dropped in on his plays to police them. He was irritated one evening to find the actors engaging in assorted misbehaviors. He sent the collective cast a telegram that read: I WAS HERE TONIGHT. WHERE WERE YOU?

Another time, he dropped in unexpectedly during the run of a play. When the curtain came down, the cast found a note from Kaufman: "11 A.M. rehearsal tomorrow to remove all improvements to the play put in since the last rehearsal."

As a technician, he was a master. In *George Washington Slept Here* there was an actress who had no lines at all. A group of men are standing in a room talking to each other. Suddenly, the girl enters wearing a picture hat and bathing suit. Very slowly, she climbs eight steps, turns the corner, and exits. Whereupon the conversation resumes. As it does, the audience laughs hilariously.

Alexander King said later that the actress complained to him that when the show toured on the road her part had been cut.

"You had no part in it," King told her. But she said that for touring they only wanted to carry four stairs instead of eight, thus depriving her of that last wiggle.

"So you see," King concluded, "you can complain even about roles that don't exist. And Kaufman's touch was fabulous, not only in such trivia but also in larger matters. Kaufman had an absolutely cast-iron notion of what a play could endure, what it could carry—as if it were a bridge—and that's what made him the greatest director of comedy in our lifetime." Eight steps, wiggle, turn, exit, start up the men, and then wait for the laughter.

The drama critic John Mason Brown showed just how much he *did* solve it when he wrote, "Both in the writing and in the production the Kaufman touch is upon every happy moment of

My Sister Eileen. What the Midas touch was worth in gold, the Kaufman touch is worth in laughter. . . . Genius is the only appropriate term to apply to him when it comes to suggesting the consummate skill of his showmanship. . . . For the moments he fills with gaiety—the Kaufman moments—when nonsense is so supreme that life comes to a temporary halt and the ridiculous and the sublime seem near to being one, are experiences to be treasured. . . . With comedy—his kind of comedy—his is without peer."

Feuer and Martin who were to produce *Guys and Dolls,* came to Kaufman with the beginnings of Abe Burrows' script.

Kaufman read it carefully, shook his head, and said, "Abe can get closer to the flavor than that."

Positively elated that Kaufman would even consider directing the musical, Burrows scrapped the four scenes he had written and started afresh. Hear Burrows on Kaufman:

I had a rule with Kaufman. I told my wife, "Look, this is my first show. I'm going to do exactly everything this man tells me because this guy does the kind of theatre I understand." And I did. From the moment he started the show, I did exactly what he told me to do. He and I never had a single argument in connection with the show. The only time we differed one or two moments was when the matter of tenderness on the stage would come up.

George loathed love scenes of any kind. First of all, love scenes are kind of dull on the stage, and George's adjustment to life was a joke. I felt a little tenderness for these raucous guys and gunmen and gamblers, and he finally gave me my way. But if he told me a thing should be cut, I'd cut it. There were moments where George would cut very deeply to see what the thing had, and then he'd say, "Perhaps we cut a bit too deeply, Abe."

143

And I'd say, "Yes, sir," but it always went back if it was really needed. So I listened to him, and out it came with that kind of spare, sparse feeling he had about writing. That's something I really learned from him.

I finished most of the first draft and then he asked me to come to Bucks County. When you worked with George in Bucks County, it was literally like Nicholas Nickelby or Oliver Twist. Because there I was in that little room, his study—where he kept all his awards, the Pulitzer Prizes and everything were there—and the room was under the eaves, so it was kind of hot, and I was working. I remember one day I was rewriting, and people were all talking merrily on the terrace and the maid comes out and says, "Lunch," and I hear my wife Carin say, "Where's Abe?" And George says, "Oh, Abe will have lunch in his room." He didn't ask me, but at that moment, another maid entered with a tray and I ate up there alone.

One time in the middle of *Guys and Dolls* he bawled me out, really cut me up. That's right. This was while we were doing the final polish before going in, and George was sitting with me on that and guiding me through every line. We were to meet at eleven and I said, "George, I might be a little late. Leonard Lyons' oldest son is being bar mitzvahed and it's at the temple and I promised I'd go." He kind of grumbled and I said, "Well, it's Leonard's first born. I've known the kid and I said I'd go." So I did.

I went to the temple and the rabbi spoke. First he looked around and he saw an audience filled with people like Oscar Hammerstein and Albert Lasker and Barney Baruch. So he decided this was a big chance, and he talked and talked. Halfway through the speech, Molnar turned to me and said, "This is a very long rabbi. If he talks ten minutes more he can bar mitzvah Warren." That's Leonard's second son.

So I didn't get to George's until twelve-thirty, and he was livid. But he wasn't angry with me for keeping him waiting. No. He said to me, "How can you be such an amateur?"

"Look," I said, "it's a bar mitzvah, you know . . ."

"You're an amateur! How can you waste your strength on foolishness?"

At first I didn't know what he was talking about. My strength didn't feel wasted. He couldn't stand it. Anything that took away from your work was sinful. Leading a social life was being an amateur to George. Eventually I got the idea, and we went to work.

With Kaufman in charge of a production, discipline in the theatre was an accepted fact. I mean nobody did what Kaufman didn't want them to do. At least, not for long.

Old Pat Rooney used to drive him crazy with the kind of laugh that he did. George loathed laughter on the stage. He used to quote Howard Lindsay: "It saves the audience the trouble." And until he got old Pat to give up that laugh, he was pretty annoyed.

He got annoyed another time, I remember. The script was his Bible and the author was to be protected. An actor named Tom Pedi added a couple of lines, and right in the middle of rehearsal I heard George call out, "Mr. Burrows!" I knew that "Mr. Burrows" meant trouble, so I hurried down the aisle toward him.

"Mr. Burrows," he said when I got to him, "would you consider giving Mr. Pedi credit as co-author?" It got very quiet, and after that Pedi never did it again.

Then, I remember George making a very brief little speech to the actors before they started rehearsing on the day of the opening. He told me he felt they should always rehearse, because they get nervous opening night and working is good for them. I've always followed that in shows

I've directed myself in the years afterward, and frankly what I say today is mostly what George said to the cast of *Guys and Dolls*.

He said, "These are a bunch of smart bastards out here tonight. This first-night audience is the smartest bunch of bastards you'll ever encounter. At least, they try to be smart. They'll try to beat you to every joke you say. And you've got to be ahead of them. You can't slow up on them." And then his final thing was, "If I don't come back to see you tonight, it's because I don't like crowds."

And I remembered. I listened. Boy, I was aglow. I was like nothing for my first show! And then the show opened, big success, and about eight weeks later I remember he called me and said, "We're rehearsing tomorrow."

"Rehearsing?" I said. "I thought we were all done. What do you mean rehearsing?"

He said, "Oh, no, it's time for a little rehearsal, and we can use a few new jokes."

So I wrote. He made me write five or six new things that hadn't really been worked out, and I did. And that was *Guys and Dolls*. And George.

In addition to casting and moving the actors about the stage, a director's responsibility includes that art form called stage design. The stage settings, the colors, the lights, the costumes are executed by others, but always under the authority of the director. Kaufman joined forces with a host of designers during the years he worked in the theatre. Two of the best are Jo Mielziner and Donald Oenslager. Each has a slightly different view of Kaufman the director.

"He worried me because his faced looked so worried," Mielziner said, "until I realized that it was just an exterior. In a way he kept me at arm's length, and yet once in a while there'd be a friendly flash of appreciation. He told me quite frankly, 'I have no visual sense.' Then he smiled and said, 'You don't mind if I bring in somebody who's gonna be my eyes?' And sure enough, the next day he brought some very charming lady, and fortunately she expressed a favorable opinion. He never would trust his own eyes."

The show Mielziner was discussing was *Of Thee I Sing*. However, he saw Kaufman when times weren't so good, too, when the notices were bad or the line at the box office just wasn't there or the star was ailing. "But I never heard him complain about the actors or the weather or the Jewish holidays or anything else."

Contradicting Mielziner slightly was Donald Oenslager. "George always had an incredible intuition or a feeling of the visual theatre. I'll always remember *Of Mice and Men*. He would say, 'Don, we want the feeling of all these people in this strange place, these people who wandered around, who were out on their farms, and it's all got to be very earthy. And yet, while they are just shacks, don't you think it can be beautiful, too?'

"The set had to move very swiftly and very easily. George was never concerned with how things moved unless they made noises. And if anything made a noise, it nearly killed him because he was so attuned to the sounds. About the barn scene, which was the final scene, George said, 'This must have a poetic quality to it.'

"I was always amazed that George could work with a musical and work with the subtlest, gayest comedy, and work with a drama like *Of Mice and Men*—and approach them all from a totally different point of view."

He was able to make these transitions not only because of who and what he was but also because of where he was working. An empty theatre had a tranquilizing and joyous effect on Kaufman. The man who was cross or silent or angry changed the moment he entered a playhouse. This was *his* ground, *his* workshop, *his* world. He functioned so easily and so well within the four walls of those high-ceilinged, musty, dark, unheated buildings that even Woollcott observed George was an entirely different person inside a theatre.

As Oenslager pointed out, Kaufman did not devote himself exclusively to musicals, or even to comedy. *Of Mice and Men* represents one of his finest jobs in guiding a play from page to stage.

He met its author, John Steinbeck, winner of the Pulitzer Prize, the Nobel Prize, and other certifications of literary genius, in the lounge of the Music Box Theatre. Both men found difficulty in speaking. Inhibition, a sense of inferiority on Kaufman's part in working with a man of Steinbeck's caliber, an identical feeling on Steinbeck's part concerning Kaufman, all were overcome when Kaufman started to lay out Steinbeck's novel as a play for Steinbeck to write.

After a series of meetings Steinbeck retired to his agent's farm in Connecticut and wrote a draft of the play. The rewrites were done at the Kaufman place in Bucks County.

Here is Steinbeck on Kaufman: "He was honest. He was easy to work with if you don't make 'easy' 'permissive.' And he was tactful. He could make you feel right when you were wrong. . . . George was the man with the most sharpness in the theatre. He made it very easy for me. I didn't realize that little things in writing made such a difference, and George taught it to me for the first time in my life. I couldn't have done *Of Mice and Men* without him."

Steinbeck said that in his opinion Kaufman was an important man in American letters. He said that because of the nature of the theatre, plays dating themselves as rapidly as they do, there was a tendency for many people to gloss over Kaufman. But, in truth, he believed Kaufman was a giant not only in the field of the theatre, but all the way around—as a man of letters of his day and as a contribution to American culture.

Steinbeck said that of all the men he had met "in terms

of working on typewriters," it was Kaufman who impressed him most.

Impressed, too, was the most influential drama critic America had yet seen. Brooks Atkinson wrote in the Sunday *Times*:

> After speaking contemptuously of the commercial theatre on many occasions, this column is prepared to eat its words this morning. *Of Mice and Men* is the quintessence of commercial theatre and it is also a masterpiece. . . . What was in the book is now to be seen and heard on the stage, admirably vitalized in the patient and subdued acting of Broderick Crawford, Wallace Ford and John F. Hamilton and in the selfless direction of Mr. Kaufman. . . .
>
> Although Mr. Kaufman is celebrated for his wit and his craftsmanlike facility in stage direction, admit *Of Mice and Men* as evidence of the fact that he can also enter into the spirit of a fine play and give it the most humble sort of expression. Apart from the casting, the performance is meticulously and affectionately modulated; the silences are as eloquent as anything Mr. Steinbeck has said in the play. . . . It is seldom that distinctive acting and individual voices merge so quietly into a whole.

Shortly after the play opened in New York in November 1937, John Steinbeck—from his home in California, where he was at work on a novel to be called *The Grapes of Wrath*—sat down and in his own hand wrote on lined paper the following letter to George Kaufman.

Los Gatos

Dear George:

As the reviews come in it becomes more and more apparent that you have done a great job. I knew you would of course but there is a curious gap between the thing in your head and the thing set down and you've jumped that gap. It's a strange kind of humbling luck we have. Carol and I have talked of it a number of times. That we—obscure people out of a place no óne ever heard of, should have our first play directed and produced by the greatest director of our time—will not bear too close inspection for fear we may catch the gods of fortune at work and catching them, anger them so they hate us. Already I have made propitiation—thrown my dear ring in the sea and I hope no big fish brings it back to me.*

To say thank you is ridiculous for you can't thank a man for good work any more than you can thank him for being himself. But one can be very glad he is himself and that is what we are—very glad that you are George Kaufman.

It doesn't matter a damn whether this show runs a long time. It came to life for one night anyway, and really to life and that's more than any one has any right to hope.

Sometimes in working—the people in my head become much more real than I am. I have had letters. It seems that for two hours you made your play far more real than its audience so that Mr. Black's loss in the market, and Mrs. Klick's hatred of the Vanderbilts disappeared from them and only the play existed. I wish I could transpose into some mathematical equation, my feeling, so that it might be a communication unmistakable and unchanging.

And that's all.

John

Kaufman was pleased with Steinbeck's letter, and cherished it. But he failed to understand why the author never came to see a performance of the play. He was annoyed when Steinbeck didn't come to the opening, and irritated when he didn't hear from Steinbeck when the play was chosen Best Play of the Year by the Drama Critics' Circle. This was behavior Kaufman

---

* See Herodotus, *The Histories*, Book Three.

simply could not comprehend. After *Of Mice and Men* had played 207 performances on Broadway, after it had toured throughout the United States and Steinbeck still never took the time to see it, Kaufman became furious. For years thereafter he decided never to exchange another word with him. Finally, it was in "21" that Steinbeck faced up to Kaufman.

"George, you haven't spoken to me in twelve years," the novelist said.

"Then it's about time," Kaufman answered. "How about dinner next Tuesday?"

From then on, they saw each other regularly.

Rather than read the opinions of others, examine the list of plays directed by George Kaufman. In themselves, they provide comment of their own.

1928 *The Front Page,* by Ben Hecht and Charles Mac-Arthur

1929 *June Moon,* by Ring Lardner and George S. Kaufman

1930 *Joseph,* by Bertram Bloch
Once in a Lifetime, by Moss Hart and George S. Kaufman

1931 *Of Thee I Sing,** by George S. Kaufman and Morrie Ryskind

1932 *Here Today,* by George Oppenheimer
Dinner at Eight, by George S. Kaufman and Edna Ferber

1933 *Let 'Em Eat Cake,** by George S. Kaufman and Morrie Ryskind
The Dark Tower, by Alexander Woollcott and George S. Kaufman

1934 *Merrily We Roll Along,* by George S. Kaufman and Moss Hart

* Musical.

*Bring On the Girls,** by George S. Kaufman and Morrie Ryskind

1935 *First Lady,* by Katharine Dayton and George S. Kaufman

1936 *Stage Door,* by George S. Kaufman and Edna Ferber
You Can't Take It With You, by Moss Hart and George S. Kaufman

1937 *Of Mice and Men,* by John Steinbeck
*I'd Rather Be Right,** by George S. Kaufman and Moss Hart

1938 *The Fabulous Invalid,* by George S. Kaufman and Moss Hart

1939 *The American Way,* by George S. Kaufman and Moss Hart
The Man Who Came to Dinner, by George S. Kaufman and Moss Hart

1940 *George Washington Slept Here,* by George S. Kaufman and Moss Hart
My Sister Eileen, by Jerome Chodorov and Joseph Fields

1941 *Mr. Big,* by Arthur Sheekman and Margaret Shane
The Land Is Bright, by George S. Kaufman and Edna Ferber

1943 *The Naked Genius,* by Gypsy Rose Lee

1944 *Over Twenty-One,* by Ruth Gordon
While the Sun Shines, by Terence Rattigan
The Late George Apley, by John P. Marquand and George S. Kaufman

1945 *Hollywood Pinafore,** by George S. Kaufman
The Next Half Hour, by Mary Chase

1946 *Park Avenue,** by Nunnally Johnson and George S. Kaufman

* Musical.

1948   *Town House,* by Gertrude Tonkonogy (from the short stories of John Cheever)

       Bravo!, by George S. Kaufman and Edna Ferber

1949   *Metropole,* by William Walden

1950   *The Enchanted,* by Jean Giraudoux (adapted by Maurice Valency)

       *Guys and Dolls,** by Abe Burrows and Jo Swerling (from the stories by Damon Runyon)

1951   *The Small Hours,* by George S. Kaufman and Leueen MacGrath

1952   *Fancy Meeting You Again,* by George S. Kaufman and Leueen MacGrath

1953   *The Solid Gold Cadillac,* by Howard Teichmann and George S. Kaufman

1955   *Silk Stockings,** by George S. Kaufman, Leueen Mac-Grath, and Abe Burrows

1957   *Romanoff and Juliet,* by Peter Ustinov

The last two productions were not directed in the manner to which Kaufman had been accustomed. The acriminious battle of *Silk Stockings* will be discussed in a later chapter.

As for *Romanoff and Juliet,* it was produced by David Merrick, presently the premier producer of legitimate theatre in the United States. For years Merrick had tried to tempt Kaufman to direct a play. "He was an absolute hero of mine," Merrick said. At last, with *Romanoff and Juliet,* an English comedy written by and starring Peter Ustinov, Merrick got what he wanted.

John Steinbeck had said, "I got George Kaufman at his prime when he was still operating scared, so I got the best of him." Merrick got him at the very end when Kaufman was sick and weak and not at all the man of whom Merrick had dreamed.

"He was totally without energy," Merrick observed. His contributions to the play were minimal. In fact, conditions reached

* Musical.

the point where Ustinov would walk down from the stage onto the orchestra floor, seat himself alongside Kaufman, and direct the play with him. Why Kaufman accepted what in former days he would have considered an outrageous insult may be credited to one of the few remaining emotions he still felt in the theatre: fear. He was afraid to let go. He was afraid that without the theatre he would cease to exist. As a result, he said nothing and accepted his lot, painful as it was.

During the last week of out-of-town tryout, Ustinov decided that what was wrong with the play was the ingenue. Each day a new girl was sent to Philadelphia from New York. Each evening she would go on. At the end of each performance Ustinov would ask for and receive her dismissal. At the end of the week George Kaufman, accompanied by David Merrick, entered Peter Ustinov's dressing room. Once there, he made "a fervent impassioned plea" to stop ruining the morale of the company by changing actresses nightly. He may have been old and long past the top of his prime as a director, but in the theatre he still knew right from catastrophe.

Having made his speech, Kaufman limped out. Ustinov looked up from his dressing table at Merrick and said: "I feel as if the Brontosaurus at the museum has just come to life and started to speak."

The differences between Kaufman and Ustinov were large ones. Ustinov had written, directed, and starred his play into a hit in London. Here now was this elderly American who was to have rewritten the play for the States and who proved incapable of rewriting or directing. The battle between youth and old age in the theatre is no different from anywhere else.

David Merrick's great contribution to the American theatre cannot be disputed. His list of credits is long, successful, and distinguished. But nothing he has done seems more honorable than his remark to Peter Ustinov when the question arose of replacing Kaufman as the director. "I would rather have a flop,"

Merrick said, "than fire George Kaufman at this stage of his life and career."

To Mr. Ustinov's credit must go the fact that he agreed with Mr. Merrick, and the last play bearing George Kaufman's name as director came into New York and ran a year.

Kaufman's own opinion of stage direction was summed up neatly in a note he wrote for John Gassner's book, *Producing the Play*.

What Is Direction, Anyhow?

Some years ago a young friend of mine, after a considerable apprenticeship in the theatre, finally directed his first New York production. The play was a failure, and that was that. No one mentioned the direction.

A few months later he directed another play. Again it was a failure, and again nothing was said about direction. Then came a success. It was a good resounding success with two popular stars in it, and the reviewers were unanimous about the direction. They said it was wonderful.

There followed three more failures—not a word, of course, about direction. Then came another success, and this time the critics went to town. It was absolutely the best direction of the season.

Now I am not aiming any shafts at the critics—that is not my point. I simply feel that there is a natural tendency to confuse the direction and the script. Good plays have a way of being well directed. I am not sure that there are three people in the land who can sit in front of a play and tell you definitely just what is direction and what is the play itself, and what is the performance. But everybody tries.

My own opinion—and I hope it will go no further or I shall certainly lose out on some jobs—is that the whole business of direction is overrated. I am not so fatheaded as to claim that it doesn't matter at all, mind you. Certainly if you put a theatrical ignoramus in charge of a fine play he will probably make a mess of it. But if a director has a competent sense of theatre and a bit of an ear he will turn out a success when the play is good and a failure when the play isn't, year in and year out.

Personally I am always a little suspicious when the director is too highly praised. A play is supposed to simulate life, and the best direction is that which is so effortless and natural that it simply isn't noticed at all. Once it begins to call attention to itself, something is wrong.

More economically and concisely, he wrapped up his idea of stage direction for Lynn Fontanne when she telephoned him one day, asking if a certain young man was a good director or not. In typical Kaufman fashion he said, "He's a good director when he has a good play. When he has a bad play, he's a bad director."

Finally, a pair of brief observations from the man who urged George Kaufman to become a stage director.

"I am really a confirmed amateur in the theatre," said Jed Harris. "But Kaufman, Kaufman was the pro."

7 One Seat in off the Aisle

How could a man who wrote so many plays, directed so many theatrical ventures, dealt so many hands of poker and bridge, went to so many luncheons and dinner parties, attended so many rehearsals and opening nights still have so much time for so many women?

The fact is: Kaufman never mentioned his affairs. But the women he knew—they were something else again. How eager most of them were to talk about their experiences with him! Most of them spoke with a candor that verged on braggadocio. Some of them spoke with their current husbands sitting in the room. A few were more modest. One lady offered to talk freely of her affair with Kaufman, and the next day her husband telephoned to explain that his wife was merely "a kid" at the time and could the story be deleted?

Verification may be found in the recorded tapes, photostated letters, and newspaper stories. Documentation is easy. Credulity is not. Here, however, is the carefully sifted truth.

As her best friend has testified, in the months following the stillborn death of her child, Beatrice Kaufman, finding no expression of physical love from her husband, began having affairs with other men on her own social level. George, lacking her confidence perhaps, turned to another sort of woman. The same George Kaufman who could not cast the prostitute properly in *The Front Page* proved more adept in his own life.

In the second or third year of his marriage, he opened a charge account with Polly Adler, the literary madame whose house was not a home. He never visited that place, preferring or insisting that the young women selected to give him pleasure for the evening meet him on Central Park West under a street lamp between 73rd and 74th Streets at an hour specified by him. Promptly, at the agreed-upon time, Kaufman would approach the prostitute, attempt to make her acquaintance, succeed, invite her to a small apartment that he kept on 73rd Street, attempt to seduce her, succeed, promise to meet her again, and politely show her out of the apartment. Romance, apparently, was the key to the scene. Nothing as sordid as money passed between them. Instead, at the end of the month a bill would be rendered and Kaufman would pay it.

A bit unusual, perhaps even bizarre, but nothing to indicate to Kaufman or to anyone else that within fifteen years he would become an internationally known lover whose name would be on the first page of almost every newspaper in the United States and Europe—not as George S. Kaufman the drama editor of the New York *Times*, not as the eminently successful playwright and director, but as the sex symbol of the Thirties.

To those who knew him best, his doctors, Kaufman was a man who could never satisfy himself either in work or in sex. Frequently, he employed one as a substitute for the other. It is of no small importance that he was compulsive in both. Childhood guilt, anxiety, and hostility clung to him throughout his life. That his brother was dead and that he was alive; that he was small and weak and that his father was strong and big;

that his mother was beautiful and his sisters were pretty and, in the case of Ruth, talented; all this while he thought of himself as unimportant, helpless, and ugly—these were the roots of his drive in a battle he could never win but never stopped fighting. Perfection was what he demanded of himself; when he found it unobtainable he was left feeling unfulfilled. No matter how good a play he wrote, the next one had to be better. No matter who the woman was tonight, tomorrow she had to be different.

It is impossible to select the precise moment when Kaufman realized that chorus girls in the Twenties went to bed with authors and directors almost as easily as ladies who were paid to do it.

A quaint custom of that day in the theatre was for the chorus to be allowed to sit in the seats of the orchestra floor during rehearsals. Those girls who were available for dinner or more made sure to place themselves one seat in off the aisle. That was the signal: one seat in off the aisle. An author or a director wishing to make conversation or more, simply slipped into the aisle seat. It was as easy as that.

When he wasn't walking around in the back of the house snapping his fingers to pick up the tempo of the dialogue, or leaping onto the stage and whispering words of advice to actors, Kaufman learned about that empty aisle seat. From that time forward, business slumped for the pros and picked up sharply for the amateurs.

Many former chorus girls connected with Kaufman musicals tell of meeting him in precisely that manner. Many of them tell convincing stories of no action whatever from him.

William Frank, Kaufman's boyhood friend from Pittsburgh, remembered clearly the following story: "Mildred Green was in the back row of a Kaufman musical and thought nobody was noticing her. They were out of town—as I remember, Asbury Park. After the performance, she dressed very leisurely,

159

and she was late getting out. As she moved through the dark alley of the theatre, a gentleman stepped up to her and said, 'Millie, let's go have a drink.' That was George. It was his show. And while they had that drink he said he was very much attracted to her, and he thought he'd get her to come home and sleep with him. And Millie said, 'I don't know why not.' So they went home. I said, 'Well, Millie, what did you see in him?' And she told me very proudly, 'He was a very romantic person, very warm, very tender. I was his mistress for two or three years.' On one drink," Mr. Frank added reflectively.

Before very long, however, he learned that actresses as well as chorus girls chose to occupy one seat in off the aisle. From then on, the floor was the limit.

He didn't dance, drive them about in automobiles, get them drunk, or throw jewelry at them. He did take them for walks and for dinners at restaurants ranging from the Automat, Childs, and Schraffts, to Sardi's, "21," the Colony, Voisin, and Pavillon.

The paradox in Kaufman the lover is that Kaufman the man was outwardly a prude of unquestionable dimension. He possessed a perfect set of manners. He appeared to be as sexually inhibited a man as the Victorian era could turn out. He almost never used profanity in conversation. Smutty jokes he referred to as "blue stories," and stayed away from them almost always. Any mention of the sexual act seemed offensive and unclean to him.

And yet, there he was, indisputably involved with women. Some thought he was ugly, some thought he was madly attractive. Some thought he was considerate, flattering, and a man who appreciated women as very few men really do.

There is no question that a great many women were attracted to him because of who and what he was: the most prolific and successful comedy writer-director of his day. That he could put a girl into a Broadway play or musical was a certainty.

That he ever did it purely for sexual reasons is highly doubtful. That he capitalized on who and what he was is undeniable.

———————

"I walked out of the stage door after a performance on the road," an actress said. "I walked to a drugstore window and looked into it. When I looked up, I saw his image reflected in the glass. He was standing very close behind me. 'How about a cup of coffee?' he asked. That's how it began."

•

Natalie Schafer, television and Broadway actress, was seated in the orchestra floor of a Boston theatre sobbing softly to herself. Her favorite scene in *Lady in the Dark*, the Moss Hart musical starring Gertrude Lawrence, had just been cut.

"I know what you're going through," a man's voice said.

She looked up and saw George Kaufman slipping into the seat next to hers. She'd never met him, but that did not deter him.

"I'm pretty much responsible for this," he continued. "That scene held up the play. It won't hurt you, being cut, because everything else you do will be better because of this cut. But I know what you must be going through."

"I want an ice cream soda," Natalie Schafer moaned.

Without a word Kaufman arose, left the theatre, and reappeared a few minutes later with a container filled with an ice cream soda. After that it was just a matter of time.

•

To Nola Chilton, a young theatre-oriented lady whom he invited to dinner, he telegraphed: MAGNIFICENT CAR WILL BE

161

AT YOUR DOOR TOMORROW, THURSDAY NIGHT, SIX THIRTY. DON'T
BE AFRAID OF WHITE SLAVERY, GET RIGHT IN.

•

A young Broadway actress based on the West Coast returned to New York and renewed her friendship with Kaufman. She was both surprised and delighted to stop at the desk
of her hotel late one night and find three handwritten messages.

"10:30 P.M." the first one read. "George Kaufman stopped
by on the chance you might be in."

"11:40 P.M. George Kaufman stopped by again."

Finally, he wrote, "1:13 A.M. George Kaufman was here
again, the old fool."

•

A leading lady whose marriage has placed her among the
very top socialites in the country reports, "One night I was
playing at the theatre and he was in the audience. During
intermission he came backstage, looked at me, and said, 'Where
can a Stage Door Johnny get your phone number?' and I told
him."

•

Joan Castle, a New York actress, was deeply in love with
Kaufman at one point in her life. They saw each other regularly
and passionately. As matters had become so intimate, she
felt she could unburden herself to him during one of those
small hours in the morning when terror takes over from reason.

Shortly after two, she telephoned him and broke down.
Although she hadn't wanted him to know, things had reached
such a state that she had to tell him; the rent on her apartment
was six months in arrears, she hadn't had a new dress in twice
that time, she was, in short, broke, she didn't have a dime in

the world, and she had been lying in bed, unable to sleep, shaking with fear.

Kaufman, always sympathetic to suffering, was mortified. He told her not to worry, he would take care of everything immediately.

Could she count on him, she wanted to know.

She most certainly could, he told her.

Soon?

Within twenty minutes, he promised her, a Western Union boy would be at her door with an envelope with what she needed and wanted.

True to his word, twenty minutes later the doorbell to her apartment rang. She answered it, and the Western Union boy handed her the envelope. Ripping it open she found not a check from George, not cash, but two sleeping pills.

At the time, she was indignant. Today, having married into a renowned and titled English family, she tells the story with amusement.

•

"He invited me to supper one night while the show was trying out in Philadelphia," Adele Racey Sardi, wife of the New York restaurateur, said. "We had a drink, something to eat. He told me I was one of the most beautiful women he'd ever met. Then he asked me where my hotel was. I was a little afraid but I told him. We got into a cab. When we got there he opened the door, helped me out, smiled, and thanked me for the evening. I felt terribly let down."

———————

Of the many ladies whose acquaintance he made, one was a West Coast movie star. She had been born Lucile Langhanke in Quincy, Illinois. Lucile Langhanke was put through the meat grinder that was Hollywood and emerged as Mary Astor.

Until he met Mary Astor, Kaufman was careful that all his relationships with women be maintained with discretion. With Miss Astor, however, the world turned upside down.

Generally, but with some exceptions, Kaufman's women tended toward a stereotype directly opposite to Bea: they were small, blonde, feminine, and they hung on his every word. Miss Astor was not small, she was not blonde, but she was extremely feminine and exceptionally bored with her life and the people who failed to fill it. Having always wanted to be a writer, Miss Astor began keeping a journal for her own personal interest and amusement. No experiments in fiction here. Mary Astor recorded the truth in her life as she saw it and lived it.

In violet ink and a perfect schoolgirl hand she penned not only her secret thoughts and innermost feelings but also a precise and detailed account of each man with whom she tumbled into bed. Yes, she was married, and had a child whom she adored; these items were duly recorded in her diary, but they did not interfere with her voracious sexual appetite.

Weary of Hollywood and her husband, she came to New York. The purple prose that follows is direct from her diary as published in newspapers and magazines throughout the world:

Thursday, January 14, 1934. Well, here it is another Year and I'm doing my usual wondering about what's going to happen to me.

To go back to that May [1933] entry—I flew East with the Gallaghers, stayed about two weeks and had a beautiful time. I did meet a man, professional, somewhat older and rather well to do only his first initial is G—George Kaufman—and I fell like a ton of bricks—as only I can fall—it was just one of those things—I met him the Friday after I arrived, at the Algonquin—Marian had told me to look him up and I had phoned him Monday—he was out of town but he phoned me Friday A.M. and made a luncheon engagement for Saturday with me—the same day I had one with Natalie . . . and in he came—he seemed very nice, made some remarks about the fact that it was lucky we had met and wouldn't have to wear a red carnation or something. That evening I had a dinner date with a young man, I've forgotten his name, at "21" and there he was again—

Saturday he called for me at the Ambassador and we went to the Casino for lunch and had a very gay time—he was so much fun—we drove back to town and sneaked in at the Music Box where his show *Of Thee I Sing* was playing, stayed a minute and then went next door where *Gay Divorce* was showing and it was very cool and pleasant and Fred Astaire was dancing so beautifully to such a beautiful number—"Night and Day" and the theatre was half empty so we stayed and he was looking at me more than the stage and I liked it.

Sunday night we had dinner and saw *International House* at the Paramount and laughed a lot and liked each other even more.

Monday I had a previous engagement with Bennett Cerf for dinner, but George called me up and said he knew about a tea party that might be fun and would I go—I would and did, but the tea party wasn't fun and we left in about fifteen minutes—it was very hot and we got a cab and drove around the park a few times and the park was—well the park—and he held my hand and said he'd like to kiss me but didn't—

Tuesday night we had dinner at "21" and on the way to see *Run Little Children* . . . he did kiss me—and I don't think either of us remembered what the show was about—afterwards, we had a drink someplace and then went to a little flat on 73rd Street where we could be alone and it was all very thrilling and beautiful—

I didn't see very much of anybody else the rest of the time—we saw every show in town, had grand fun together and went frequently to 73rd Street. I remember one morning about 4:00 we had a sandwich at Reuben's and it was just getting daylight so we drove through the park in an open cab and the street lights went out and the birds started singing and it was cool and dewey and pretty heavenly.

The evening I left we had dinner at "21" and a bottle of lovely wine—he had a car and drove me to the airport, kissed me good-by.

Monday, January 18th. That was six months ago and it's still pretty good—we write to each other often—about every two weeks—flowers and telegrams for Christmas and New Year's—once when Franklyn was away on a hunting trip he called me long distance and we talked for half an hour—his last letter finished with "think of me, my darling, because I certainly think of you. If it's lasted this long on both sides it must be something pretty good—too good to let drop."

The "Franklyn" mentioned above was Miss Astor's husband, Dr. Franklyn Thorpe. According to other pages of the diary, a good deal of Dr. Thorpe's hunting was in the company of Hollywood's favorite leading man of that day, Clark Gable. Dr. Thorpe, along with Miss Astor, purchased a sixty-four-foot schooner and sailed the Pacific. It was not the outdoor life she wanted, however, as the next entry concerning Kaufman discloses.

In the usual high sense of banter . . . he had never used the phrase "I love you" with me—not even as a prop—a phrase, a caress—He said that he was trying to be square with me.

166

Another time he said, "I wish I were madly in love with you, but those things just can't be arranged—I haven't been in love for many years and I doubt very much if I can again ever."

All of which makes me a little sad. I would like to have him love me.

1935. And Kaufman was off to Hollywood to write A *Night at the Opera*. Although he was pleased to renew his friendship with Miss Astor, he was quite unprepared for anything else.

I called for George at the Beverly-Wilshire at seven. He was very pleasant but a little jittery and strained, I noticed. In the car on the way to the Trocadero, I said, "Feeling lowish?"

"Mm—yeah—I'll tell you about it."

We went downstairs to the bar, sat down at a table and ordered drinks.

"Shall I wait for you to have a drink or shall I plunge right in?"

I was pretty mystified and worried and said, "Plunge in, I'm dying of curiosity."

"I've had a visit from your husband." I practically went through the floor.

Franklyn called on him about eleven o'clock Sunday morning, they talked for about half an hour in which Franklyn stated the reason for his visit, shook hands and parted—all very pleasantly.

He told George that he knew that he could not completely fulfill my life, that I needed other interests, but the sacredness of marriage, the child was at stake and George must be willing to take his share of the responsibility involved. What he meant by that, specifically, or what he wanted George to do exactly, George couldn't find out.

What he expected to gain from the interview is more

than I can figure. He doesn't know yet that I know about it. It seems to me that probably in all honesty, he loves me and wants to keep me at all costs and probably wanted to frighten George into breaking off with me.

I told George that if he wanted to get out—he could—his answer was very nice, "I'll have no farewell scenes with you, Miss A. I don't want that."

Certainly he didn't want that. No farewell scenes with Miss Astor. No obligatory scene with her husband. Neither of them was in his style of writing or in his style of living.

George fled Hollywood as quickly as he could manage. He returned to that well ordered New York home that Beatrice ran so well. The furniture glistened with polish, the air was filled with those delightful odors that the German cook in the kitchen seemed intent on perpetuating. Here, safe from everything, George still was a wreck from his western visit. According to Edna Ferber, Beatrice found him nervously twisting a napkin on the morning after he came back from the Coast.

"You haven't finished your breakfast," Bea observed.

George made sure their daughter had been taken to school and the servants were out of ear's reach before he spoke.

"I'm in trouble," he said, according to Bea, who had good reason to recall this talk in a Paris hotel room the next year.

"You shouldn't have gone to Hollywood. It's not for you," she comforted him.

"It certainly isn't. And that's where the trouble is."

"All that is behind you," Bea said.

"I'm afraid it isn't. I'm also afraid, Beatrice, this may involve you."

"Me?" Bea protested. "I barely stopped in Hollywood last time I was there."

"Beatrice," George said as he stood up, "I've just come back from playing that scene with the leading lady's husband."

Bea didn't understand.

"The leading lady is Mary Astor and her husband is really her husband. And honest to God he paid me a visit."

Having heard that much, Bea sat down heavily and listened to the entire story. By that stage in their marriage they kept few secrets from one another. When he concluded, she consoled him, saying, "It will all blow over."

For once, Bea Kaufman was completely wrong.

All of the dirt could have remained under the carpet had not Miss Astor consented to an uncontested divorce from her husband in 1935. The result of this divorce gave custody of their child to the husband along with sixty thousand dollars' worth of negotiable securities and real estate.

The next year, Miss Astor changed her mind and instructed her attorney to bring suit in court to set aside the divorce, grant her an annulment, and award her the child, the securities, and the real estate. To counter this action, her husband brought a second suit, entered Mary Astor's diary as evidence before the court, and leaked large portions of her journal to the press.

The parties met in Superior Court, Judge Goodwin J. Knight presiding. From mid-July to mid-August, 1936, a daily volume of scandal would flow. It was so juicy, so loaded with names, so intimate, so far beyond anything the newspapers had ever printed before that almost every event in the United States paled before it.

According to the August 17, 1936, issue of *Time* magazine:

[Miss Astor's husband's] attorneys wheeled into action the most formidable instrument for destroying a film character by sexual innuendo that California had seen since the 1922 Fatty Arbuckle case.

However, no screen lover but a sad-eyed dramatist was cast as Mary Astor's No. 1 partner-in-sin.

Browsing through the diary, her husband's lawyers found

that she had recorded experiencing a "thrilling ecstasy" in the company of George S. Kaufman. "He fits me perfectly," she wrote, recalling "many exquisite moments . . . twenty—count them, diary, twenty . . . I don't see how he does it . . . he is perfect."

One New York newspaper, stunned by the astronomical count given by Miss Astor, "twenty—count them, diary, twenty"—added that she was "perhaps referring to the number of clubs she and Kaufman visited one night." But the columnists of the country knew that Kaufman wasn't a nightclub regular.

Miss Astor, according to the stories fed to the press and according to the testimony in court, listed her gentlemen friends and compiled a list of her "top ten" lovers. Leading the field by several lengths was Kaufman.

The New York *American*, "A Paper for People Who Think," quoted Mary Astor as having written in her diary in 1934, "I am still in a haze—a nice rosy glow. If I thought the business with George was half hearted I was crazy. It's beautiful, glorious—and I hope is my last love—I can't top it with anything in my experience. Nor do I want to . . . Only ten days but enough for me to remember for the rest of my life."

The *Daily News* had her writing, "And how I hated to come back home and have to shift into low gear. There's more of it —but it's too dangerous to put even in this very revealing document—someday perhaps I'll be free to put it *all* down—in twenty years from now—perhaps."

Roughly twenty years later, Mary Astor did write her autobiography, but by then she charged that much of the diary had been fabricated by newsmen.

Kaufman, unaware of Miss Astor's legal activities, had returned to Hollywood to work with Moss Hart. Called as a witness by the husband's lawyer, he failed to appear in court. A bench warrant was promptly issued by Judge Knight.

In retrospect, it is hard to come by a more comical situation than the sight of the sheriff's deputies giving chase to the harassed Kaufman through Hollywood. Out of the Beverly-Wilshire he escaped to a home rented by his collaborator Moss Hart. The deputies pursued. A yacht owned by Irving Thalberg and Norma Shearer got Kaufman off the mainland and onto the island of Catalina. The deputies pursued by plane. Back on the yacht went Kaufman—with Carmel Myers, a Hollywood actress, who for the entire voyage played "The Music Goes Round and Round" over and over again on the ukulele.

"It was so maddening, I was ready to throw myself overboard and let the sharks finish me," Kaufman confided to Harpo Marx.

Back flew the deputies. As they rang the bell to Moss Hart's front door, the near-hysterical Kaufman went out the back door and hid in the bushes across the way. To the deputies, Hart shrugged and denied knowledge of Kaufman's immediate whereabouts.

Next day, well-disguised with bandages covering his face and blankets around his body, he was hoisted onto a stretcher and placed aboard a train bound east for New York.

"I slept most of the way," Kaufman claimed later. "That's the only way to travel."

"I'll put this man Kaufman in jail," thundered Judge Knight, "if we can find him."

By then, the train bearing "Public Lover No. 1" as he was labeled by headline writers across the country, was in New York State.

Not daring to meet the press at Grand Central Station, Kaufman got off the Twentieth Century at Harmon, New York, and was driven into New York City and hidden away with his sister Ruth. That night, while she was reading in bed, a plaintive voice called, "May I come in and talk a while?"

"Of course," she answered, and there in the doorway stood her brother, America's current sex symbol, wearing floppy bedroom slippers, the ever-present eyeglasses, and a white cotton night-shirt that ended just above his knobby knees. His sister recol-lected that when she grinned he managed a small self-conscious smile.

The size of the headlines was not to be believed. With the Spanish Civil War at its height, with John L. Lewis and his United Mine Workers bolting the A.F. of L. to form the C.I.O., with Hitler hard at work preparing for World War II only three years and two weeks away, the nation's press wallowed joyfully in the "mis-step diary" story.

The tabloids devoted entire pages to it. Five-column headlines in five-column papers appeared day after day. Eight-column headlines in eight-column papers also were run. On August 11, 1936, the two biggest headlines atop the front page of the New York *Times* were CORN CROP WORST SINCE '81 and WARRANT OUT FOR KAUFMAN.

Distressed by such coverage, Kaufman wired his wife's rela-tives in Rochester: DON'T BELIEVE WHAT YOU READ IN THE NEW YORK TABLOIDS. On receipt of the telegram, the family naturally raced out and bought every available Manhattan newspaper. For days, required reading in the Bakrow and Adler households were the reports of the carryings-on between George and Mary Astor. "I used to talk about my famous nephew," one of Bea's uncles said. "Now I talk about my infamous nephew." The children in the family thought it was a huge joke.

At the height of the diary furor, when George was being hailed in the press as the nation's top lover, Jean Dixon, one of Kaufman's favorite Broadway actresses, who kept their relation-ship on a strictly professional basis, received a note from a friend. "If what you've always said is true, that you never went to bed with G.S.K.," the note read, "I'll bet you're sorry now."

Broadway reaction was understandable. Kaufman had always been seen in the company of attractive young women, but then so were most directors and producers. It was part of the profession. As for his being a sex symbol, it was difficult to imagine. He was so cold, so aloof, so austere, so untouched and untouchable, so antipathetic toward love scenes on stage that participation in an actual love scene seemed totally out of character for Kaufman. And yet, there it was in print, a new episode each morning, a new episode each night.

Being an old newspaperman, Kaufman was horrified that his own kind should turn against him. Still, he was able to grasp that the pressure on the reporters was too great to be ignored. Reluctantly, he agreed to meet them in the library of his town house at 14 East 94th Street on Friday morning, August 14, 1936. He was clad in gray slacks and a blue shirt without a necktie, his hair was disheveled, his face was pale, and his hand shook nervously as he ran his fingers through his rumpled locks. His voice, a newspaper reporter noted, was the voice of a man who recognized the end had come and had prepared to make the best of it.

He said he fled Hollywood, driving to San Bernardino, and there flagged the Santa Fe to Chicago. Nobody spotted him in the Windy City, "Though I didn't wear smoked glasses," he added. He took the Twentieth Century, the crack Chicago-to-New York train, east-bound.

"I assure you," he told the assembled press, "it would not have been worth a reporter's while to have seen me in California, or a pleasure, either. I could not have uttered six coherent words. Unfortunately, I am of a very nervous temperament and I took this hard."

"I have one piece of news for the Great American Public," he announced. "I do *not* keep a diary myself."

He followed that by saying he had lost seven pounds and that he hadn't slept well. Then he took an envelope out of his hip pocket and began reading.

"Being a little nervous and quite unaccustomed to extemporary speaking, I've made a few notes on what I think I can talk about." His voice quavered. "There must be more important things [in the news], at least two or three, than anything I can possibly say. I've been in the public eye long enough and the public is probably as glad to get me out of it as I am to get out."

"Do you feel the Public Lover Number One position justified?" a reporter asked.

"I don't think I ought to answer that," Kaufman said. He mopped his forehead with a handkerchief frequently.

Another question was, what did he resent most in the recent case?

"The only thing I resent in this whole thing is that some news writer referred to me as a middle-aged playwright. Probably that's because I *am* a middle-aged playwright," Kaufman said. He was, at that time, forty-six years old.

"I haven't been out yet," he told reporters. "I feel very nervous about the thought of walking, even as far as the corner." Then he remarked suddenly, "I miss my wife."

"Have you been in touch with Mrs. Kaufman?" he was asked.

"Constantly. At great expense, too, on the trans-Atlantic telephone."

"Any—er—trouble?"

"Not in the least," Kaufman replied promptly. "She's been not only sympathetic but comforting. But I never had any doubts of that. Put that a little delicately, if you will."

Prior to leaving London for New York, Bea courageously if inaccurately told the press, "I knew all about this case before it caught the limelight. I know Mary Astor. I know her well. My husband met her just about this time a year ago. I was in Honolulu. He was working in Hollywood. They had a flirtation. I can't see there's any terrible harm in that.

"Is it unusual for a husband to flirt with an actress?

"We have been married twenty years. We are adults, leading

our lives in adult fashion. George is a good husband. I love him very much. He is in love with me despite the things that may have happened.

"When I get to New York, George will be there to meet me. . . . She kept a diary. Very stupid, that."

Red-eyed from crying and lack of sleep, Bea arrived in New York. She had been correct. George was there to meet her. Weaving her way through the working press, she waved farewell to her shipboard companions, Mr. and Mrs. Irving Berlin.

"How'm I doing, Irving?" she called out in an attempt at lightness she did not feel.

"Just great, kid," came the reply.

When she met George they refused to pose for kisses for the photographers. They gave no statements to the waiting press, which was there in numbers large enough to greet a reigning monarch. Instead, they hurried away in a taxicab.

Bea got in first. Then Howard Reinheimer, George's friend and lawyer for many years. Finally, George stepped in quickly and snapped at the cabbie. "Drive on. Just drive on!" He didn't want the reporters to catch the address.

"I'd rather not go to the house," George said. "There'll be newsmen there."

"Come to my office," Reinheimer suggested.

"George," Beatrice said, turning to her husband. "One of the reporters on the dock told me you held a news conference yesterday."

"I had to. They hounded me."

"I thought you'd at least wait for me," Beatrice said. "We could have done it so well together . . ."

"I'm too nervous to know what I'm doing," he replied.

"You look terrible, George."

When they arrived at Reinheimer's office, Kaufman finally faced his wife. "I feel rotten about this, Bea."

For the first time since she stepped off the gangplank of the ship, Bea's face softened and, slowly, that smile that radiated such warmth and encouragement came out. She walked over and took his hand.

Twenty-four hours later she issued a formal statement through her lawyer. "Mr. Kaufman and I are pursuing the usual routine of our lives. We have no intention of changing its order. Naturally, we both regret that an incident which must have occurred in the lives of many adults was made the focus of public interest. We honestly wish to be permitted again the peace and privacy of ordinary individuals."

By February 1, 1937, Walter Winchell wrote and had set up in type at the *Daily Mirror*, the following item: ". . . It is common gab that the George S. Kaufmans will become Renotables, perhaps six months hence. The charge—'humiliation.'" And then, because he was not positively certain, he stamped the item "DO NOT USE, UNLESS VERIFIED."

During the first few days following Bea's arrival, she grew increasingly bitter with most of her friends. They kept calling or stopping by to ask her when she was going to Reno to get her divorce.

Instead, in less than a month Bea had found Barley Sheaf Farm near Holicong, Pennsylvania. Although they continued to maintain their residence in New York City, by October 1 she had moved her family down to Bucks County. Bea found a girls' school close by for her daughter, had a study constructed in the house so that George could work without interruption, and she herself began a collection of Early American antiques.

A few months later, Kaufman returned to Hollywood, where he faced Judge Knight in the latter's chambers. Amiably, jokingly, Kaufman made his apologies to the court. Judge Knight thought him "a witty, winning fellow," fined him five hundred dollars, and as far as the public prints and records were concerned, the Astor diary episode was over.

To Beatrice Kaufman the effect of the scandal was galling.

She and George had put up with each other's peccadillos for years, but the affairs had always been conducted with delicacy and consideration for the public image of their marriage. The Mary Astor diary proclaimed to the world the hollowness of Bea's union with George. On the surface, Bea still laughed and gave parties, but as Ira Gershwin's wife Lee told me, "She was gay, adorable, and heartbreaking. Her personal life was always with her, and even in her gaiety you could sense the hurt."

To George, the resultant notoriety from the diary caused him temporary humiliation and shame. Guilt for the embarrassment he brought Bea showed itself after her death. Carrying her picture in a leather frame, he placed it in his room wherever he traveled. It was something he had never done before. "He made her into a saint," offered a lady who doesn't want her name used because she has a jealous husband. "If you ask me, I think he fell in love with her all over again." His sensitivity regarding the Astor episode continued for many years. On my fortieth birthday, I began keeping a diary. When he heard about it, Kaufman said, "Be careful. You've just struck a nerve."

Many years later, Miss Astor, in a telephone interview, stated simply, "George Kaufman? I don't want to talk about him. He caused me a lot of trouble once."

Aftershocks from the Astor diary were many, and continued for years. "Women I scarcely recognize keep coming up to me," Kaufman told Leland Hayward. "Sometimes I don't even know them at all." Did this embarrass Kaufman? Was he bothered or flattered by it?

"George's greatest weakness was women," reflected one of his female friends who insisted on remaining unnamed. "The number of women he saw was—well—legion. At the same time he was going around with me, he was seeing I don't know how many others. He would not limit himself to one girl. It wasn't a matter of loyalty or fidelity. It's just that there were so many women who wanted him and he made them feel so important and did such marvelous things for their egos—he simply couldn't help it."

There is no defense for promiscuity, if indeed today's moral code requires defense for such action. All that remains is the ultimate question: how good a lover was George S. Kaufman?

"He was very square," Joan Castle believed. "He was not like a continental lover. He was not skilled or versed in any way."

"He was the kind of man I'd go over a cliff for," Mary Astor wrote.

"George used to give perfume to the chorus gypsies," a former Kaufman chorus girl remembered, "and sometimes he had several in the same company. He was not always wise in his choice of scent, and the girls would exchange the perfumes among themselves. You know, 'What did you get? I'll trade mine for yours.' It became an interoffice joke."

"He was sensational," a leading lady in a Kaufman play declared. "I mean tender and considerate and always careful to do everything that was sweet and that women like—the flowers, the perfume, the candy, the notes, the attention. He really went all the way, like a school kid. I loved him for it." Still, Kaufman offered them a greater and deeper attraction.

A world-famous musical comedy star now retired from the stage admitted, "His great appeal, and he certainly had it, was that he really understood and liked women. Most men don't. Just in his interest in the things that most men are a little bored with, such as what you wear and the details about your appearance and his sensitivity about what you felt and his listening to the things you say. Most men don't listen to women, they merely tolerate their conversation; but George listened."

He did more than listen. Long after the affairs were over he kept in touch with many of the women who had shared his bed. He was genuinely concerned about them and he cared. If they made successful marriages and soared high in the world, or if times were tight and they were a little strapped for cash, George always was in communication with them. Neither his first nor second wife knew anything about those little notes he used to send. I have seen and xeroxed dozens of such notes to a dozen different ladies. "Apply externally. Do not inhale." "Do something with this. After all, that's why checks were invented." "For God's sake, don't let this disturb you. Can happen to anybody. What the hell is money?" Cash, checks, they really didn't matter. What was important to each of those women was that long after the physical relationship was ended, George Kaufman still remembered them.

"George, George," an elderly woman cried as she came face to face with him in an aisle during the intermission of an opening night. "I think of you so often."

"Of course you do," he smiled down into her upturned face, "and I think of you, too, always."

Ruth Goetz, who accompanied George to the theatre and witnessed that touching little episode, added that once they were outside, George said, "I'm sorry, Ruth, but I'm sure you're aware I couldn't introduce you, because I couldn't think of her name."

Symbolic of his relationships with women is a sealed envelope in the J. Pierpont Morgan Library in New York. It was put there by an international star whose credits take up two and a half columns in *Who's Who in the American Theatre*. Written on the face of the envelope is: "To be opened fifty years from the above date. Contents: 68 tender and intimate pieces of correspondence from George S. Kaufman, 1938–1953."

During the tryout of *Park Avenue*, Nunnally Johnson, the gifted author and film producer, was dining in Philadelphia with some people from the *Saturday Evening Post*. Moss Hart stopped by the table to say hello. When he left, one of the women said, "I'll never forget Billie Dove's diary and Moss Hart."

"I can't wait to relieve George," Johnson thought to himself.

When he saw George, however, and told him that at least part of the American public had substituted Billie Dove, a silent screen actress, for Mary Astor, and somehow Moss for George, Kaufman shrugged, shook his head, and looked more than a little disappointed. "People from the *Saturday Evening Post* said that? I may just have to cancel my subscription."

The "Madeline" to whom the "Good Boy" wrote was Madeline Hurlock, first wife of Marc Connelly and second wife of Robert E. Sherwood.

To Madeline
from a Good Boy—
George

Hits would make him handsome; meanwhile he glared through his glasses as his older sister Helen and his younger sister Ruth stole the show.

*Boys' and girls' dancing class, Pittsburgh, Pennsylvania, circa 1899.
The "Good Boy" is in the top row, second from the right.*

*The humor columnist for the
Washington Times (1913) sported
a bow tie, a watch fob, and, to crown
it all, a pompadour.*

The drama editor of the New York Tribune, *1916.*

1925: The New York Times *drama staff. Left to right, George Kaufman, drama editor; Ted Sweedy, copy boy; Brooks Atkinson, critic; Sam Zolotow and John Byram, reporters.*

Atlantic City was where tired
businessmen took their secretaries
during the Twenties; however,
Kaufman took his wife Bea there,
and Julius Tannen, a Broadway
comedian—plus many of his plays
for initial tryouts.

Costume parties were most definitely in with the Kaufman set. Here, at an affair
honoring Admiral Dewey, are, left to right, Margaret Leech Pulitzer,
Marc Connelly, Russel Crouse, Thomas Finletter (later, Secretary of the Air Force),
and Emily Kimbrough, author of Our Hearts Were Young and Gay.

Beatrice. Woollcott, Moss Hart, and Harpo Marx called her "Lamb Girl."

The man who gave Kaufman his start, F.P.A.

Sooner or later "everybody" visited Neshobe Island, Alexander Woollcott's New England suzerain. Here, left to right, are Harpo Marx, Irene Castle, Alfred Lunt, Woollcott, and Lynn Fontanne.

Kaufman loved to masquerade as Abe Lincoln. The "Peggy" to whom he dedicated this photograph was Margaret Leech Pulitzer.

At the Algonquin Round Table, as drawn by Hirschfeld (clockwise, from the bottom left): Robert E. Sherwood, Dorothy Parker, Robert Benchley, Alexander Woollcott, Heywood Broun, Marc Connelly, Franklin P. Adams, Edna Ferber, and George Kaufman. In the background, left to right, the Lunts, Frank Crowninshield, and host Frank Case.

Edna Ferber. This gifted, stern-faced spinster was the collaborator who most intimidated Kaufman.

In the office of Sam H. Harris in the Music Box Theatre gathered the men who put together the satire about Franklin D. Roosevelt, I'd Rather Be Right. Left to right are Harris; Lorenz Hart, lyricist; Richard Rodgers, composer; Hart and Kaufman, authors; and George M. Cohan, the star.

The woman who kept the diary, Mary Astor.

Barley Sheaf Farm, the estate in Bucks County, Pennsylvania, to which Beatrice Kaufman retreated with her husband and daughter following the diary scandal.

RIGHT: *The second time he won the Pulitzer Prize, 1937.* BELOW: *In Boston for an opening: Moss Hart and the original man who came to dinner, Alexander Woollcott.*

Singing in the New Year (left to right): Charles Friedman, Moss Hart, Bea Kaufman,
Frank Sinatra, "Yip" Harburg, Fred Saidy, and (in back, center) Harold Arlen;
at the piano, Ethel Merman. Bea had the photograph cropped to include only
Frank Sinatra and herself, and sent it out as a Christmas card.

An early shot of George Kaufman
the father with his daughter Anne.

Men at work:
Kaufman and Hart.

Men at play:
Woollcott and Harpo.

Croquet was the game.
Kaufman was in form;
Harpo was in costume.

At the Stork Club: Kaufman, Kitty Carlisle Hart, and her husband,
Kaufman's favorite collaborator.

1949: George S. Kaufman and
the woman who became his
second wife, Leueen McGrath.

"This Is Show Business": Sam Levinson (who had replaced Abe Burrows),
Clifton Fadiman, Jacqueline Susann, and the Old Curmudgeon.

ABOVE: *On location deep in Hollywood: Nunnally Johnson;*
Gene Fowler, Jr.; Gene Fowler, Sr.; Kaufman the Director; Ella Raines;
Peter Lind Hayes. BELOW: *Uncertainty, apprehension, and confidence*
at a three-handed poker game in Hollywood, as seen in Rupert Hughes,
biographer, novelist, and short-story writer; George Jessel, actor,
comedian, and man-about-town; and, of course, the Card Player himself.

ABOVE: *Father and daughter aboard the* Queen Mary, 1956.
BELOW: *The last picture of George S. Kaufman. He inscribed it*
"From Adam Kaufman and his friend—George."

8 *Annie's Father*

HER MOTHER CALLED HER "BUTTON" AND HER FATHER CALLED her "Poke." Legally, she was obtained from the Louise Wise Adoption Center in New York, in 1925, and officially she was called Anne Kaufman. The name "Button" was a generally accepted term of endearment for a little one. The name "Poke," which her father used throughout his life, was a contraction of "slow-poke." Whenever he called her "Anne," or wrote, "Dear Anne," he was either angry with her or about to deliver a message of the utmost seriousness.

She arrived, at the age of three months, in the Kaufman household at 158 West 58th Street—and, characteristic of that household, Beatrice proceeded to rent an apartment next to the one she and George shared for their new daughter and her nurse.

George's daughter believes she was raised as a rather typical child, but this scarcely could have been the case. Typical children do not find themselves mentioned in F.P.A.'s "Diary of Our Own Samuel Pepys." "Anne, as sweet a child at five months of age as I ever saw," F.P.A. wrote, "and ever in a merry mood and laughing as unlike George as might be."

Nor do typical children receive first visits from top-seeded theatrical talent such as Ruth Gordon. At Miss Gordon's first visit, Anne was an infant propped up against the back of a couch holding the *Times* and laughing. Miss Gordon thought this child would be very good for George Kaufman, as she apparently provided both of the things George wanted most: someone to read the newspaper for which he wrote, and someone to laugh.

A pretty picture, but one that was mostly for company.

The home in which Anne grew up was a strange place for a child. On the one hand, there was so much social activity; on the other hand, there was practically no family relationship. She might just as well have lived in a first-class hotel for all the cuddling and cooing she received.

Bea, as mentioned earlier, never won a prize for being the Ideal American Mother. George didn't have to stand in line for an award either. He didn't even pretend to like small children, his own or anyone else's. He was quickly bored by stories about other people's kids, tried not to talk about Anne too much, and had a positive loathing for persons who handed out snapshots of their offspring.

When she was three years old, she went into her father's room and looked up at him.

"Go, Poke," he said. "I'm not in the mood for you today."

"I'm not in the mood for you today, either, Daddy," she answered.

He liked that. He liked fast answers from his daughter just as much as he liked them from the character women or the leading ladies in his plays.

Her bedtime generally coincided with the hour the Kaufmans and guests sat down to dinner. George enjoyed having his pretty little girl come in and say good night. He would allow her to stand next to him, and would beam at the bright manner she employed in chatting with the grown-ups. Ten minutes of this and he would kiss her and send her off to bed.

Bea had practically no time at all for her daughter. On Sundays, she'd scream, "You've *got* to do something with her."

So George, the dutiful parent, took the small child to one of his bridge clubs where they played serious bridge, hour after hour. Anne learned the virtues of silence, learned how to clear the mints off the nearby plates, and learned a loathing for cards that remains with her to this day.

She grew up among a procession of opening nights in the theatre, none of which she was allowed to attend and all of which were her father's. But in 1934 her mother had an opening night, and Anne was so keyed up by it that she sent a bouquet and printed the following note on a Postal Telegraph blank:

The Great Night

Dear Mother,

Room one to the right on the third floor. These flowers will tell you how much your little girl has been thinking about your play, tonight, before going to sleep and has wished for you the greatest success.

Hug and kisses,

Anne

Bea was so moved by that little epistle that she kept it forever in her scrapbook.

Anne was raised by a succession of nurses, governesses, and mam'selles in a series of fashionable town houses and elegant apartments. "There was one gala party when I was little where Daddy and Moss Hart dressed as liveried footmen, wore white powdered wigs, and announced the names of the guests as they came in. There was a way to sit at the top of the stairs," Anne remembered, "where I could look down without having any-body see me."

From that vantage point she watched as the great and near-great of the world came to her parents' frequent parties: George Bernard Shaw, Fiorello La Guardia, Robert Benchley, Somerset Maugham, Donald Ogden Stewart, S. N. Behrman, Sidney Howard, Beatrice Lillie, Peggy Pulitzer, Ethel Barrymore, Bennett Cerf, Gilbert Seldes, Edmund Wilson, George Backer, Margalo Gillmore, Peggy Wood, Vincent Astor, Damon Runyon.

As is the case with many only children, she was shy and quiet with her contemporaries. With adults, however, she was far more comfortable. Whenever there were parlor games, her father chose her first to be on his side. By the time she was thirteen, she was quick and highly intelligent, and that's the way he wanted his daughter to be.

Her mother said, "Oh, she's an adolescent. I'd like to put her away so nobody could see her for three or four years."

Anne went from one to another of five private schools: Walden, Lincoln, Todd Hunter, Dalton, and Holmquist. Even in this, Anne hardly could be considered an average child, for what average child has a letter of recommendation written to the headmistress of her school by so exalted a personage as Alexander Woollcott? With a sense of humor typical of him, Woollcott wrote, "I implore you to accept this unfortunate child and remove her from her shocking environment."

As she grew older, Anne thought of herself as introverted but a relatively good student. Her schoolmates thought of her as shy, lonely, and quiet. She had dark hair, a dark complexion, and dark, somber, saucer eyes.

Anne met Mary Astor the summer before the famous diary went into court in violet ink and came out in 72-point type in the newspapers. George was working in Hollywood, and after a trip to Hawaii with her mother and the current mam'selle,

Anne stopped at the Beverly Hills Hotel and visited Daddy. Daddy took her to the motion picture studio, where she met not only Miss Astor but Miss Astor's daughter Marilyn. The two little girls got along beautifully. Next year, when the girls in her school asked if she knew Miss Astor, Anne answered affirmatively. Anything else they wanted to know was in the newspapers.

The key to George's relationship with his daughter was that he treated her as a grown-up. He often took her to the theatre; not just to children's shows, which he tolerated in a fashion quite unexpected of him, but to adult theatricals, which both of them enjoyed. Anne spent one Thanksgiving Day going up to New Haven with George to see a musical they both knew was a flop.

"I think this is a terrible way to spend Thanksgiving," Anne complained. "I'm not even going to have any turkey."

"Just wait!" George answered.

Anne's feelings for her father can be seen in the letter she wrote him on his fifty-first birthday in 1940:

Dearest Daddy;

Well, sir, here we are again. Every year at this time I want to write you a really nice letter, and every year I'm just as much at a loss as I was the year before. In between times I can make up gobs of them—I remember things we do together; funny things you say; but those aren't reasons for writing people birthday letters—those are just a few reasons for liking you. Others are hard to say—hard even to define in thinking terms to oneself. I'm growing up a little every year but not enough to make you feel any older. In six years I'll still be flunking the same math tests I flunked last year—so that is unchanged. The football games with Dick will be no different than seeing *Life With Father* with you —probably not as much fun. And I still can't fold letters and put them into envelopes—I won't even try with this one. If Father William could stand on his head at 80, so can you!

Happy Birthday, Daddy,
LOTS OF LOVE
POKY

Oh, Daddy could be fun, Daddy could be charming, or, if he chose, Daddy could be a disciplinarian.

Ruth Goetz, their Bucks County neighbor, recalls that when Anne was fourteen or fifteen years old she came down to the pool in Bucks County wearing "a darling little bathing suit that I thought was simply charming on her. It was a little bra and short panties, and when George saw it he went into a rage. 'Go back to the house and get into something decent!'"

In short, for a man who led so free a life, he was strict with his daughter. America's Number One Lover, it turned out, could be a moral tyrant at home.

The key to Anne's relationship with her father was in the saving grace of her sense of humor. Without it, he would have ignored her. With it, he paid as careful attention to her as to anyone else who had the temerity to speak up to him. As a result, Anne rather quickly developed standards of courtesy, good manners, keen observation, and the ability to keep prattle to a minimum.

In return for this adult-like behavioral pattern, Anne was granted the privilege, at fifteen or sixteen, of attending rehearsals conducted by her father. There she met a procession of stage managers, assistant stage managers, and actors, all or most of whom seemed quite eligible to a datable young girl. Although Anne was amenable, what assistant stage manager or what bit player was ready to take out George S. Kaufman's only daughter?

Saint Subber, who then was one of those assistant stage managers, not only dated her but wanted very much to marry Anne.

One of the obstacles, of course, was George himself, "because," as Saint Subber said, "he was an enormous figure to any young man who wanted to marry her. Because you weren't marrying Anne, you were also marrying George."

In her teens, Anne was a smaller, trimmer, prettier version of her mother. Although her father's wit was something she came by rather easily, it did her no good one afternoon when she dropped into the office of one of his old friends. Deciding that Anne was now grown up enough to make a pass at, the old friend chased her around his desk with relish for a good five minutes.

And then the phone rang and, of course, it was George. While he talked, Anne straightened her blouse and fixed her hair—and had to laugh, hearing the old friend say, "George! Guess who just walked in? Little Annie."

Before she was finished with high school she was casting about for a college. Watch how George S. Kaufman, skilled playwright, consummate director, master of 44th Street, wrote to influence his only child:

Anne Darling:
More and more, as we inquire about the University of Chicago, it doesn't seem to be at all the place that you would be happy in.

Last night we had dinner with Edna [Ferber], who spent a large hunk of her life in Chicago—not, to be sure, at the University, but close enough to be familiar with it. Also she is familiar with its more recent history. It stands for exactly the kind of things that you hate—the things that you find so distasteful at Holmquist. Its leadership is reactionary, and inevitably that reaction seeps down through the teaching ranks. It is a great rich institution with all the flaws and the restricted thinking that great rich institutions are likely to have . . . As your Mother has already pointed out, there would be no campus life, nothing of the atmosphere that is supposed to go with college life, and which I know you would find so congenial.

If, on top of this, it offered certain courses in which you were passionately interested, and which could be got no-where else, then we would still think it was right for you to go there. But it doesn't. It seems to have nothing at all to offer you . . . And I forgot the Chicago weather. Simply frightful, *all* the time. *That* wouldn't matter either if there were compensations.

What about Wisconsin, which came under discussion? It is apparently a fine school. I'm not trying to sell it to you—look over some others. But don't deliberately pick the worst one.

My love darling.

Daddy

Kaufman knew no more about the University of Chicago than about handling a daughter. But observe his second letter to Anne, written a short time later:

Well, Poky, I hear you got in at Chicago. I thought of sending you, by way of congratulation, a copy of my letter to you telling you why you shouldn't go there, but maybe you remember it. At least I have discovered how to get you to do *anything*—just write a good strong letter the other way.

But I'm delighted, darling. Your college career will be what you yourself make it. I know you'll find friends wher-ever you go, and I have a hunch you're going to work. But, particularly, I'm pleased because that's what you wanted. Maybe some day you can explain the Chicago Elevated System to me.

And my love, in quantities.

Daddy

Kaufman's hunches were limited to the theatre. Anne, though admitted, never attended the University of Chicago. On completing high school, she thought of herself as so mature that she skipped college and got married.

Although he paid for a medium-sized wedding, arranged by Beatrice at the Hampshire House in New York City, George's reaction to his daughter's marriage was decidedly frigid. The groom, John Booth, a graduate of the Lawrenceville School and Columbia University, was a soldier during World War II. Within six months he was shipped overseas, and Anne moved back into her parents' home.

It was during this period that Kaufman wrote his brother-in-law, Leonard Bakrow: "Your sister is an alternate mass of ambition and inaction—one day she wants to go right over and settle the war and then she thinks nothing would be more pleasant than staying in bed until further notice. In between she has Anne to contend with—a married daughter is just as much trouble as an unmarried daughter—although the nature of the trouble changes a little. You can't quite tell her what to do any more, but you can still fight with her."

When her husband returned to the States, Anne divorced him. George was indifferent to the entire proceeding, believing as he did that it was wrong for his daughter to have gotten married. He neither reproached her nor comforted her. His silence showed everyone concerned precisely where he stood.

On Anne's twenty-first birthday, however, Kaufman revealed how deep his love was for his only child as well as for his recently deceased wife. "Poky Darling," he penned in his own handwriting,

I cannot say all that is in my heart for you. So here are two small gifts to speak for me.

As for the locket, I hope that the first picture that goes

into it will be your mother's. As for the check, it is to buy whatever you want.

My love and congratulations, darling, and also my high hopes.

Daddy

June 23rd, 1946

In May of 1947, Anne Kaufman incurred more of her father's displeasure by marrying for a second time. In place of the posh Hampshire House, a small quiet wedding was held at Barley Sheaf Farm in Bucks County.

Her first husband had been a newspaperman in civilian life, a member of the Sunday department of the New York *Times.* Anne's second husband was also a journalist. Bruce Colen was an editor *of Holiday* magazine. Over and beyond that, he committed the unpardonable act of making George S. Kaufman a grandfather. This single feat, scarcely a dozen years after the Astor diary episode, might have put a lesser man out of the running. But not Kaufman. He chose largely to ignore this entire incident and its issue, and Anne gratified him by securing a second divorce after five years of married life.

By then, of course, Beatrice had been dead for seven years, and his daughter had learned in some detail about her father's romantic conquests. On first hearing of the apartment on West 73rd Street, which he still rented and used regularly, her initial reaction was, "I wonder if Mummy furnished it?"

To get her second divorce, Anne accompanied one of her father's favorite lady friends to Las Vegas. The friend also was in the market for a divorce. After they had been pronounced single again, Anne and her father's friend both went to Hollywood, where they joined George, who by then was quite welcome in the state of California, because the judge in the "misstep diary" case was now Governor Goodwin Knight.

It was at this point in their relationship that Anne and her father became extremely close. She functioned as his official hostess, traveling companion, and confidante.

He was slightly puzzled by the fact that she refused to play cards, but he was more than pleased with her actions on the croquet court and with her quick, agile manner in the intricacies of parlor games.

By now, Anne knew her father well enough never to keep him waiting, never to use four-letter words, never to display an inordinate amount of emotion. Theirs was a close arrangement. He didn't have to tell her he loved her. She knew it.

She was not prepared, therefore, for the announcement that her father and a girl only a few years older than herself were going to marry. Leueen MacGrath, the blonde, beautiful, British actress, had swept New York off its collective feet, George Kaufman included. While theirs was not an overnight courtship, Anne had never considered that anyone except herself would succeed to the role of hostess in the Kaufman home. However, in 1949, six months after he met Miss MacGrath, George married her.

Although Anne arranged the wedding, she discovered that she was jealous of her new stepmother. Lulu, as Anne took to calling Leueen, put an end to the jealousy by having Anne around the Kaufman household as much as Anne cared to be around. The result was twofold: she saw even more of her father, and she became Lulu's friend.

Four years after Leueen and George were married, they sold the estate in Bucks County to buy a town house in London. Number 17 Blomfield Road was a beautifully quaint place, but so ancient it required the services of an architect, who happened to be Sigmund Freud's grandson. In the summers, Leueen would fly over to supervise the rebuilding or the reopening of the house. George preferred ships. He also enjoyed the company of his daughter on such voyages.

On one crossing, Anne entered the ship's ping-pong tournament, and while she was eliminated in the first round, she had the satisfaction of having her own cheering section, which was composed of George and the English actress Hermione Gingold. She was amused to see that her father and Miss Gingold had made pennants and banners, which they waved as they cheered enthusiastically for her.

In April of 1960, "after a whirlwind courtship of ten years," Anne married a third husband. This time it was no one from so transient a world as journalism but someone steady from the solid and conservative area known as the theatre. Irving Schneider, general manager for Irene Selznick when that lady was producing plays on Broadway, proved a good and lasting husband to Anne.

George, who was not well enough to be present for the brief ceremony, actually shook Irving's hand when the bride and groom presented themselves later at George's penthouse. Later, when his doctor paid him a visit, George said warmly, "She's a lovely girl and I hope this one sticks. I hope it takes just like a vaccination."

As a father-in-law to Irving, he was courteous if somewhat aloof. Only once did Irving Schneider feel the Kaufman wrath, and that was before his marriage to Anne.

Early in the 1950's he was visiting in Bucks County. One morning, he took a telephone call after breakfast. It was from Mrs. Selznick in New York City, and Irving, not knowing that George himself was expecting an important call, stayed on the telephone for half an hour. Maybe more. When he came back into the room, Irving noticed that his girl's father looked pasty white, that he was tight-lipped and grim. It wasn't until Anne told him that he understood that George was furious.

For the remainder of the morning, throughout a most uncomfortable lunch, clear into the afternoon, George refused to cast even a snarl in Irving's direction. Finally, that evening, as they drove over to Moss and Kitty Hart's for dinner, Kaufman turned to him. "From the length of your phone conversation," he said, "I gather nothing is new."

To wind it up: George was as good a father as George could be. Considering the work he accomplished and the life he led, Anne came out of her father's house with the assurance of one of George S. Kaufman's "off-the-cuff" heroines. She is charming and chic as Bea would have wanted. She is amusing and astute as George would have wished. She is her own person: Irving's wife and Betsy's mother. Still, a great many people continue to think of her as Annie Kaufman, George's daughter.

9 *The Card Player*

At an age when most young boys are playing ball, George S. Kaufman was playing cards. He continued to indulge in this pastime almost to the very end of his life.

Card playing held three important meanings for him: first, it provided a field for his fiercely competitive spirit, a spirit in which hostility may be expressed through use of the mind rather than coordination of the body; second, beginning with the Press Club in Washington, D.C., cards meant money to George, and money meant a release from the grinding, shabby poverty of the last years in Pittsburgh and the boarding houses of Paterson; last, card playing provided him with an audience outside the theatre.

In an autobiographical sketch of himself, Kaufman wrote, "Playing stud poker at the National Press Club was what hardened my character."

In 1920, when his salary on the New York *Times* had been raised from thirty-six dollars to forty-eight dollars per week, George and Beatrice Kaufman moved into a luxury apartment on West 58th Street. The monthly rent on that apartment was five hundred dollars. This was before the opening of *Dulcy* and the influx of big money. How, then, did they manage this bit of economic magic?

From "The Diary of Our Own Samuel Pepys," Sunday, November 6, 1921: ". . . thence to G. Kaufman's, and played cards and lost so little that H. Ross said it was a moral victory."

Kaufman was not a card sharp. He was, however, the best poker player in New York at that time and probably the best amateur bridge player in the country.

Sam Zolotow, who, as office boy at the *Times* was privately recompensed by Kaufman to pay Kaufman's bills and balance his checkbook, often wondered where those large sums of cash came from that were deposited so frequently in the Kaufman account in the Bank of New York.

Kaufman was a man with a highly compartmentalized mind. As a playwright, he could and did work on several plays during the week. As a card player, he could and did participate in five or six card games during a seven-day stretch. Almost every day of his adult life he played in a variety of poker or bridge games, with an occasional nod to social gin rummy.

Poker began in Washington. It continued in New York in two major games. The first and largest was named originally by F.P.A. in his Pepys' Diary as the Thanatopsis Pleasure and Literary Club. Down through the years, the chroniclers of this group altered its name. It was, at various times and in various magazines, columns, and books The Thanatopsis Inside Straight Poker Club, The Thanatopsis Inside Straight Chowder and Marching Society, as well as a host of offshoots. In all instances the word Thanatopsis was used. An outgrowth of the Algonquin Round Table, the club met at five o'clock on Saturday afternoons and played until the late dawn of Sunday morning.

In addition to Franklin P. Adams, who was a poor poker player, there were, as previously noted, Harold Ross, also a poor poker player; Marc Connelly, a poor player; Heywood Broun, Robert Benchley, Alexander Woollcott and Gerald Brooks, poor players all; Herbert Bayard Swope, a good poker player; Harpo Marx, who by his own admission was a pretty fair poker player; and George S. Kaufman, who by everyone's admission was the best honest poker player in town. He was also the game's unofficial but highly efficient secretary and book-keeper.

A great many other names drifted in and out of the game, and the game itself floated from the Elbow Room, which later became the Barberry Room, to the Colony Restaurant, and back to the Algonquin Hotel. It became so large in numbers, so popular as a fashionable place to be seen and heard, and eventually its stakes so high that an offshoot was formed called the Hoyle Club.

Found regularly at the Hoyle Club's table, or, if the game was so large, two tables, were Russel Crouse, playwright and poor poker player; Theron Bamburger, press agent and poor poker player; Alfred de Liagre, theatrical producer and poor poker player; Bernie Hart, brother of Moss Hart and poor poker player, and, needless to add, George Kaufman, of whose ability no more need be added.

In the Thanatopsis Club a player could lose anywhere from a thousand to several thousand dollars of an evening. At the Hoyle Club substitute hundred for thousand and the result was the same.

Heywood Broun sat down one evening with a fine fat balance in his checking account, and by dawn's early light had lost every cent he and his wife had intended to use to purchase a home. When he returned to his apartment, Mrs. Broun, on hearing the dolorous news, refused to speak to him for three weeks.

This is the same Heywood Broun who, after a divorce from Ruth Hale, brought a young chorus girl to kibitz at the Thanatopsis table. On being introduced to Kaufman, the young lady acknowledged the introduction by saying, "Pleased to meetcha, Mr. Kaufman."

The gentleman in question did not bother to look up. Staring hard at his cards, he said, "Oh. A dancer."

It must be understood that for those in both poker clubs the purpose was not only to relax and tempt Lady Luck; the other object was to get off as good a line as possible. Delivered adroitly, the line might be accepted as humor; delivered less deftly, it would be considered a wisecrack; but delivered with consummate skill it could be construed as a witticism, the best of which survive to this day. Many were spoken by Kaufman.

Harpo Marx made an astute observation of Kaufman, not only as the card player but as the story teller. "He was a good player," Harpo said. "He always had a story to tell, but he never told it unless he was dealing. He'd be holding the cards, smart? So he got his point over all the time."

To the Thanatopsis Club came Charles Chaplin on the night his new film opened in New York. *The Gold Rush* was packing them in, and the Thanatopsis brethren were in a rush to relieve the great motion picture comedian of the gold coming his way. This was easy, as Chaplin proved to be an inept poker player. He was also inept at repartee. His single topic of discussion was his blood pressure. Soon, everyone was discussing everyone's blood pressure. But Chaplin, who had introduced the subject, was determined to have the last word on it.

"Mine," said Chaplin, "is down to a hundred and eight."

"I don't know whether to buy the common or the preferred," Kaufman said.

•

During a game where his luck had been running poorly for the entire evening, Kaufman finally turned his cards face up on the table. Mostly, the hand consisted of two's and three's.

"I'm going," Kaufman said as he stood up. "I've been trey-deuced."

•

At the Hoyle Club one evening, Theron Bamburger was particularly garrulous. Taking as much of the press agent's chatter as he could, Kaufman finally said, "Bamburger, don't you ever have an unexpressed thought?"

•

As unofficial scorekeeper, Kaufman kept track, in a small black pocket-sized notebook, of who lost how much and what sums were owed to which players. A major debtor was Marc Connelly. Shortly after *The Green Pastures* hit it big, Connelly met a group of the poker-playing fraternity on the street. He acknowledged at once that he owed each of them something, but how much he couldn't tell, and since he couldn't tell . . . The inference was that payment would have to be deferred. Before he got any further, Kaufman had the book out of his pocket and was reciting, "Seven hundred and fifty dollars to Swope, three hundred and sixty-six dollars to . . ."

•

Not all of the games were played at the clubs. Whenever there were enough hands, a game was started at the Kaufmans'. It was to such a game that Frank Adams brought a young New York gentleman who was interested in something other than the family baking business. He was seated, he recalled, next to a young man with wild hair and dirty fingernails. By the end of the game, the young man had more than dirty fingernails. His name was Harold Ross and he had the backing of the man seated next to him, Raoul Fleischmann, in a project called the *New Yorker* magazine. More than that, he had the promise of contributions from F.P.A., Robert Benchley, Ring Lardner, Aleck Woollcott, and of course, the host, George Kaufman.

•

Before bridge became fashionable, whist was the socially accepted game. At the Swopes' on weekends, they played whist all night, all the next day, and on into the second night. Kaufman was quick to come up with an axiom relating to time.

"It's too early for the winners to leave and too late for the losers to stay."

•

Gin rummy was a game that Kaufman tolerated as a social necessity and at which he excelled. The following two instances illustrate Kaufman the gin player; they also show the depth of his competitive spirit and provide an insight into the Kaufman who was not always witty and gay.

During the ten years in which I worked with Kaufman, we played cards only once: gin rummy at his place in Bucks County. While he tolerated me, he was inordinately fond of my wife. Her early training in gin rummy taught her to turn her discard face down prior to knocking or going gin. The one time we played with Kaufman, she continually beat him. Not only was he a poor loser, as both Ira Gershwin and Howard Dietz have testified, but his mind was geared to memorizing every card that was played.

He was not only furious at being beaten but incensed at her turning down her card. After asking her not to do this, and after she, out of long habit, continued, he pointed to the back of her gin card on the table and roared, "Damn it, Evelyn, you don't think I'm going to steal it, do you!" It was the only time in a decade that he had ever been anything but gracious to her. *But he had to know what the hidden card was!*

Still, she got off luckier than Moss Hart's wife Kitty. At a similar game in the same place, Mrs. Hart admitted making "a terrible misplay, and he reached across the table and gave me a smart slap on the jaw. I didn't say anything. Nobody else did. I don't think anybody saw it, it was so fast. It surprised me tremendously because he always seemed so gentle. You know, in his mannerisms, in the way he used his hands and in the way he touched objects he was very gentle."

No one, living or dead, has left any record of being struck by George S. Kaufman save for the wife of his dearest friend. What that single slap boils down to may be interpreted many ways, not the least of which is that Kaufman was a professional, whether at whist, gin, bridge, poker, theatre, or newsroom. He could bear mistakes, but he was wholly intolerant of foolishness at the card table, in a news story, or on the stage. He expected of everyone what he demanded of himself: the best.

The best is what Kaufman chose to play every afternoon at New York's two outstanding bridge clubs, the Cavendish and the Regency. No suckers, no set-ups, no easy marks for him. He sought out and played with the top professionals of his day—Jacoby, Culbertson, Goren. Not only the money but the challenge of pitting his mind against theirs gratified Kaufman.

"The best amateur bridge player in America," is what Ely Culbertson said of George Kaufman.

"He was good enough to be a pro," said Charles Goren. When Goren's book, *Better Bridge for Better Players* was first published, it included an amusing foreword by Kaufman. A choice sampling follows:

> As for the choice of seats—how to select the winning chairs—that is a matter on which science is now working, and I may have some very interesting news for you in a future article. For the present, I can only say that some highly promising results have been obtained with rabbits, but as yet I can only hint at the possibilities. Eventually, I am sure, it will be possible to predict with complete accuracy which way the cards will be running on a given afternoon or evening, and when this happens no one will ever lose a rubber.

It is difficult indeed to imagine that anyone could be intrepid enough to stand behind George Kaufman as he played bridge. And yet, there must have been some such persons with the audacity to do it. In the *New Yorker* magazine, Kaufman wrote his answer to them in the short story "The Great Kibitzer's Strike of 1926."

> . . . a player named Jymes, or Hymes, or something— the records are unfortunately vague—concealed a Queen of Spades from a kibitzer, known simply as Commander Smith, during the play of the hand . . . On the following night, Smith didn't show up. It was the first night he had missed in eleven years, but still no one was worried; it was simply assumed that he was dead. This had happened before to kibitzers, and the procedure in such cases was well established. One of the players would deal and say,

"Did you notice that Bill Clunk died last night? One spade," and his partner when it came to his turn, would say, "Yes, I did. Two spades." Or diamonds, or hearts, or whatever it might be. So the players would kitty out three dollars for flowers, and that would be that. (How times have changed! Under today's rules, the death of a kibitzer calls for the cessation of play for a full ten seconds, and the next four hands are automatically doubled.)

———————

At the Regency Club one afternoon, Kaufman shuddered at the atrocious playing of a fellow member. When the hand was finished, the bungler sensed disapproval in Kaufman's silence.

"All right, George," he protested, "how would you have played it?"

Kaufman answered, "Under an assumed name."

•

After an exasperating session for George, his partner arose and announced he was going to the men's room.

"Fine," Kaufman spat, "this is the first time this afternoon I'll know what you have in your hand."

•

In a game which was played at three cents a point, Kaufman once said, "I'd like to have a review of the bidding—*with the original intonations.*"

•

In one hand, George bid one club. The bidding came around for the fourth time and it was still one club.

His opponent said of George's partner, "He's not even trying."

And George replied, "Oh, he's very trying."

•

Once when Mankiewicz was his partner and blew the hand,
Kaufman said, "Herman, I know you learned to play bridge
today, but what *time* today?"

•

When he grew ill and infirm, his memory began to falter.
It was then that Kaufman, rather than embarrass himself,
stopped playing cards. For a while, he would go down to the
Regency at the end of each afternoon and stand behind a
player's chair and watch. But Kaufman did not have the personality of a spectator. Either he was in or he was out. Two
years before he died, he gave up cards. When he did that, he
surrendered a very definite slice of his life.

His attitude toward cards may be summed up in four words.

In the days when he was still speaking to Jed Harris, he
said to him, "We caught So-and-So cheating last night."

Harris was amazed that the man Kaufman named, a multi-
millionaire, a public figure of great importance, should risk his
reputation for a few dollars.

"Why did he do it?" Harris asked.

"He wanted to win!"

———

Dig deep beneath the outer layers of Kaufman's character,
and there lay a fierce determination to succeed. Victory seemed
to solve so many of his problems: his ego was bolstered by it,

his fears of poverty were temporarily allayed, his shyness and his faint sense of inferiority both disappeared with success at cards, with women, or in the theatre.

There was an earnestness to say nothing of absolute truthfulness in a line he once dropped at the card table, spoken with the usual light Kaufman touch.

"I'd rather be a poor winner," he said, "than any kind of loser."

10 *The Man Who Hated Hollywood*

GEORGE KAUFMAN WAS NOT A FRESH-AIR FIEND. NOR WAS HE A sunshine bug. Palm trees left him indifferent, and the only kind of cocoanut he liked was the one the Marx Brothers were in. The upshot was that he hated Hollywood and loved to ridicule it.

He rather liked the intimate confines of the Garden of Allah, the "in" place for theatrical people to stay back in the Thirties, but he abhorred the way writers were treated at the studios. In the New York theatre, the writer was the single most important person on the production staff. In Hollywood, Kaufman distinctly believed writers were too often ignored or insulted in the making of pictures.

In 1929 he wrote the movie version of *Cocoanuts* with Morrie Ryskind. The picture was successful. They filmed *Animal Crackers* the same year, after which the Marx Brothers and Ryskind went to California. Kaufman, however, remained steadfastly in New York, fearful of the lemon trees and the tennis courts in the backyards of Beverly Hills.

As the drama editor of the New York *Times*, Kaufman

was the first reporter to see Samuel Goldwyn after that tycoon left that other tycoon, Jesse Lasky. The *Times* generally did not bother with news of motion pictures in those days, but this was a story good enough to bring out Kaufman.

Goldwyn was so impressed with him that he hired Kaufman and Robert E. Sherwood to write the screenplay for *Roman Scandals*, starring Eddie Cantor. In 1934 Kaufman, who had heard how Hollywood treated authors, insisted that a clause be written into his contract stipulating that he, Kaufman, would not have to meet with or listen to Cantor's view of the story. On the signing of the contract there was much trumpeting by Goldwyn's press department. Kaufman was coming to Hollywood for an extended stay. He went, and he and Sherwood, old friends from New York, finished off the first draft of the screenplay in short order.

When Cantor learned that a story conference was to be held, he went to Arthur Hornblow, the director, and begged to be allowed to sit in on it. Hornblow contacted Goldwyn, who gave permission, provided Cantor simply sat and listened.

At the story conference the next day, Kaufman, as was his custom in New York, read the script aloud. At its conclusion, Cantor asked if he might be permitted to make a single comment regarding the script. Goldwyn nodded, and three hours later Cantor finished, having talked his way into an entirely new story.

Kaufman arose and, without a single word, left the conference. Shortly thereafter Goldwyn received a letter from Kaufman. It contained two salient points: (1) "My contract has a clause which permits me to work free of Cantor," and (2) "I am finished with this job."

In 1934 Kaufman and Sherwood sued Goldwyn for the remainder of the money due them for services rendered on *Roman Scandals*. They won their case.

Despite their law suit, Sam Goldwyn and George Kaufman became great friends. Goldwyn once approached Kaufman with what Goldwyn considered an intriguing proposal.

"I've got a proposition for you," Goldwyn began, "I want you to work for me. You see, I've been looking for a man who's smart, who knows what's what, a clever guy who could take over all my responsibilities for six months, a year. So what do you say?"

"I say this," was Kaufman's answer. "I've been looking for the same guy myself."

Goldwyn paid Kaufman the highest tribute a Hollywood producer can offer a writer. "He had the art of working very hard," Goldwyn said. "He had no swimming pool."

In 1935, Hollywood—not to be outdone by New York—found its own Boy Genius. Irving Thalberg, as the presiding oracle at MGM, realized that the Marx Brothers had just finished two rather ordinary pictures. The Marx Brothers assured him it was their material. The best man to write their material was in New York, and no one but no one could get George S. Kaufman back to Hollywood.

"I can," the Boy Genius is claimed to have said. What's more, he did. But that's why he was being paid to be a Boy Genius. How did he do it? Easy. He guaranteed Kaufman a hundred thousand dollars to write a single picture.

Now remember, in 1935, when veterans were selling apples for a nickel and other good men were raking leaves for the W.P.A., $100,000 was an honest-to-God one hundred thousand dollars. So in between writing and staging *First Lady* with Katharine Dayton and *Stage Door* with Edna Ferber, Kaufman rode out to Hollywood and wrote *A Night at the Opera* for Thalberg, the Marx Brothers, and MGM.

Once at the studio Kaufman was given the treatment that,

five years earlier, in *Once in a Lifetime*, he and Moss Hart had predicted would be the lot of playwrights in Hollywood.

Many of filmland's wits had sport with the institution of Waiting for Irving (Thalberg), but it remained for George Kaufman, who also served his time on what was known as the million-dollar bench, to originate the line, "On a clear day you can see Thalberg."

When Thalberg finally consented to meet with him, he fired a series of inquiries at Kaufman regarding the projected *A Night at the Opera*. As creative head of MGM, Thalberg was a busy man. His queries came with the speed of a telegrapher's key.

Kaufman sat and listened patiently. Finally he spoke. "Mr. Thalberg, I came here to write for the Marx Brothers," he said, "not to play Twenty Questions."

"I brought you here at a pretty fancy price just to answer those questions, Mr. Kaufman. How soon can I have an outline?"

"I don't know," Kaufman told him.

"Monday?"

"I told you. I don't know."

"Wednesday?" the producer persisted.

Kaufman pinched an ear lobe several times before answering him.

"Mr. Thalberg, do you want it Wednesday or good?"

That was more than enough for Thalberg. They became close friends, as close as anyone in Hollywood could be to George Kaufman.

When Thalberg's wife Norma Shearer went into the hospital to have her baby, Thalberg engaged an adjoining suite. While Miss Shearer waited in one room, Thalberg played bridge throughout the night in the next room. The first player he invited was George Kaufman.

But to Kaufman, playing bridge in Hollywood was like almost everything else in Hollywood: childish.

Once, George and Howard Dietz were matched against Moss Hart and Charley Lederer. The score was so one-sided that Lederer suggested he and Hart be given the advantage of looking in each other's hands. Kaufman agreed and he and Dietz still beat Lederer and Hart.

•

By the time the bridge games were played and the parties attended, Kaufman and Ryskind finished the script of A *Night at the Opera*. At the end of the film, Kitty Carlisle and Allan Jones are singing together onstage. As the duet draws to a climax, Harpo and Chico run from one side of the stage to the other, followed closely by the police. Then there is a shot of Groucho and the stately Margaret Dumont in a box at the opera house. Observing the contretemps on the stage, Miss Dumont demands, "What's that?" Groucho peers myopically and replies, "Either there are cops in *Il Trovatore* or the jig is up!"

There was so much laughter at the previews as a result of that one line, audiences couldn't hear how the picture ended. Before it was generally released, Groucho's line was cut. Old Hollywood observers still believe it was the funniest line in the picture. Even without it, A *Night at the Opera* became a spectacular success artistically as well as financially. In its first run it made a profit of over three million dollars—this in a day when admission to picture shows usually ranged from twenty-five to forty cents.

•

Rosalie Stewart, a Broadway emigré, stopped Kaufman in the commissary at MGM one day to congratulate him on the good work he'd done on the Marx Brothers picture. After he thanked her, the former Broadway producer, currently a Hollywood author's agent, asked Kaufman if he remembered her brother, Stewart Stewart, in New York. George remembered him, whereupon Rosalie confessed that their family name had been Muckenfus, but they had changed it.

"You mean your brother's name," George demanded, "was Muckenfus Muckenfus?"

•

The sunshine and the outdoor living, the lush gardens and the roll of the surf at Malibu were all distracting elements from the form of life to which he'd grown accustomed back East.

When he was in Hollywood he complained he never had time for books. Standing on a street corner with Leonard Lyons, he watched two airplanes writing in the sky urging people to drink Pepsi-Cola.

"That's the only thing I've read since I've been out here," Kaufman told Lyons.

•

Lyons met him not only on the street but occasionally caught him at one of the larger social gatherings. After Lana Turner was "discovered" and made into a film star, a raft of other girls standing behind counters and waiting on tables were also "found" by Hollywood. At a Beverly Hills party, a Warner Brothers talent scout was bragging about the good taste and shrewd instinct of his employers. Kaufman looked at him with disdain. "They don't want actresses," he said, "they want waitresses."

•

At an early Hollywood dinner party, an English author was shredding the reputation of a Broadway actress, capping it with, "She's her own worst enemy."

To which Kaufman quietly added, "Not while you're alive."

•

In addition to parties, another irritant was the fact that *everyone* drove automobiles *everywhere*. Kaufman, of course, had to have a chauffeur.

Once, while he was being driven about Hollywood by a chauffeur, a policeman stopped the car for going through a red light. Kaufman sat impatiently, reading a newspaper, while the officer wrote out the summons. When his ensuing harangue to the chauffeur proved too much, Kaufman leaned forward, showing the front page of the newspaper to the policeman. It listed the statistics on unsolved crimes in Los Angeles. Then he addressed the cop.

"Two weeks ago, all of my clothes were stolen from my hotel room," he said to the man in blue. "I called the police and they said they'd be in touch. That was two weeks ago. And *now*," Kaufman said, pointing to the summons, "they've finally gotten in touch with me!"

•

Over the hill from Hollywood is Palm Springs, and that is where he made his most famous remark about Moss Hart.

Hart, out on the desert for the first time, decided to go western in a fashion that only Hart could pull off. Always the retailer's best friend, Hart showed up in a pair of frightfully expensive Texas boots, chaps, jeans, a beautifully hammered silver belt buckle, an elegant elkskin vest, and Stetson's best twenty-gallon hat.

One glance was all Kaufman needed.

"Hi-yo, Platinum," he said.

•

With Hart, in 1936, Kaufman wrote the play *You Can't Take It With You* in Hollywood, and just as they finished it the Mary Astor episode broke. Local papers reported that Kaufman had slipped out of California incognito, bound in bandages and blankets almost as tightly as a mummy.

No wonder, then, that despite the Pulitzer Prize that *You Can't Take It With You* won, Kaufman always disliked the play and its unpleasant associations. He refused to adapt it for the screen, and the film went on to win the 1938 Oscar for the best picture of the year.

When he returned to Hollywood the next year and made his peace with the court, Kaufman quite understandably did not go near Mary Astor. The Broadway leading lady Jean Dixon, on the Coast for her honeymoon, met him. Daring to comment on the lack of press that accompanied this Kaufman visit, she teased, "Well, I haven't seen any of your ads in the papers lately."

George stiffened. "When a building falls on you once, you don't take a chance of it happening again," he told her.

•

The Hollywood prince Adolph Zukor once offered a trifling thirty thousand for the movie rights to a Kaufman play. Kaufman shot back a telegram offering Zukor forty thousand for Paramount Pictures.

•

Although he returned to Hollywood in 1940, it was not as a film maker. His old friend Alexander Woollcott was starring in the play *The Man Who Came to Dinner,* and was stricken with a severe case of laryngitis. Kaufman rode the railroad clear out to California to play Sheridan Whiteside. At a time when most Americans were flying, why no plane for Kaufman? He was afraid of them.

When his lawyer drew up a will providing for the possibility that George and Beatrice might perish in the same airplane accident, he said, "We could die in the same airplane accident only if I were walking down a country road and the plane Beatrice was in crashed and fell on me."

•

After a farewell dinner given in honor of his friend S. N. Behrman's departure from Hollywood, Kaufman was surprised to see the guest of honor still at the studio a week later.

"Ah," Kaufman said, "forgotten but not gone."

Many years after that, Behrman repeated the remark to President John F. Kennedy, and Kennedy asked if he might use it.

"It's not mine, it's George Kaufman's."

"Whoever it is," the president said, "it will come in very handy in the corridors of the White House."

•

During World War II, Kaufman found himself in a gin-rummy game with his Hollywood friend Charley Lederer. Lederer was absent-mindedly humming a tune of Sir Arthur Sullivan's with words of his own making: "Oh, he nodded his head and never said no, and now he's the head of the studio."

"Where'd you get that?" Kaufman asked.

"I just made it up."

"Will you sell it?"

Lederer allowed as how he ought not sell anything that trivial, but Kaufman insisted he wanted this to be a business transaction. Lederer said he couldn't take money for such an idle thought, but if Kaufman wanted to use it, and if what use he made of it turned out well, Kaufman could buy Lederer's wife a bauble.

George Kaufman wrote down the terms and had Lederer sign the paper. When the deed was done, Kaufman announced, "You've just given me a brilliant idea for a show I'm going to call *Hollywood Pinafore*."

Hollywood Pinafore proved to be one of his biggest and most costly failures.

Shortly after the war, he saw Lederer again. Without giving him a chance to utter a sound, Kaufman ran over to him, clamped his hand over Lederer's mouth, and hissed, "For God's sake don't sing anything!"

•

His reputation as a Hollywood lover sometimes proved inhibiting and uncomfortable.

When he was asked by a West Coast hostess to bring Hedy Lamarr to a dinner party, he and the chauffeur did just that. Hedy Lamarr in those days was a reigning beauty and a sex symbol on her own. The hostess had imagined a perfect match.

Promptly at the allocated hour, Kaufman's limousine rolled into Miss Lamarr's driveway. The chauffeur opened the rear door. Mr. Kaufman got out and rang Miss Lamarr's doorbell.

A maid answered and stared at him. "Are *you* Mr. Kaufman?" she said in a voice that registered deep disappointment.

Kaufman choked up, swallowed twice, and managed a faint nod of his head.

"She'll be right down," the maid said.

Hedy Lamarr at the height of her career was a movie star of the first magnitude. The brilliance of her beauty, the carriage of her head and body, to say nothing of the fact that she had been the first actress to romp in the nude in the Austrian film *Ecstasy* made her someone very special.

Not wanting to crack her makeup, she favored Kaufman with a slight parting of the lips, which was intended to pass as a smile.

He and the chauffeur helped her into the limousine. She sat in one corner, he sat in the other corner. She waited for him to be gay and charming. Instead he was, thanks to her maid, morose and silent. Not a word was exchanged.

At dinner, they were seated at opposite ends of the table. When it was time to take her home, he approached Miss Lamarr and raised his eyebrows. Miss Lamarr got the message and her wrap.

In the limousine again, she sat in one corner of the back seat and he sat in the other. They proceeded to her home in the same silence as they had come.

By the time he saw her to her door, Miss Lamarr was so furious with him that she didn't even say good night.

"That's a night I'd like to live over again," George told me, "if I could just eliminate the goddamn maid."

He didn't return to California professionally until 1947, and then it was to direct *The Senator Was Indiscreet*. Al Lewis, a Broadway producer who had become an indentured servant in

Hollywood, received the first telephone call shortly after Kaufman arrived.

"Will you please come over here?" Kaufman said in his Hollywood voice, which was quite often impatient, angry, and tighter than usual. "I'm in a little office, if you're able to find it. I've just arrived at Universal Studios, and I've just had a man who pretended he was an executive but who sounded like a janitor say, 'Mr. Kaufman, this is where you're going to go.' And it's big enough for a typewriter but not for me *and* a typewriter. And where is Nunnally Johnson?"

Nunnally Johnson, Kaufman's friend and collaborator on a Broadway musical, was the producer of the film Kaufman was to direct.

"The only reason he came out here," Johnson said, "was that he had nothing to do in New York at the time. His life here was skimpy. You rarely saw George in Hollywood. You just heard about his being here."

Although he had been directing plays for twenty years, Kaufman was leery of the technical side of the film industry. To compensate for this, Nunnally Johnson hired Gene Fowler, Jr. Fowler was to look after the mechanical end of the picture; all Kaufman had to do was to concentrate on the actors. Together they made a team that worked well.

He chose William Powell to play the title role and found him to be a charming man and an excellent actor. Ella Raines was cast opposite Powell, and Kaufman had nothing but kind words to say about her.

"He had one of the greatest ears," Fowler said. "He would sit and not look at the actors, just listen. We would do fourteen or fifteen takes and he wouldn't look at them once."

Although Fowler didn't know it, this was not dissimilar to the way Kaufman directed a play.

Fowler would call "Action!" or "Cut!" and Kaufman didn't

seem to mind it. He didn't have that ego associated with Hollywood motion picture directors. He was more than ready to delegate authority, especially in those areas in which he was unsure of himself. He even felt guilty about the money he was drawing down and frequently said to Fowler, "I'm getting paid more than I deserve."

Each evening Fowler would stop by the Garden of Allah, where Kaufman was staying, and map out the next day's shooting. He noticed that nightly there was a different attractive woman in the Kaufman suite. "Whoever she was," Fowler said, "Kaufman disclaimed her airily, as though she were there merely to turn down the bed or change the towels."

The few friends with whom he associated in California were limited to New York theatrical or literary figures: the Marx Brothers, Robert Benchley, Robert Sherwood, plus a few transplanted and now permanent citizens of the Golden Bear State: Sam Goldwyn, Charley Brackett, Charley Lederer, and of course Nunnally Johnson.

The work day was long, though, and George wasn't used to getting up early in the morning. Nunnally listened to him complain about how hard he was laboring on the picture.

"Look at that beautiful girl walking there," Nunnally said.

"Six weeks ago," Kaufman answered, "I would have turned around."

What Kaufman liked about the picture was its subject matter. *The Senator Was Indiscreet* was about a lame-duck politician who was equipped to do nothing except be president of the United States. The senator was Kaufman's kind of character— the bumbler, the innocent, the inoffensive fellow. At best, or at worst, depending on which side you took, it was a mild, engaging spoof of American politics.

He was totally unprepared, therefore, for what happened when the picture was released. The late Senator Joseph McCarthy of Wisconsin was just beginning his witch hunt. He denounced the film with numerous epithets ranging from "un-American" to downright "traitorous."

Kaufman watched in horror as name after name was added to the dreaded Hollywood Blacklist. Actors, authors, directors, producers were thrown out of work and left to go hungry or worse simply because one person might have said something of a quasi-sensitive nature to somebody else. Hearsay, not evidence, ruled. Guilty or innocent, everyone in the path of the Red Wave became a victim.

As he never joined anything, needless to say, George escaped all this, but he was shocked and offended, and fled Hollywood forever. It wasn't Senator McCarthy who drove him out. It was his contempt for those Hollywood executives who kowtowed to McCarthy and permitted him to get away with such tactics.

At least, that was what George gave as an excuse. In reality, it wasn't his kind of town, it wasn't his kind of work, it wasn't his kind of craft.

In Hollywood, his own personality was completely incorrect for motion picture production. To a large degree, that process is mechanical, and Kaufman had a lifelong battle with inanimate objects. He would walk across a room and always be sure that chairs deliberately got in his way. The mechanical aspects of Hollywood were abhorrent to him. The pace, the early morning calls for shooting, the cutting, the rushes, the moviola, the splicing, the dubbing—all matters so important to the production of a first-rate film were, in his mind, contemptible.

In Hollywood, after a day of shooting, they would come to Kaufman and ask him to look at the dailies.

"What's that?" he inquired.

When it was explained to him, he said, "I don't want to see any pieces, I want to see the whole picture when it's finished."

"Well, you're the director," he'd be told. "You've got to choose the shots you want."

"Let the cutter do that," Kaufman would say.

He was never a man for Sunset and Vine. He believed he belonged on Broadway. He sensed an impermanence to Hollywood, and time has proven him right.

11 *Leueen's Gentleman*

FOLLOWING THE DEATH OF HIS WIFE BEATRICE, GEORGE KAUF-
man became more of an introvert than ever. Bitter and angry at
those friends of theirs who did not attend her funeral, he began
to see fewer people. Those whom he did see worried about him.
He dropped out of his two poker clubs. He showed less and less
interest in work. Writing was no longer compelling. Directing
was no longer gratifying. He would get between his sheets in the
evening, sleep the night, and spend all day in his small room.
When asked why he did this, he said, "I have nothing to do,
nowhere to go, I might as well stay in bed." He looked poorly,
sounded bad, and felt worse.

The time from Beatrice's death in 1945 until he began collaborating with a new partner in 1951 was the most unpro-
ductive period in his adult life. He wrote only one musical,
Park Avenue, with Nunnally Johnson, and one play, *Bravo!*,
with Edna Ferber. Both were failures, but that new collaborator
—she wasn't just a smash hit—turned out to be the love of his
life.

Late one afternoon toward the autumn of 1948, Ruth Goetz

gave a cocktail party for an English actress friend, Peggy Ashcroft. It was one of those theatrical affairs that New Yorkers manage so easily, one of those "everyone was there" assemblies. Among those present was Mr. Kaufman. This was highly unusual, as Kaufman did not care for cocktail parties, and following the death of his wife he had forsaken large areas of the social life. But Ruth Goetz and her husband Gus were particularly dear to him, so he arrived. And stood in the corner. And spoke to almost no one.

Then there swept into the room a fellow player of Miss Ashcroft's, an absolutely dazzling young woman, so striking that almost all of the men at the party, according to those who were there, rushed to her side. Except George Kaufman. He took off one pair of glasses and put on another pair, and gazed at her.

She was really something to look at. Petite, blonde, brown-eyed. Her figure was even more delicate than her face; her waist was so small that any grown man could put his two hands around it.

She was making her first appearance in New York at the Martin Beck Theatre, in a play by Robert Morley and Noel Langley entitled *Edward, My Son.* She, Mr. Morley, and the play had opened the previous year in London to great critical acclaim and popular appeal. While doing the play in London, she and Spencer Tracy had made the film version for MGM. Then she and Robert Morley, Peggy Ashcroft, Ian Hunter, Torin Thatcher, and others had come to New York and repeated the success scored in London.

Mr. Morley of course was the star, and rightly received the lion's share of the notices, but the critics found in the young woman who was playing his highly efficient secretary as well as his highly infatuating mistress a beautiful woman and an excellent actress.

Dylan Thomas had once said of her, "She looks like a lascivious choirboy." He was exactly right. She favored clothes that lived up to the Irish poet's description; her daytime dresses emphasized broad, white yoke collars and white cuffs. Her eyes sparkled with healthy animal excitement, while her highly cultured British accent was delivered in a soft academic whisper. She spoke French with as much ease as she spoke English. And while she was no more athletic than a cloisonné doll, which she rather resembled, she seemed to float across a room rather than walk.

Her name was Leueen MacGrath. Leueen was an Irish word for a small coin. MacGrath was pronounced more like McGraw.

Kaufman saw her at Ruth Goetz's cocktail party but didn't say a word to her. That was in late October or early November. In May, around the same time that Aly Khan married Rita Hayworth, George S. Kaufman married the daughter of Major Walter Michael Anthony MacGrath, D.S.O., M.C., Croix de Guerre.

MacGrath, an English Irishman, part-time mining engineer, part-time soldier, had traveled from the Balkans to India and back again, marrying Jean Martin, fathering a daughter, and fighting with His Majesty's British Expeditionary Force in France, gaining the above-mentioned decorations.

A daughter, Leueen Emily, was born July 3, 1914, in London. She had a continental education—Sacré Coeur in Lausanne, Farnborough Convent College, and Les Tourelles in Brussels—and studied at the Royal Academy of Dramatic Art. Her first stage appearance was at the Garrick Theatre in London on April 17, 1933. From walk-ons, she rose through a series of ingenue roles to the rarefied height of leading lady.

In World War II, she drove an ambulance through the streets of London during the blitzes and the V-1s and V-2s. If there was a wide-open chink in the beautiful armor she had built about herself, it was the recollection of the fires and explosions and screams and cries of death brought on by the Nazis. She could and did shake visibly whenever the subject of wartime London arose.

To aid her fortune as an actress, she acquired a sort of trademark. At a time when almost all women wore short hair and had it curled in a dozen fashions, she wore her straight blond hair well below her shoulders.

As for men, she always had many more than she could handle. As for husbands, she had two before George Kaufman and two after him. Of the first two and the last two, little need be said. It was how Kaufman landed Leueen when she was at the height of her beauty and the top of her career that is of interest.

For a man who had been directing plays since 1928, moving a few friends around so that he could meet someone who caught his eye was no great challenge to Kaufman. From his rather aloof vantage point at Ruth Goetz's cocktail party, Kaufman picked up assorted pieces of information. Peggy Ashcroft had left the company of *Edward, My Son*. Peggy Ashcroft was planning to dine that evening with Ruth and Garson Kanin. Peggy Ashcroft was going to a press party with Leueen MacGrath after the theatre that night.

The easiest thing in the world was to invite the Kanins to dinner; they would bring Miss Ashcroft; if Miss MacGrath wanted to meet Miss Ashcroft later . . . Easy? Of course.

The Kanins came to dinner at George Kaufman's apartment at 410 Park Avenue. They brought Peggy Ashcroft. At eleven o'clock, Miss Ashcroft telephoned the theatre to tell Miss MacGrath where she was. The press department at MGM had provided Miss MacGrath with a limousine and chauffeur.

"Have her meet you here," Kaufman said.

Miss Ashcroft, a first-rate professional actress, did as directed.

Miss MacGrath, also a first-rate professional actress, did as directed. Within half an hour after the curtain fell she was at 410 Park Avenue, and as the small gathering of Miss Gordon,

Miss Ashcroft, Mr. Kanin, and Mr. Kaufman seemed so much more interesting than a large press party, Miss MacGrath spent the remainder of the evening there.

Next morning, one of the Kaufman servants brought him a book. It was the bound copy of a play by Philip Barry. On the flyleaf was the name Leueen MacGrath and her hotel.

"I left it behind," Miss MacGrath recalled. "I don't think intentionally . . . but maybe."

Kaufman went directly to his typewriter and pecked off a note to the effect that he was perfectly prepared to return her book, but only on the condition that she have dinner with him.

On receipt of the hand-delivered note, Miss MacGrath called him and explained that she needed the play, as she had been asked to do it for television.

"Dinner, tonight. My place," he pronounced.

That evening and for several evenings after that, they dined together.

Kaufman, who had known more women than most sultans, real or fictitious, never made a move in Miss MacGrath's direction.

Finally, one evening as they were having a late supper at "21," he peered over the rims of his glasses and said, "Well, Miss M., is it yes or is it no?"

She smiled and continued nibbling away at her salad.

The next morning, the great telegram-sender shot off a simple message of ninety-nine words. It read:

WHERE ARE YOU? WHERE ARE YOU? WHERE ARE YOU?
WHERE ARE YOU? WHERE ARE YOU? WHERE ARE YOU?
WHERE ARE YOU? WHERE ARE YOU? WHERE ARE YOU?
WHERE ARE YOU? WHERE ARE YOU? WHERE ARE YOU?
WHERE ARE YOU? WHERE ARE YOU? WHERE ARE YOU?
WHERE ARE YOU? WHERE ARE YOU? WHERE ARE YOU?
WHERE ARE YOU? WHERE ARE YOU? WHERE ARE YOU?

WHERE ARE YOU? WHERE ARE YOU? WHERE ARE YOU?
WHERE ARE YOU? WHERE ARE YOU? WHERE ARE YOU?
WHERE ARE YOU? WHERE ARE YOU? WHERE ARE YOU?
WHERE ARE YOU? WHERE ARE YOU? WHERE ARE YOU?

GEORGE

The notion of George S. Kaufman trying to find a motel room in Miami Beach for himself and a girl is difficult to contemplate. And yet there he was with Leueen—wanting to go to one of the islands in the Caribbean but unable to because she, a British subject, had forgotten to get a re-entry permit. So there they were in Miami Beach, trying to get away for a long weekend together.

One motel, the Green Heron, seemed rather sleazy, but on viewing a few others, worse yet, they decided to find out if they could get in. Kaufman the sophisticate, Kaufman the debonair, Kaufman the fellow of few but precise words telephoned the Green Heron from a gas station.

"Hello," he mumbled into the phone, "I am the people who were there before."

"Somehow he got the bungalow," Leueen recalled fondly, "and it turned out to be just the place both of us had wanted, and he and I knew we were very much in love."

Leueen wished it to continue that way. She was smitten with an enchanting, important figure in the theatre. He amused her, he was tender, confident, commanding; his place in the social order in which he lived was unchallenged. Wealth and success were never qualities that Leueen sought out, but they were as much a part of George as the comb he carried in his jacket pocket. True, he was considerably older, but age counted for nothing at that point in her life.

George wanted romance on a much more permanent basis. He was in love with a young woman who moved and spoke with a dash and candor he had never found in any female. The woman he had been waiting for all his life had suddenly materialized. As a result, he said something that none of the very many ladies he had known had heard him say.

They were at his apartment having dinner, when he stopped eating and said, "Well, you know, we really should be married."

"I honestly don't know," Leueen answered. "I think it might be wonderful, but I honestly don't know. I think we should live with each other until we're sure."

George, however, was not to be denied. It was a bride he wanted, not a mistress, and it was a bride he got.

The Justice of the Peace in Doylestown, Pennsylvania, was by matter of business an automobile salesman; as an elected official, however, he was vested with the right to perform the marriage ceremony. He exercised that right at Barley Sheaf Farm when he joined Leueen MacGrath and George Kaufman together as man and wife on May 26, 1949.

They honeymooned that spring and summer at the farm, surrounded by the personal and household possessions that had been Bea's. Leueen slept in Bea's bed, on Bea's monogrammed linens, dried her hands with Bea's hand towels. The wastebasket in her bedroom was initialed B.B.K. The silver at the dining table was similarly engraved. Visitors were reminded of Daphne du Maurier's novel *Rebecca*. Leueen apparently experienced no qualms.

If all of these memories of Bea did not bother her, they most assuredly had an effect on George. Late one night when he was unable to sleep, he came into her bedroom and confessed to a fear that had dogged him from the early years of his first marriage. He was afraid that, as with Bea, after a year he would be unable to make love to her.

Leueen brushed the confession aside as late-night nonsense, but her husband grew increasingly earnest. If that should happen he wanted her to find contentment with other men. She was a young and healthy woman, and complete abstention from sexual activity was not a fate he wished her to endure.

Again she tried to brush this talk away, but George insisted that in the future she recall his wishes. He kissed her gently, turned off her light, and left her bedroom. The house still seemed to belong to Bea.

The tinkling name of Leueen sounded affected and on the brassy side to some of Kaufman's friends. The thought of a man marrying someone so many years younger rarely sits well with those parties who have an interest in that man himself.

Edna Ferber, while gracious and outwardly hospitable to the new Mrs. Kaufman, said that it was as if George were in the third grade, falling hopelessly in love with the beautiful girl with pink skin and long blond curls who sat across the aisle from him.

A disconcerting moment occurred for his daughter Anne when she and her own daughter Betsy were standing in front of a Philadelphia movie house. There, on an easel, blown up to heroic proportions, was a photograph advertising the movie *Edward, My Son*. The camera and the artist who retouched the photograph showed Leueen's lips slightly parted and larger and more concupiscent than they ever were. Her eyelids were heavily made up and half closed, her hair hung in a sultry fashion, and the cleavage was not to be believed. Betsy recognized her at once.

"Look Mommy," she called out, "there's Grandma!"

Thornton Wilder found Leueen enchanting. "She was very tender, like a dove who may have injured one wing."

Those who were closest to him realized that it was a magical marriage for George. All his life he had wanted to pour out affection and tenderness to one woman, and finally he had found her.

Mrs. Richard Rodgers contrasted Kaufman's two marriages: "They were certainly different. I remember one time when George and Leueen came to spend a weekend at our house up in Connecticut. It was cool and Leueen had forgotten her sweater," Mrs. Rodgers said. "The guest room was two flights up and George ran up to get it for her. Well, I couldn't have imagined him doing this for Beatrice. He really waited on Leueen, he adored her in a different way. He was almost like a boy in love with her. I never felt this in his relationship with Beatrice. I think he would have let Beatrice walk up the stairs herself to get whatever it was she had forgotten."

Moss Hart, who had known Beatrice as well as anyone, always said that Leueen was the only woman George really loved.

The scoffers, the sneerers, those who said the ugly things about her—never in front of Kaufman, of course—had to sulk in the back ranks of his friends.

As for Kaufman himself, his second marriage turned him from a dour, sour man to one who laughed and chortled and constantly thought of what things he might do to please his bride.

There were many.

The last apartment Beatrice had furnished for her husband was at 410 Park Avenue. No one ever questioned Beatrice's taste. The apartment was, nevertheless, very large, very dark and if not heavily Teutonic in flavor then at least splendidly Victorian.

The new Mrs. Kaufman did not wish to live on Park Avenue. She expressed a fondness for cottages. As the number of cottages on the fashionable East Side of the island of Manhattan is nonexistent, she settled for a facsimile of a cottage. It was the penthouse of 1035 Park Avenue.

Dorothy Hammerstein, wife of the famed author and lyricist, was a talented interior decorator who helped Leueen furnish the apartment. She found that her client preferred white walls, thick white rugs, and a combination of English and French furniture.

To everyone's amazement, George even went shopping with his new wife. In the drapery department of Bloomingdale's, while Leueen was elbow-deep in materials and fabrics, George stood isolated and forlorn. Taking pity on him, a salesman approached and asked if he might be of help. "Maybe you can," George answered. "Do you have any good second-act curtains here?"

Household help, too, was changed. The German servants whom George had endured with custom and comfort during the years with Beatrice were replaced by a French couple—Jean the butler and Rose the cook. Previously, they had been in the employ of Winthrop Rockefeller.

Far from being unhappy with these changes in his life-style, George welcomed Leueen's efforts warmly. He even worked out two standard jokes about Rose.

"She's been over here so long she's forgotten how to speak French, and since she never learned to speak English, she's unable to talk at all."

The second Rose story concerned fudge, a candy that Kaufman had learned to make with his sister Ruth in Pittsburgh, that he still made, and of which he considered himself the world's foremost manufacturer. Discovering that the master liked fudge, Rose began preparing plates of it. George claimed it couldn't compare to his. As visitors reached out to take a piece of the cook's fudge, Kaufman would deliver his second Rose line. "There's a problem here," he would say. "If we don't eat it, she'll be insulted. On the other hand, if we *do*, she'll make more."

He made no jokes about Jean. Au contraire. Jean was silver-haired, and carried himself with a haughtiness reserved for a man of position. Imagine the effect on Leueen's English friends who came to dinner at 1035 Park Avenue. They were greeted at the door by an elderly man, distinguished enough to be one of America's foremost theatrical authors, so they chirped and chimed about how happy they were to meet Mr. Kaufman— and then, at the dinner table, to have the man whom they had greeted as Mr. Kaufman serve the meat and the vegetables and remove the used dishes!

Kaufman enjoyed it all thoroughly. He learned to like those English friends just as easily as he learned to like the French wine Leueen had served at lunch and dinner. When they dined in restaurants, he positively beamed when his wife would take the wine list and order in flawless French a chateau wine and specify the vintage year.

Leueen pulled off another miracle. George heartily disliked all animals. As far as he was concerned, they belonged in the same category as waiters and cab drivers.

Dorothy Parker had once come to the farm with a rather large dog. Kaufman objected to its being brought into the house. Mrs. Parker grew nasty. Kaufman grew nastier. Mrs. Parker and the dog left in a huff. The dog, Kaufman related, never said a word to him.

That's how he wanted it with dogs.

And yet when Leueen arrived home one day with a Siamese kitten, George glared at it suspiciously and said, "We'll call him Adam and let him stay until he grows into a cat." Leueen was delighted. After a pause, George added, "It's too bad he has my nose instead of yours."

Adam grew from a frolicking little kitten to quite an imperious cat. He walked about on George Kaufman like a Lilliputian general on a defenseless Gulliver. Everybody waited for the day when George would tell off Adam. Instead, they became great friends. Visitors were astonished to see Adam dip his paw into the same jar of bacon rinds from which George ate. Kaufman not only permitted this but also allowed Adam to interrupt a Kaufman story by leaping from the coffee table or the mantel onto Kaufman's lap. George would wince and grimace but never complain.

The only joke Kaufman couldn't resist making about Adam was on the day the cat was "altered" by a veterinarian. George borrowed Strickland Gillilan's old line, "Adam had 'em."

Marrying Leueen provided many more dividends. His fear of heights disappeared. The wide terraces that ran around four sides of the penthouse were guarded by high enough walls, but an earlier Kaufman would have been sick with fear if he had to step outside, let alone walk to the edge and look over. Now, he was not only secure, he could jest about it. When a collaborator who was waiting for Kaufman was found leaning over Park Avenue, Kaufman crept up behind and whispered, "Don't jump. The second act can be fixed."

More importantly, his drive to participate in the theatre returned. A few months after he married Leueen, Max Gordon had him directing again. The play, *Metropole*, did not succeed, but George was back at work. He followed that immediately by directing Giraudoux's *The Enchanted*. No luck there, either. It was an even more bitter pill to swallow because Leueen played the leading lady.

In the summer of 1950 his wife enticed him not only to England but to the south of France. His friends were astounded. For a man who had been on record for so long as being opposed to travel, airplanes, and foreign food, it was obvious that only Leueen could have gotten him out of the country. And even then, when he went abroad for the summer, he took a large supply of his favorite oatmeal with him, not trusting those fancy European chefs to come up with the kind of breakfast he expected.

On his return, he plunged into work directing what proved to be a typical Kaufman musical comedy. *Guys and Dolls*, with book by Abe Burrows and score by Frank Loesser, was the most successful musical Kaufman had directed since *Of Thee I Sing*.

231

Now he had everything: Leueen and a hit. Just as his cup ran over, he had his first stroke.

Leueen knew she was married to an "older man," but after the stroke, she realized how ill and how old he really was. Though never in front of him, she wept frequently. Her appetite disappeared and she began to lose weight immediately. As for George, he was too frightened to discuss what had happened to him, but now and then he would get up the courage to say, "I haven't felt well since . . . my illness. The symptoms are terrible—too terrible to talk about."

When George Kaufman came out of the hospital, to cover his anxiety of the present and his fear of the future, he began to work almost at once on a play with his wife. To those who knew little or nothing, it appeared to be a case of an older man pleasing his pretty young wife. In many instances this was true. When it came to a matter as important as work, Kaufman was far too professional to allow sentiment, even emotion, to interfere. To those who knew them intimately, George and Leueen had been literary collaborators since the first weeks of their marriage.

During the war Leueen had written a play. A friend had taken it out of the country, and it had been produced in Sweden. After she and Kaufman were married, she confessed this little indiscretion to him, and he was delighted. Their first work was a film scenario. It did not sell. Thereafter, they spent their afternoons and evenings discussing ideas for plays, television scripts, films. Kaufman, it must be recalled, was that compulsive writer and Leueen was a woman of talent and humor, with a thorough knowledge of the stage.

Their first work to be presented on Broadway was in 1951— *The Small Hours*, a drama concerned with the problem of loneliness. Fate and the critics decided it should not last long.

The next year, Kaufman and MacGrath were back on Broadway with a new comedy called *Fancy Meeting You Again*. It starred Leueen and Walter Matthau.

Prior to its pre-Broadway tour, Kaufman suffered another slight stroke. This left the rewriting squarely up to Leueen. She did it, and well, too, for by the time the show played Philadelphia and Boston, word had filtered back to New York that "a sleeper" was coming in.

A comedy about reincarnation, the play had a large dog appearing near its final curtain. The animal was the reincarnation of Leueen, and it was to greet Walter Matthau very lovingly at the end. Instead of rehearsing on the day of the opening, Kaufman gave the cast time off, insisting that Matthau get to know the animal better. Following that advice, Matthau romped with the dog in Central Park—romped too much, in fact, for during the afternoon the dog got into Matthau's path, the actor fell, the dog barked, and the actor got up with the ligaments of an ankle severely strained.

In Hollywood movies about the theatre, the understudy always goes on for the ailing star on opening nights. What nobody in Hollywood seems willing to recognize is that understudies are almost *never* rehearsed until well after the show has opened. (If it closes on Saturday night, why bother to rehearse the understudies?)

Into the stage door of the Royale Theatre on that opening night hobbled Walter Matthau, his ankle swollen; he could walk only with pain, which increased with the passing minutes. A doctor was summoned, and he solved everything immediately. One shot of novocaine into the ankle and Matthau could walk, jump, kick up his heels. The pain was gone.

Accordingly, the curtain arose. Miss MacGrath was alone on stage at the rise. Enter Mr. Matthau.

Miss MacGrath threw him his first cue. Mr. Matthau, who then, as now, was known for his exquisite sense of timing, merely stood there.

Again Miss MacGrath spoke her line. Again Mr. Matthau looked at her.

What neither of them knew, what the doctor had not known, was that Walter Matthau is very allergic to novocaine.

By the time he got around to speaking his line, Leueen had decided that this was going to make George even more ill. Standing in the back of the house, Kaufman watched the scene. He was apprehensive, but not to the degree his wife was. By now she had imagined that a failure on the stage that night would kill her husband, so with an energy verging on the frantic she began to overact, hoping to compensate for Walter Matthau's allergy and thus spare George's life.

It was to have been a very light comedy. It was not. At least not on the night that counted.

Three years later, in 1955, George and Leueen tried again with a musical, *Silk Stockings*. Nothing about it seemed to go well. So bitter were their experiences with producers Cy Feuer and Ernest Martin that they determined not to remain in New York for the opening night.

"It would be an act of kindness if you and Evelyn joined us in getting out of town," he said. So my wife and I met them in Atlantic City. We stayed at the Shelburne Hotel. The dining room was half empty, and the orchestra was playing slowly and innocuously. Outside, a gentle but substantial snowfall turned the boardwalk into something as soft and as white as a wedding cake.

We had a cocktail and two bottles of wine with dinner, and afterwards went on to stingers. It was the only time in my life I saw George Kaufman drunk. As he rose from the table, he swayed across the floor. At a hand signal from Leueen, I took him by his good right arm and helped him to his room. Once there, he lowered himself onto his bed. I took off his jacket and shoes and covered him with a blanket. As I was about to turn off the light and leave him, he stopped me. "This is the worst night of my life," he said.

It was not. The notices were good, the musical ran; what had gotten through to George S. Kaufman was the realization that he was old, and too infirm to fight back. This was the first time in his life that he'd left New York because a show of his was opening, and it hurt and he was ashamed before his wife. The age difference between them suddenly mattered. Not too many years ago, George S. Kaufman would have reduced Feuer and Martin to whatever size he saw fit, and he'd have done it with no more than a dozen words. On that night in Atlantic City time was running out for him, and he knew it.

What George had told Leueen on that sleepless night early in their honeymoon was no longer a fear. For some time it had been a reality. The most he could do to show his love for her was to murmur words of endearment. The man who had never been able to write a good love scene suddenly found him-self looking at his wife and saying, "My darling," with more tenderness and genuine feeling than any actor had ever used on a stage. Still, they were only words, and George suffered in the knowledge that he was depriving her, just as he had been afraid he would, of a complete life.

"Energy was something I never thought about until it left me," he told a friend. "Now I get it from a pill. It lasts about three or four hours and then I'm really through. I hate to take the stuff, but it's the only way I can get up enough steam to do the kind of writing I want to do."

The "stuff" was Dexamyl, and after its energizing effect was over, George would retreat to his bedroom thoroughly depleted. Attendance at social events was out of the question for him. Leueen, who was willing to sit home, have a quiet dinner, and turn in early, now found that George was accepting countless invitations to cocktail parties, dinners, and suppers on her behalf.

"I'm not up to it, but I'm sure Leueen would love to come," he would say or write, whichever the case demanded.

He had always been more than generous with her about the clothing she wore. Now, he insisted that she buy the most elegant gowns from the most fashionable designers of New York, Paris, and Rome.

She would come into his bedroom before leaving for the evening, turn around for his approval of her dress and accessories, kiss him, and then leave. Generally, he would be awake when she returned home, and together they would sit and revel in the latest chatter she had overheard.

It seemed inevitable that George should insist that she go to the theatre with younger men. Alan Campbell, who recently had been separated from Dorothy Parker; Wyatt Cooper, who would soon marry Gloria Vanderbilt; Charles Addams, the *New Yorker* cartoonist; and other elegant and intelligent young men acted as her escorts. It was a matter of time before she found someone else, or perhaps before someone found her.

George was both understanding and human about her seeing other men. On the one hand, he encouraged it. On the other, he became predictably jealous. Often, when she appeared in plays, she would drop by after a performance to spend the rest of the evening with friends. At eleven-thirty, quarter-of-twelve, the phone would ring.

"Is Leueen there?" he would ask.

"She's here, George."

She'd rush to pick up the phone, reassure him that she was all right, and tell him to sleep well.

At two o'clock one morning, our doorbell rang. When the door was opened, to everyone's astonishment, there stood George Kaufman, leaning on his cane, looking grim and embarrassed, but determined to see the incident through.

"Leueen phoned a while ago and said she might stop by here," he said.

"She's here. Come in, George."

The relief on his face was immediate. Once inside, however, his expression changed again. A newspaper reporter, the son of one of the men with whom George founded the Dramatists Guild, sat on a couch next to Leueen. He had been a dinner guest who had stayed on, not knowing that Leueen would drop in, but that made no difference. George sat stiffly, gripping his cane until his knuckles shone white. It was only after Elmer Rice's son Robert left that George relaxed and suggested that they go home.

His jealousy embarrassed him and the next day he was apologetic about it. "Damn fool way to behave," he said. "But people don't always have complete control over their feelings. I was lonesome last night, so I got out of my bed, got into my clothes, and there I was."

For her part, Leueen would awaken early in the mornings and slip out onto the terrace and walk to his bedroom window. George generally slept later than she did, and she would stand there waiting to see him breathe, to see him move, living in fear of his death. George, who had been such a father figure to so many people, was now viewed with the anguish of a mother by his wife.

There could be no question that this was scarcely the ideal life for a woman in her early forties. But she was able to find an escape from it in her work in the theatre—the perfect solution. Her latest play was by the English author Graham Greene. *The Potting Shed*, which opened in 1957, carried three names starred above its title: Dame Sybil Thorndike, Robert Flemyng, and Leueen MacGrath. The play, the cast, and the director all received excellent notices.

The director was thirty-two and strongly attracted to his leading lady. Although she discouraged him, he pursued her, and then the inevitable occurred: a love affair.

Her husband had made it quite clear that he would remain tolerant of a series of discreet liaisons, but Leueen could not bear the idea of betraying George. The whispered words, the hidden moments, the secret places—all of it was without principle and she knew it. And more than that, she knew what she had to do. Rather than offend George with a series of ugly little lies, she determined that the break had to be clean and quick and as painless as possible.

Bearing his health in mind, she telephoned George's physician and asked for an appointment. Once in Dr. Greenspan's office, Leueen discussed her situation frankly and inquired whether telling George she was leaving would further injure his health. The doctor did not believe it would.

Accordingly, she arranged to meet Anne Kaufman at Greenspan's office. In age, the two women were close enough to be sisters, and their relationship was quite similar. Each had a deep emotional attachment for the other.

On the way to the apartment, Leueen explained to Anne what she intended to do. To keep up his spirits or at least to be around should he need anything, Anne agreed to accompany her.

At 12:30 P.M. on February 26, 1957, they arrived at the Kaufman apartment. Anne waited in the living room. Leueen went back to George's bedroom. She spoke with him as forthrightly as she could manage. Tears welled up in her eyes as she looked at him. He was sitting in his bed; his face was colorless. As gently as she could, she explained what had happened to her. In all candor she believed it best that she move out immediately. Finally, could he forgive this almost unforgivable action of hers? He nodded his head. And she left.

Early in the afternoon, Moss and Kitty Hart and my wife and I received identical letters. Each was delivered by hand. Each said:

It is momentarily confidential, but I want to tell you, among the first, that Leueen and I are going to be divorced.

Our ages are so far apart—and she is entitled to a life with a younger man.

This is just a quick note—my love to you both.

George

Very late that night—my diary recorded the time as 2:52 A.M.—George telephoned.

"I couldn't sleep," he said. "Evidently you can't either or you wouldn't be answering the phone."

I agreed he was right.

"You got my note? About Leueen?"

We had.

"I didn't want you two to read about it in the papers first. So damn much of my life keeps turning up in the newspapers."

I said I was sorry about Leueen.

"I am, too," he answered.

Was there anything we could do?

"If you could make this conversation just a little duller, it might put me to sleep."

I laughed. We talked until 3:06 A.M., and I noted that he seemed jollier than when he first called.

At 3:08 A.M. the phone rang again.

"Are you still writing in that diary?" he asked.

I told him I was.

"Well, don't stop until you get something bright for me to get off on!"

And the phone clicked in my ear.

George Kaufman gave a great deal and received a great deal in his marriage to Leueen MacGrath; he enjoyed the giving even more than the receiving.

Still, there were those people who could only talk about what she had taken. (The clothes on her back and a few toilet articles in a small suitcase were what she had taken when she left him.) People carped that he had sold the farm in Bucks County to buy her a town house in London. (True, but it was his decision to do both.) People spoke of her during those first weeks as though she were the original fallen woman.

She, however, would sneak out of her new home and telephone the Kaufman apartment to learn if he was well or if there was anything he needed or wanted.

When she flew down to Mexico and returned divorced but unmarried, the tongues wagged in overtime. It was only when he began to hear that she was unhappy that George became agitated. When she left her young man, George got me on the phone at once and begged me to urge her to return to England. By the time I got the plane ticket, she went back to him.

The second time she left him, she stayed with her close friend Sue Lowe, who had produced *The Enchanted*. George found her and packed her off to London before she could change her mind. After a few months, she returned to New York, and George had her met at the airport by limousine. She was brought directly back to 1035 Park Avenue, where George had arranged a small dinner for her homecoming. Everyone behaved as though she'd just been away on a holiday. Everyone except one miserable creature: Adam the cat.

Every night for weeks after Leueen had left the house, Adam would wait for her beside the front door. With the patience of an old friend, he waited and waited for her. And then, one morning he turned away from the front door, walked down the hall to George's room, jumped onto George's bed, and from then on he was George's cat. When Leueen did return, it was too late. Adam never forgave her.

Everybody else did. Especially George. He asked all of their friends to convince Leueen to marry him again. Leueen felt to do so would cause more talk and more pain.

So George, like everyone else, settled for what he got. And what he got was something of a warm and dutiful second daughter. Very often she spent the night in her old bedroom so she could be near him if he needed help. She was at lunch, she was at dinner, she was at after-theatre parties. And she kept up a gracious household touch begun when she first married him: fresh flowers every day. George, who had never been introduced to flowers, let alone known them by name, had grown quite used to them—if Leueen was near.

At this writing, she is acting and living in London. She still believes the high point of her personal life was the days she spent as Mrs. George S. Kaufman.

Who is to doubt her?

12 *The Correspondent*

THE LETTERS HE WROTE WERE GENERALLY BRISK, AND FREquently without salutations or the amenities of farewell. More often than not, the concluding sentence would be followed by the word "George." In later years, he contracted that to a typed "G" or a quickly scribbled initial.

To members of his family, however, and to those close to him, he often wrote longer, funnier, and newsier communications.

Of the hundreds of Kaufman letters in existence, the following have been chosen chiefly to illustrate the many and varied sides of his personality.

The first letter was sent to his younger sister Ruth during the 1930–31 season, when he was appearing as an actor in *Once in a Lifetime*. The nation was on what was then termed "the brink of economic disaster," but not Kaufman. He was acting in a hit, getting half of the authors' royalties, the director's royalty, and half of the producer's profits.

GEORGE S. KAUFMAN
158 EAST 63rd STREET
NEW YORK CITY

Friday

Dear Ruth:

Kaufman is my name—cloaks and suits. Or, in these times, one cloak and one suit. Anyhow, one pair of pants.

Up at the house last evening I read your son's letter—the cadet, I mean. There was also one from Frank, and in my own house there is a good deal of goings-on about this school and that—so I gather that another generation is really growing up. To say nothing of me. . . . Anne, we hope, will get into Lincoln School next year—Walden seems to be a series of fist fights, with everything but referees. . . . Have you a birthday? Congratulations.

I have been doing no work these several weeks, owing to the fact that my current collaborator decided to go off and have a baby. No, not Ferber—*what* a scare you gave me!* Meanwhile I'm just an actor—it's a good deal like going to the office, and I find that I don't mind it a bit. I shall stay on for a few months longer—I'm a little reluctant about breaking up a winning combination, and then there *was* that one woman who came to the box-office and bought tickets on condition that I would appear.

I could go on and tell you about my going to Mrs. Vincent Astor's for lunch yesterday, but she and I decided that you hoi polloi had better not be told too much about how we folks carry on. We're a little afraid of a social revolution. So you just go right on eating cake, will you?

And in the interstices give my love to yourself, the twins, and Mr. F. They make a very nice family.

* *Ryskind.* [Kaufman's footnote]

243

In the summer of 1931, shortly after the Gershwin brothers received the first act of the Kaufman-Ryskind script, *Of Thee I Sing*, Kaufman wrote them the following letter.

GEORGE S. KAUFMAN
158 EAST 63rd STREET
NEW YORK CITY

Tuesday

Dear George and Ira:

One important thing. "Sweeping the Country" just can't come at the end of Madison Square Garden—that scene obviously climaxes with a reprise of "Of Thee I Sing" and if you tried to go on to the other number you would die. We need it badly *before* Madison Square Garden—it fits perfectly and bridges the time gap from the contest to the end of the campaign. I hope that will suit you. It means, of course, taking the martial strain out of *Of Thee I Sing*, but I imagine you are going to fool with that song anyhow. I still lean to a straight love song, and preferably without those two syllables at the end of the title phrase.

We can meet you any time, preferably when you have things half in mind and are ready for a detailed lyric discussion.

We are taking a brief rest before Act 2, but have done a lot of preparatory work on it and looks to me as though it would be a more amusing act than the other.

It's the show after this that's worrying me.

George

He dropped the next letter into George Gershwin's box in the Ritz Hotel in Boston. *Of Thee I Sing* had opened to unanimous rave notices at the Erlanger Theatre in the late fall of 1931, but Kaufman was far from satisfied. Georgie Hale was the choreographer for the production, and what follows is what Kaufman thought about him.

Dear George:

Georgie Hale has talked to me about his failure to get newspaper attention on his dances, and thinks it's the billing. The truth is that his dances are the conventional formations, and are not good enough to get notices.

They are worth nothing to the show, either artistically or at the box-office. It is not Hale's fault, but the nature of the show. They are the one note that keeps the show from being fresh.

I think every so-called "hot" step should come out. Line-ups of 16 girls, the hot stuff in the second act opening —all baloney. Never saved or helped a show yet, and everybody is sick and tired of it.

Now tear that up into little pieces, and here are minor notes:

Please make all possible musical cuts. I shall continue to cut the book, even where it is fairly good, because the show is between 30 and 40 minutes too long.

"On That Point Nobody Budges" is sung entirely too often.

The rearrangement of the first act finale should get at least two minutes out of it. Should we talk this one over before you write it anew?

George Kaufman

George, who always preferred to work on holidays, spent New Year's Eve in New York with Edna Ferber. As 1932 came in, so did an idea for a play. They called it *Dinner at Eight*. It was finished in June, and opened in New York in October 1932.

By the end of that year, George and his assistant director

Robert Sinclair went to London to stage the play. Miss Ferber followed two weeks later.

The following five letters were sent from London (Claridge's); the "Dearest" to whom they were addressed was Beatrice Kaufman.

Sunday

Dearest:

Ten in the evening, and just back from a visit to Elsie Disney, who has a house at Maidenhead, where she is taking care of an invalid sister. Very pleasant, and very cold. Mrs. D., whom you may recall, is engaged to a French count, and has been for two years, pending a dispensation from the Pope, on account of her divorce.

Otherwise what? Most of what I write you in these letters is necessarily unimportant, because anything vital, of which there is also little, you would learn via cable or phone. . . . My life is very simple, although I could make it otherwise, if I may say so with all modesty. To-night there was a supper at Lady Colefax's, to which I sent regrets, and I shall also sidestep a dinner at Lilly's next Tuesday. The last she gave was deadly. . . . I go to Crockford's a good deal, and have finally hit my stride and am losing. Everyone there is a Lady or a Lord or a Baron or something—I learn the last names and occasionally make the mistake of prefixing a Mister. But I don't do it any more—I refer to them as "my partner" or "my opponent," to play safe. They are a seedy bunch, and the club itself, of course, cannot touch the new Culbertson layout. . . . I put in two heavy days of rehearsal, Friday and Saturday, and I think the company will be superb. At this writing we are short a Max. . . . Dismally cold and wet to-day, and me all bundled up in a railway carriage, traveling to Maidenhead. It was one of those where they lock you in, and I felt sure no one would open the door when we got there. However, I pounded on the window and got out. I got my first glimpses of English countryside under bad conditions. But I do know I would definitely not like to be a permanent resident of this fair land. I am too inherently American. . . . *To the Ladies* got marvelous, in most cases, notices. I am mailing them to Marc. Incidentally, Lyn Harding told me about Marc in London some years ago—holding forth on the Sacco and Vanzetti case in the Garrick Club, and being quite floored by an Englishman who had really read about the case. . . . Carol Goodner is making movies all day, and when I asked her why she said that for five years she was supposed to be the best kept woman in London, and now they've separated, and she is busy paying the bills that were run up. It's a lesson to all girls. . . . Sorry to hear about the Gershwin show, but of course it was inevitable. They may patch it together for a few months, but it will never be more than that. Did you see *Variety's* Page 1 story about my income? It reached me just as *Of Thee I Sing* lost eleven hundred dollars. . . . Am lunching with Jack Warner to-morrow if I can make it. He will be here for weeks and weeks—I'm so annoyed. . . . I shall give a few Christmas presents here—Joyce and Adrienne Massey, and Lilly . . . Edna has been in bed for two days with a cold, but is all right now. The Paris *Herald* carried an item saying that Miss Ferber was in London and staying at Christie's, which, as you know, is famous for its antiques. Miss Ferber was a little pained. . . . Starting with noon rehearsals to-morrow—up to now it has been eleven. I have done all the directing up to now, Bob being busy with production detail. Edna, Bob and I are doing the whole thing—casting, production, clothes, and all. We never see Cochran.

I hope you and Poky are well, and can't tell you how much I would like to see you both. Take care of yourselves till I return, and even after that. Loads and loads of love.

G.

Elsie Disney was an English actress; Lady Colefax was the founder of a first-rate interior decorating establishment in London; Lilly was the wife of the novelist Paul Hyde Bonner; Marc was Kaufman's old collaborator Marc Connelly; Lyn Harding was an English actor; Carol Goodner was an American actress working in London; The headline in Variety *was "George Kaufman, Author, Making Big Money on Street—Now $7,000 Wkly." Jack Warner was the Warner of Warner Brothers, the motion picture producers; Adrienne Massey was married to the actor Raymond Massey; the Gershwin show was* Pardon My English, *which lasted for forty-three performances; Joyce Barbour was a young woman to whom Kaufman became quite attached; Bob was Robert Sinclair; Poky was the nickname he used for his daughter. And the Pope was Pius XI.*

Dearest:

Monday night, and just home from the Bonners' dinner. There are really a good many Bonner invitations, and it's hard to get out of them. Woollcott got in to-day, and was there to-night, bigger than life. Otherwise rather dull.* The old gentleman had a great time in Russia, and is full of it. Says he had a marvelous letter from you, and is sailing home in time for his birthday party, or is it yours? Anyhow, I think we go together on the *Europa*, due in New York about Jan. 12. . . . And now just to dip around into this item and that. There are oodles of people here— you meet them generally at the Savoy after theatre, but other places as well. I am settling down into a pleasant

* *The party, I mean.* [Kaufman's footnote]

life. Home early to-night, and took Eno's, and wrote a
bunch of postcards, and now this letter to you. With
strength, I shall also write the folks to-night. . . . Edna is
behaving splendidly so far, although showing occasional
signs of strain. Lady Colefax is helping with our production, and that is rather hard on Edna, for Lady C. is a
trial. We may fire her . . . This afternoon I ran into
Doug Fairbanks and Harold Lloyd and the Eddie Gould-
ings. They are friends of Mrs. Dupont, whom I think you
know. She was in Benchley's boat party, and is now here
for a week—we theatred together the other night, and will
again some time this week. I may see *To the Ladies* to-night.
It's a sort of provincial production in an outlying theatre,
for two weeks only, unless they move it to the West End,
of which there is not a chance. *Lifetime* will probably also
go on, but if so I shall leave Bob to do the honors. There
is also a Paris production of *Dinner* in prospect, and
Alex reports that somebody important in Moscow wants
to do *Of Thee I Sing*. . . . Enough of that. I spent 50
minutes in a toy shop to-day, trying to get what I wanted
for Anne. It couldn't be done, so I bought a doll and a
trunk. It is quite elaborate, and will not be on this boat.
In another ten days, however, you had better have Myra
make inquiries at the customs. I enclose the bill—the thing
itself cost just under £6, as you can see. All of which I tell
you for customs purposes, so save the bill. . . . I have
learned to drink coffee and hot milk, and like it. As I
cabled you, I played at Crockford's, and won £30. Got
your cable about the Adams child, and sent a wire to them.
Also am denying the rumor that Esther is pregnant again.
. . . They have nice big bath towels in this hotel, which
envelop one all the way down. What chance for New
York? They must be fifteen feet by twelve. . . . Went to

opening of *Another Language*, with Bart and Edna—very good, but only a moderate success. Everyone predicts success for us here, but I am paying no attention. Last night at the Masseys I met Lonsdale and Roland Squires—very nice. . . . Joyce is unhappy—her show probably goes to New York, but she does not. Heigh-ho—there is always something for that kid. Paul Bonner has written half a play, and is annoyed because Lilly doesn't like it. So I volunteered to read it. I hear it's not so good. Romney Brent got a wire telling him he had a flop, and was getting stewed at Mary Ellis's to celebrate yesterday. . . . Everyone is so hospitable that I am a little embarrassed. Lonsdale asked me for dinner this week; the Masseys and the Bonners and the Marshalls and everybody keep at it. I can send the ladies flowers and invite them to the opening, and that's about all. Certainly I can't give a party. . . . I miss you, dearest, and love you, and shall be very happy to be back. I'm already looking forward to it, so I can imagine my joy by Jan. 12. . . . If I buy many clothes or presents I may cable you for some money—I didn't bring a great deal. . . . See you soon.

S.

Woollcott was the literary critic, author, lecturer, radio personality, and world traveler; the Europa *was a ship in the service of the North German Lloyd Line; Eno's was a laxative oil that Kaufman took according to directions; Doug Fairbanks and Harold Lloyd were the great Hollywood film stars; Eddie Goulding was an old film director; Mrs. Dupont was one of the Duponts; Benchley was Robert Benchley of the Algonquin Round Table,* Vanity Fair *magazine, and Hollywood; Anne was his daughter; Myra was Myra Hampton Streger, his secretary and casting director; Esther was F.P.A.'s wife; Bart was the*

Hollywood picture star Herbert Marshall; Edna was Mr. Mar-
shall's wife and a star in her own right, Edna Best; Lonsdale was
the British playwright Frederick Lonsdale, who wrote The Last
of Mrs. Cheyney; *Roland Squires may have been the British*
actor Ronald Squire; Romney Brent was the American actor,
who was making his first appearance on the London stage in
Words and Music; *Mary Ellis was an American actress living*
in England.

The signature was not "G" for George but "S" for Sniggy,
the first documented evidence of Kaufman's silly nickname.

Thursday the 15th
Around 7

Dearest:—

Nu! . . . I've been out doing a little Christmas shopping
with Munson. Found a cute miniature chest of drawers for
Lilly—old, and just about eight inches high, the whole
thing. And a trinket for Adrienne, which leaves me still
Alex and Joyce and Edna. As we were looking into a window
and considering something for Woollcott, the old fool came
along the street with Rebecca West. I have not seen him
for several days, and Munson reports that he is very social.
She says he has changed, which I find hard to believe.
Says he bandies big names around and seems really impressed by them, etc. To-morrow Cochran is giving a
lunch for Woollcott at Ciro's but I may miss it because of
rehearsals. . . . And I bought something for you. I hope
you like it. It's a 1780 dressing mirror, with inlaid stand—
the original glass, and the whole thing very beautiful, to my
way of thinking. It will not catch the *Europa*, so you may
not get it for Christmas. Anyhow, you will have to pay something at the other end—cost of packing and shipment. I
didn't pay, because they tell me sometimes they collect at
both ends. They will mail you a consular invoice, and

proof of antiquity, etc. So there will be no duty. . . . Edna still sick in bed with a bad throat, after four or five days. And having lots of fun with English doctors, who arrive with instruments all jumbled together in a bag, and try to use them on her without sterilizing them. Jack Warner is also sick in bed—he and I and Lady Sackville were to have gone to theatre to-morrow night, but it's off. He goes to Knole for Christmas, although Sackville is dying or something. But there is a rule that Jack goes there for Christmas, no matter who dies. . . . I am getting to know my London pretty well. I drift around odd corners and know just where I am, and I talk glibly of "Two bob" to taxi drivers, and all that sort of thing. . . . We have been in rehearsal a week now, and I really work at it pretty hard. There will be a Coast production in the Spring, but Bob will do all that. It's not yet quite set, but I think it will go through. Your Sniggy, however, will stay in New York indefinitely. . . . I'm spending most of the week-end with Elsie Disney, either in London or the country. . . . This is my first letter*—I ought to write four or five, but I wanted to be sure to get one off to you. . . .

LATER: Have just been to see Edna, who has finally got a good doctor, and will be all right in another day. Sybil Bolitho was there—I forgot to tell you that she is helping with our clothes, and I see a lot of her. I like her very much—it is the first time that I have been on anything but an artificial basis with her. She seems a different person from the girl I used to meet in New York. We are having quite a lot of clothes trouble, with squawking by Irene Vanbrugh and other of our actresses. But I think, from what I hear, that the show will be beautifully dressed. . . . Have seen very little of the Masseys and the Bonners lately, but they know I am busy, I think. . . . Somehow I never get

* I mean this evening. [Kaufman's footnote]

dinner in this town. It's now 8-30 and I haven't eaten. Presently I shall go around to Crockford's, and eat over there. . . . Thanks for the *Variety* piece about me. It doesn't matter—people forget those things very quickly . . . Saw Gloria Swanson at the Ritz to-day, and ran into Adele Astaire the other evening. Or maybe I reported that before. Like you, it is hard to know what I've said and what I haven't. . . . Not much longer, dearest. I'll be home three weeks after you get this letter, if I have figured correctly. . . . Just got a note from Lilly inviting me for lunch on Christmas Day, with the four kids. In the evening I go to Joyce's, with a tree and everything. It's not like being with our Poky, but at least I shall not be lonely. . . . Plenty of love, my dear. See you soon.

G.

It is the considered opinion of George Kaufman's daughter that whenever her father mentioned a woman by her last name in his letters, "generally, they were more than 'friends.'" Hence, "I've been out doing a little Christmas shopping with Munson." Rebecca West was the noted English author and companion of H. G. Wells. (In truth, her name was Cecily Isabel Fairfield, but she chose the pseudonym from the name of a role in the Henrik Ibsen play Rosmersholm, *in which she once acted.) Cochran was Charles Cochran, the London theatrical producer who presented the Kaufman-Ferber play* Dinner at Eight. *Lady Sackville could have been any one of the many Sackvilles who run through English history and literature. Sybil Bolitho was the wife of the English writer William Bolitho. Irene Vanbrugh was a London actress. Gloria Swanson was the American actress. Adele Astaire was the American actress and dancer, sister of Fred Astaire, and was just about to marry the English nobleman Lord Charles Cavendish.*

Monday night.

Dearest:

Let me see . . . Sailing into the home stretch, with scenery in a few days and the boat not much later. If only Vanbrugh and Lyn Harding would learn a few lines I would be happier. Mr. Woollcott has reconsidered, and is not sailing with me. He goes about ten days later with Philip Guedalla and Lilly Bonner, chiefly Lilly, I imagine. . . . Ferber is about well again, having had quite a siege. On top of everything a London paper, in chronicling her Mexican adventure, spoke of "Miss Ferber and her author-husband, Marc Connelly." Honestly. . . . Spent Sunday in Maidenhead with Disney and her sister, and went through a house built in 1450. Hardly restored at all, and the original windows, and still lived in, and quite thrilling. Cromwell lived in it once. Then drove home late at night in a hired Daimler, feeling that every car we met was going to bump into us. Four glaring headlights on every auto, and left side driving, all quite nerve-racking. . . . Have seen very little of Warner, owing to his illness, but can't put it off much longer. Saw *Children in Uniform* on Saturday night— the play—and what a play! If I could only have got it for New York! Go to the opening—if they do it halfway right it will be tremendous. . . . Haven't worn my heavy socks, because it would mean heavy ones all the time. Brought my oil along, and it has kept me from having anything like a cold. . . . Cochran gave a lunch for Alex at Ciro's on Saturday, with all the critics there. Met Charles Morgan, and sat next to Golding, who wrote *Magnolia Street*. Cochran is doing a play made out of it, and I gathered that I could have Mr. Golding for collaborator with very little effort. I never read the book, of course, and weakly was afraid to tell Golding that, and got myself in for a great detailed discussion about different scenes in it. I have so little sense.

Had an invitation to lunch at Sybil Colefax's to-morrow, but just had to decline. Keynes and Lopokova are to be there—too bad. My life is full of ladies—in the titled sense, I mean. It is pretty hard to meet just an ordinary woman. . . . Sinclair and Romney Brent had dinner with me here in the room: Bob is taking the troupe for to-night's rehearsal, and I will do it to-morrow. . . . Bought your perfume to-day—nice big bottles, and also a few small ones for general distribution. Christmas lasts for five days over here, and I just have to ask the troupe to work on all except Christmas Day. If it were New York I would work Christmas too, but I don't dare over here.

That's all, my darling—I shall be so happy to see you and Poky again. Wagonloads of love, and then some.

Your

S.

(*Without a doubt*)

Philip Guedalla was the English historian and essayist. Keynes was John Maynard Keynes, British economist, author, and later Director of the Bank of England. Charles Morgan was an English novelist and drama critic of the London Times. *Lopokova was Lydia Lopokova, Russian-born dancer and actress; she married John Maynard Keynes, and when that gentleman was made the First Baron of Tilton, she had the good fortune to become Baroness Tilton.*

Sunday night

Dearest:

Just between Christmas gatherings. Lunch at the Bonners, with the three oldest kids and Sinclair and Woollcott and Rebecca West and her husband. Quite pleasant. Wooll-cott sails on the *Bremen* on the 15th—Home the 20th, maybe the 21st.

Then early this evening I went to the Bird-Barbours—very depressing. It was the first time I had been in their place, and it was rather saddening. It was just family, except for Alex and Romney and me, and I was glad to have an excuse to get away. My excuse was that I am going on to a third place, which I am, but I am writing this letter in between. From here I go to some people named Mocotta, whom I met at Crockford's. They keep some sort of open house on Christmas Day, and there will be a bridge game for Baby. So that will be all right, I imagine.

Later: Very pleasant bridge game, in which I lost about £8. The bridge here is not very good, by the way—Crockford's cannot come within a mile of the Cavendish, for example. But their bridge manners are so good as to be painful; one always says "Thank you" to one's partner when the dummy goes down. At first I thought they were kidding, especially when the dummy did not contain a trick, but I gradually have discovered that they are never kidding, no matter what they do or say. No remark is too absurd to be taken literally by them, and I have finally got myself to the point of not saying anything except what I mean. A partner's play is never criticized, no matter what. In some ways that is better than our free-spoken system, and in other ways not.

Joyce was taken with flu in the middle of her matinee Saturday, just to complicate her Christmas. I gave her a few nice presents, and am bringing home a quantity of perfume, as well as some other things that I shall pick up. Please bring some cash to the boat for customs—I'll remind you of that again by radio. About three hundred dollars. Glad to hear the deposits are growing, but of course you had to pay something these three weeks just ending. It will be better again from now on, however. I still have no idea for a play. Incidentally, I know that Edna does not want to work with me again. We threshed out the whole thing again, with no great bitterness, and Edna doing most of the talking. She is so sure that she is right in everything she says—it must be wonderful to be like that. Never is there the possibility in her mind that anything she thinks or says could be less than gospel. I shall talk to Alex about a play before I leave. Or, that failing and Morrie yielding nothing, I shall write a simple comedy for next season, along purely comical lines. I think I could do that, although I still have no notion. That's not quite true—I have a slight lead.

So anxious to see you, my dearest, to say nothing of our Poky. I shall follow close on the heels of this letter—about a week—no, two weeks. I shall probably write one more letter, a week hence.

To-morrow is Boxing Day, a great holiday here, but our cast has to work, which annoys them a good deal. . . . Jack Warner says I will be invited to Knole for a luncheon, if old Sackville is well enough. Probably I shall be unable to go, even if invited. Certainly if uninvited.

My love, darling.

S.

What is significant about this letter is the renewal of the running feud between Kaufman and Edna Ferber. This hardy perennial bloomed more often than annually, and usually, it remained for Beatrice to patch things up.

Although Miss Ferber was certain she would never do another

257

play with Kaufman, they did in fact write three more works for the theatre, not the least of which was Stage Door.

George first met Kitty Carlisle on the sound stage of *A Night at the Opera*, where she was playing a very young leading lady. At the time, he was more than occupied with Mary Astor. That did not, however, keep him from noticing the beautiful Miss Carlisle.

Even before the diary case broke, George wrote her. The envelope is dated February 7, 1936. This was long before his friend and collaborator met her and made her Mrs. Moss Hart.

GEORGE S. KAUFMAN

14 EAST 94th STREET

NEW YORK CITY

Dear Kitty Carlisle—

I've regretted not seeing you, and now I hear you've been ill, and now I'm going South, and anyhow you're going into a show, and —. Oh, well, have a drink with me some time.

George Kaufman

Even before her daughter turned out to have married the lion of Broadway, Bea's mother was considered to be the snob of the family. After George made it, she was almost unapproachable.

George, however, was a sentimentalist of surprising proportion, especially as regards the sick and the elderly. In 1939, on his mother-in-law's seventy-fifth birthday, he wrote these three verses for her. The quality of the poetry may be judged by the reader.

258

To, and About, Mother Bakrow

She looks upon a gentle world,
Where angry lips are never curled.
No one is ever mean or small—
She only sees the best in all.
She really thinks the Japanese
Are trying very hard to please.
A feminine Diogenes,
Discovering our honesties.

If someone starts reciting "Trees,"
  Or plays the pianola,
She says, "What handling of the keys!
What wondrous miracles are these!"
She sees in every piece of cheese
  The rarest Gorgonzola.

To her there are no Pharisees
To plunge us into agonies;
With each one's generosities
  She always acquiesces.
In one and all she thinks she sees
The very lovely qualities
    That she herself possesses.

                        George

"Mossie" was the term of endearment he used for Moss Hart. In January of 1944, Kaufman wrote his friend and colleague, who was then on the West Coast.

The Woollcott book to which Kaufman alludes was a collection of Woollcott's letters that Bea edited with Joe Hennessey, Woollcott's secretary, chauffeur, bookkeeper, and friend.

GEORGE S. KAUFMAN
410 PARK AVENUE
NEW YORK CITY

Wednesday

Dear Mossie:

A very fine letter, Mr. M., and that's good enough for me.
I don't like to think of your being out there all that time,
including making another picture, but after you make the
capital gains deal maybe you'll be in a jail somewhere in
the East, and we can see something of each other. . . .

In the other room Beatrice is pounding away on the
Woollcott book—it seems to call for a surprising amount of
work, just putting some letters together, and every once
in a while I am asked a theatrical question, such as what
year John O. Hewitt played King Lear at the Old Vic.

Our little charade is an unbelievable smash, considering
that it ain't much of a play. Yesterday I sat at one of those
Dramatists' Guild meetings for about nine hours, and
Edward Childs Carpenter came up and made a speech
about the play, saying that he was surprised that the critics
missed the play's theme. I said yes and meant it, because
the play does have something to hint at about these times
and the shifting social values. Oh, no, said Carpenter—the
the theme is the way that woman sticks to her man all
through. And the critics never mentioned it, he said. I have
a suspicion that this is the reason Edward Childs Carpenter
is Edward Childs Carpenter, but I didn't say so.

Mr. Morrie Ryskind and I exchanged letters about what
Of Thee I Sing should be like in the movies, and the
result is a slight change of our plans. The change is that

we are not selling it at all. Morrie sees it as a fine spring-board to attack the present administration, so we are simply calling the whole thing off. Consequently I shall not be coming to California. . . .

Every time I stage a show people look in the papers and say, "Oh, yes, *that* bastard is still around," and I get fifty bad scripts. Try as I do to duck, I cannot say No to Terry Helburn and people like that, and it's awful. I shouldn't complain, because it would be worse, in a way, if I didn't get them. Incidentally, Billy Rose has quite an exciting idea for an unusual show—revue, I suppose it is—with seven stars and Stokowski in the pit, to open the Ziegfeld. I may function as a kind of director-writer in a half-assed way, and if you have three days we might do a sketch and a half when you return. You could have it acted by six stars, anyhow.

Yesterday I saw Atwater. Looks fine, but she had some shenanigans with her throat in Chicago, as you know. (She said she had been talking to you.) I only hope that the doctors are telling her the truth.

I was, strangely enough, simply devastated by the killing of Clare Luce's daughter. . . . Come on back before those automobiles or something get you. . . . On this cheerful note I depart.

The best.

George

John O. Hewitt was a British character actor. "Our little charade" was The Late George Apley, *which Kaufman and John P. Marquand adapted for the stage from Marquand's Pulitzer Prize novel of the same name. Edward Childs Carpenter was an American playwright and member of the Drama-*

tists Guild Council, of which Kaufman was vice-president. Terry Helburn was the co-founder of the Theatre Guild, Billy Rose was the producer and financier, and the show to which Kaufman referred was a revue to be called Seven Lively Arts *and from which Kaufman eventually removed his name. Stokowski was Leopold Stokowski, the symphony conductor. Atwater was Edith Atwater, a New York actress and longtime Kaufman friend.*

It pleased him to write amusing letters almost as much as it pleased him to write amusing plays. This one is to his brother-in-law, Leonard Bakrow, in Rochester. The envelope is dated March 9, 1944.

GEORGE S. KAUFMAN

410 PARK AVENUE

NEW YORK CITY

Thursday

Dear Leonard:

Well, I got into the elevator very brightly yesterday, ready to face the world, and the elevator man said, "I hear that man in Ten South died last night." This gave me something of a turn, because I know the man in Ten South very well. In fact, I *am* the man in Ten South. "Me?" I said to the elevator man, feeling around the back to see if my behind was still there. "Oh, no," he said, "I meant Twelve South."

Naturally this started me off fine—from there on it was all down hill.

I got wonderful reports of you from Beatrice—in fact it seems that this letter to the hospital will barely catch you there. She said you looked quite your usual self, your eyes

262

were shining brightly, and that in not too long a time you would be again 100%, no discount. All good news.

She and Anne came back in a crowded coach, riding on one sandwich or something like that, but there are no visible signs that it did them any harm. In fact, I think something like that is good for a person once in a while, so long as it doesn't happen to me.

Did you hear about the father who was boasting of the skill of his son, who was a chemist? "He takes a gallon of hydrogen," he said, "and a gallon of oxygen, and he makes water." "I should think he would," said his friend.

It's a democracy, after all. Michael Todd, whom you may have heard of as a play producer, is going into the Navy. Having seen Billy in a sailor suit, I can hardly wait to see Todd. He is 36 years old, and Jewish, and if they show him to the Germans the war will stop pronto.

Big intermission there while I actually worked for nearly twenty minutes. After that, of course, I laid down for an hour and had a massage. Tough life.

Remember me to everybody—especially yourself, Edith and Billy. And again I say, I'm delighted to have heard such good news about you.

George

He wrote to his good friends and neighbors Ruth and Augustus Goetz about their play *Franklin Street*, which he had directed. It tried out in Wilmington, Delaware, and this was his manner of attempting to ease the pain of not having the play come into New York.

GEORGE S. KAUFMAN
410 PARK AVENUE
NEW YORK CITY

Tuesday

Dear Goetzes:

I had a chance to dispose of the movie rights to *Franklin Street* the other night, so I thought I'd better do it. This was in a dream induced by two sleeping pills, which is the reason I went right ahead without communicating with you.

This was in a large store which seemed to handle a good many things besides movie rights—shirts, nails, custard, everything. I had a good deal of trouble getting waited on. "Miss, would you mind . . . Miss, I've been waiting longer than . . . I think it's my turn now, Miss." But once I got attention everything went very nicely. I sold it an act at a time, which is a new idea that I rather like. The first act went for $30,000, and the second act for $60,000, which I thought was doing pretty well. The girl who was waiting on me knew all about these two acts, but the third act was all new to her. However, she took my word for it. I said there were two very nice situations in it, and that it should bring $35,000. I remember her saying, "Well, as long as we've got the other two . . ."

Don't bother to thank me for this—anyone in my place would have done the same. I imagine they're delivering the money, like Saks.

And incidentally, how's tricks?

George

He could hide sentiment rather well, but the emotion of losing his dear friend Herman Mankiewicz brought this touching, warm letter of condolence to Herman's widow, early in March 1953.

Monday, March 10

Sarah Dear:

Inevitably my quick and shocked telegram did not begin to convey what was in my mind and heart, and I don't know if these few lines will.

Joe had prepared me some months ago, but still I was hard hit by it and terribly saddened. I've thought much about you since then—Irving Lazar told me on the phone a few days afterwards that you were being your expected sturdy self.

I have resented all the Mank stories in print, because they have not done him justice—badly told, always—disgracefully, sometimes. I have been telling them a lot myself—but picking my audience with care, because Herman had a rare mind and a wit so razor-sharp and subtle that it was not meant for everyone. (Subconsciously I flatter myself by implying that I was one of the rare spirits that appreciated him to the full, but damn it! I *was*.)

Memories of our working together—a play, a movie, The *Times* . . . gorgeous memories, some of them, and a few exasperating ones, too. But always shot through with his fantastic and brilliant humor.

That's all, and little enough. But I just want you to know that I will think of him for a long, long time, and that I hope you'll find a peaceful and happy life.

My love to you and the family.

George

Joe was Herman's brother, Joe Mankiewicz, a most successful Hollywood author, director, and producer. Irving Lazar was the famous West Coast representative of Kaufman, Hart, and other New York theatre and literary figures.

To his utter dismay, his portable typewriter broke down aboard the *Queen Elizabeth* during the spring of 1954. As a consequence, he was reduced to writing with a pencil.

". . . instead of a hand grenade, how about a small capsule containing a lethal gas?" is a reference to a horrid little melodrama he and I were working on. It was to have starred Miss MacGrath. Mercifully, it was confined to the bottom of a trunk.

Aldous Huxley, of course, was the English author. During this crossing, he and Kaufman became such good friends that the next summer Huxley was given use of the Kaufman apartment in New York. He broke Kaufman's air conditioner, Kaufman's standard typewriter, and had a serious personality conflict with the Kaufman cat, but he left a most polite thank-you note.

> Cunard Line
> R.M.S. "Queen Elizabeth"

Dear Howard—

My oatmeal was too liquid the first morning, so I had them make it thicker. So the steward came in afterwards, and asked: "How were your oats this morning, sir?" . . . I have done no work, but that is no excuse for you. At the end, instead of a hand grenade, how about a small capsule containing a lethal gas? It goes back to your original idea in a more plausible form. . . . As Anne probably has informed you, I have been switched by radiogram to the Hyde Park, where I shall tell them that a strange American with two heads and one small brain will arrive in June . . . I started off my first evening aboard by leaning over to run the bath, fully clothed, and of course turning on the shower instead. . . . This is being written in pencil, third night out, because I am sitting in the bar waiting for Aldous Huxley. Hot diggedy! The only thing we have in common is Shepard Traube, who put on *The Gioconda Smile*. . . . Peggy Webster is aboard—does that fascinate you? We meet only on boats, Peggy and I—never on land.

I finished reading that English comedy—or didn't I mention it to you?—and decided not to do it. In fact, I have decided not to do *any*thing for about 27 years. You go ahead and write the plays and I'll put my name on them— if I don't have to write *that*.

The Glenn Miller Story is being shown aboard to-night, but not to me. I'm waiting for the Gilbert Miller Story. . . . A kiss to Evelyn.

George

Shepard Traube was the New York producer. Margaret "Peggy" Webster was the American director. Gilbert Miller was the international producer-director.

The following thoughtful note to Moss Hart is undated, but *My Fair Lady*, which Hart directed, opened on March 15, 1956.

GEORGE S. KAUFMAN
1035 PARK AVENUE
NEW YORK CITY

Wednesday

A letter, Mossie, instead of a telegram.

I find myself feeling very emotional about *My Fair*

Lady, and that, I need hardly add, is due to your participation. Of course I'm looking forward to the opening with great excitement, and thanks greatly, first, for the wonderful seats. I'm sure it will be one hell of a night.

You've apparently done a wonderful job, and I'm sure you will get gigantic credit.

Anyhow, this is just a letter from a full heart, so far as you are concerned.

Love and luck and everything, and come-to-England.

George

Max was his producer, Max Gordon. Clurman was the New York director and drama critic of the *Nation,* Harold Clurman. And Dorothy Tutin is the English actress for whom Kaufman fought to be included in the Queen's Birthday Honors, not only for her fine talent but also because he wanted to continue to use Annie's line about her. This letter was written in 1957.

GEORGE S. KAUFMAN,

17, BLOMFIELD ROAD,

LONDON, W. 9.

CUNNINGHAM 4411.

May 18

Dear Howard:

Not much to tell—the trip was rather rough and Scotland was cold. Ditto London. Anne and I fought our way home through a snowfall after theatre last night, wet and cold, and Anne said: "Really, Daddy, couldn't you have met a nice Italian actress?"

Max keeps me advised on what there is of business. Leueen's play is impressive in total, but I fear rather special, and maybe just not good enough. Her part, ditto, is not quite good enough. I shall deliver your messages and dollars. Clurman summed up the play shrewdly after a week on tour. He said: "This is a bum play—none of the women in it will sleep with me." There's dramatic criticism for you . . . Anne is looking forward to the day when the star of *The Lark*, Dorothy Tutin, gets an honor from the Queen and is known as Dame Tutin.

What are *you* looking forward to? Don't tell me—I'm staying here for the summer.

Love.

George

Rodney was my daughter's cat. More importantly, he was on a corresponding basis with the Kaufman cat, Adam.

GEORGE S. KAUFMAN,

17, BLOMFIELD ROAD,

LONDON, W. 9.

CUNNINGHAM 4411.

Saturday

Dear Howard:

If you think you are as big a hypochrondriac as I am I will spot you any three diseases you name and beat you with one leg tied behind me, which is where it will damned soon be.

And if you think our play is not funny you had better prepare to make it so, because it is unlikely to come out of me.

That will be all until the day after I get home, when—all things being equal, which they certainly aren't and I never heard anything so silly as that supposition—for

269

example I suppose pencils and marshmallows are equal—or you and Rodney—you know he is your superior in every way, and I would thank you to send him up to work with me and you stay home and meow—well, you know how this sentence finishes. If not, *Rodney does know.*

G.

Unfortunately, I never made it to England while he was there. It is the second paragraph of this letter, written in the summer of 1955, that is most interesting. On and off, Kaufman expounded his theory of collaboration. People who have wondered why he chose to collaborate in almost all of his theatrical works will find a ready answer in that paragraph.

GEORGE S. KAUFMAN,

17, BLOMFIELD ROAD,

LONDON, W. 9.

CUNNINGHAM 4411.

Tuesday

Dear Howard:

Random thoughts on life·

First, your cable just read to me over the phone, and it sounds as though you might be coming, and that would be just wonderful. You will love it, even if I make you work every day. That is, you will not love the work, but when you're not working, and just hanging around with Princess Meg.

A thought on collaboration: It is marriage without sex, and subject to many vexations. But pay no attention to them, because in one respect at least it is wonderful. The total result is frequently far more than the combined abilities of two people might give you—one person feeds

270

the other, and in some way something absolutely great comes out of it—much better than the two talents added together. It is like geometrical progression, if you ever got that far in school. The two people often fly far above their talents, and if I don't know about collaboration who the hell does?

My back is killing me—I was off to the osteopath to-day and am going again to-morrow, and if you come over I will take you along and watch me suffer. I am reading seven books at various times of night, and thinking about our opus the rest of the time. I am sure a few weeks together will straighten our scenario—there is so much good stuff planned for Act 2 that we can take our pick. Unless I'm crazy, and don't bother to express an opinion on that.

To-night I will make sure that Leueen comes right home to bed—I will go down and get her and bring her back by the hair. Curtains ring down at ten o'clock here—wonderful!

The weather is good and the town is waiting for you. Come on.

G.

She has been up late for a week—too long a story to write you. So come over and hear it.

The play he mentions is another one we consigned to the darkness of a trunk.

The postscript in Kaufman's own hand refers to the fact that the couple who had been working for them had taken their silver, their linen, their clothes, and then fled the country.

The spring of 1956 found Kaufman writing from London, where he was engaged in the adaptation of *The Lipstick Wars*, a satire of the cosmetic industry that never reached the stage. His collaborator was Dorothy Parker's husband Alan Campbell.

Although his speech, as previously noted, was singularly free of profanity, letter writing apparently severed his inhibitions; to wit:

GEORGE S. KAUFMAN,

17, BLOMFIELD ROAD,

LONDON, W. 9.

CUNNINGHAM 4411.

June 28

Dear Mossie (and especially Kitty. Aside to Kitty: Save your money from that television show—we're all going to need it some day)

Well, you have been through something, and I can only say that it takes a strong man. We all (certainly I) have a way of clinging to shows with a sort of lightning-may-strike point of view, even when we feel dubious or disinclined, but eventually the axe must fall. Me, I've done it again and again. In fact, I may be doing it now—I have an uneasy feeling that the show I'm on with Alan is rather dated—those twin targets at which I have aimed so many times—business and politics, whereas they want pajamas and baseball. I know that doesn't make sense, but you can't have everything. Hell, you can't have *any*thing. But you will go down in history—maybe ahead of it.

Excited at the prospect of your coming over here—we'll certainly still be here in September—and I'll look up boats home right away. I can't speak for Leueen, or even definitely for myself—I might stay till November if Leueen is ready to go back then. Her play dawdles and dawdles, but is finally showing signs of life.

Anne flew back from Sweden yesterday and will be in New York on July 10. Schafer is here, working in *Anas-*

tasia, and Margalo came over the other day. . . . Our life is more or less quiet—Leueen sees her many friends, but is naturally restless under inaction. I have been working and resting, and little else. I mean it when I say I think our show may be old-fashioned—it is hard to change one's style. On the theory that credit should be given when credit is deserved, I have prepared a credit list for the program, as follows:

By George S. Kaufman, plus glucose, lecithin, Bemax, Serpisal, Anesolysene, nutrilite, lipotaine, Equanil, Empirin, Veganin, Codeine, dramamine, Doctors E. B. Greenspan, L. S. Kubie, John Janvrin, C. L. Johnson, Vitamins B1-2-3-4-5-6-7-8-9-10-11 and 12, Laboratory staff of Mt. Sinai Hospital, phenobarbital, seconal, nembutal, tuinal, and FUCKITALL

—AND—

Alan Campbell.

Still have a few shows ahead of us to see—two of the current revues, *Waltz of the Toreadors,* which Leueen has seen but I haven't, a dramatization of *Cards of Identity,* which we were to have gone to this evening, but my watch stopped while I was playing bridge, and now it's pouring, so we were lucky. It's now nine o'clock, and we'll go down and pick up a cold supper—it's the staff's night out, and anyhow there is a small crisis there—they must go back to Italy and the sun for four weeks because the cook is ill. This is after all winter as a vacation. Oo-la-la, or whatever the Italian for oo-la-la is.

This is rather a pedestrian effort after your throbbing letter, Mossie. If I am not being impertinent I hope you are going to write a straight play now—I like to think of you being at work and I like to think of eventually seeing the play.

273

We miss you like blazes, and will fall on your necks. However, we promise to fall right off again, so you won't have to keep us there.

All kinds of love—French, Italian, everything.

G.

We should go back on either the *Lizzie* or the *United States*—not the *Mary*, which rolls too much. Let me know your preference and a possible date. And how many people will you be? And everything.

Same Fellow

Kitty, of course, was Moss Hart's wife Kitty Carlisle, and the television program referred to was the Goodson-Todman panel show "To Tell The Truth." What Hart had "been through" was an idea for a musical that didn't work out. This led Kaufman to "hope you are going to write a straight play now." Hart never did.

Anne, needless to add, was his daughter. The play Leueen was restless about was Jean Giraudoux's Tiger at the Gates, *adapted by Christopher Fry. It had been a solid hit in London and was about to be brought to New York, where it also scored with both critics and public. The doctors referred to are his New York internist Dr. Edward Greenspan, one of his psychoanalysts Dr. Laurence Kubie, and his London physician Dr. John Janvrin; C. L. Johnson remains a mystery. The "pajamas and baseball" reference was to* The Pajama Game *and* Damn Yankees, *the first two musicals that were co-produced by a newcomer named Harold Prince.*

The volume of mail received by George S. Kaufman was mountainous. Aside from constant communications from his collaborators, producers, actors, and individuals asking him to rewrite plays, direct plays, cast them in plays, were letters from diverse correspondents: William Allen White, the Kansas news-

274

paper editor; Henry L. Stimson, Secretary of War during World War II; Alfred E. Smith, Governor of New York and candidate for the presidency in 1928; William Lyon Phelps, the Yale English professor and writer; James Hilton, the English novelist who wrote *Goodbye, Mr. Chips* and *Lost Horizon;* Booth Tarkington, author of *Penrod, Alice Adams,* and *The Magnificent Ambersons;* three of the four Marx Brothers; Theodore Dreiser, the novelist who wrote *Sister Carrie* and *An American Tragedy;* Fred Allen, the humorist and radio and television star; Walter Damrosch, conductor of the New York Symphony Orchestra; Adolphe Menjou, the Hollywood actor; Oswald Garrison Villard, one-time publisher of the New York *Post* and the *Nation;* James Farley, F. D. Roosevelt's early campaign manager and postmaster general; Otto H. Kahn, the financier and patron of the arts; Neysa McMein the painter; Ina Claire the actress, and Alexander Woollcott, about whom enough has been written in this book.

There were many others, of course. Some were fan letters, some were requests, others had to do with the day-to-day work Kaufman and his fellow writers found themselves in. Kaufman did not throw these letters aside. Carefully and promptly he answered them all. Social letters pleased him; business correspondence irritated him. In one of his edgier moments he sent a reminder to a collaborator regarding a small item of business, instructing him what to do and how to do it. He signed the note: "Kaufman (everybody's secretary)."

13 *The Relative*

"Sight unseen," George Kaufman used to say, "I'll trade my relatives for yours."

Actually, the line was a pose, for Kaufman was a reasonably devoted and kind relative. His father and mother always had his respect and, if needed, his money. His father, who could give excellent advice to everyone except himself, laid down a tenet that the son followed for the better part of his life. "George," the elder Kaufman told him, "just because you can write plays doesn't mean you're a businessman who knows how to handle investments. Besides, everybody in show business ends up broke. So if you're smart, you'll take only what you need and let some professional, like a bank, handle the rest of it." Kaufman followed that parental advice and ended up a long way from broke.

His mother once, quite inadvertently, gave him an idea that turned out profitably. Edna Ferber recalled that when his parents were living on West 86th Street, George walked into the apartment one afternoon while his mother was having a card party.

He stood unobserved in the entrance hall and listened to all those women talking and talking and not playing cards. Being a highly impatient card player himself, George was struck by the fact that instead of devoting themselves to the game, his mother's friends merely indulged in conversation. That night, he sat down and wrote in a single session what remains to this day one of the most popular one-act plays in the United States, *If Men Played Cards as Women Do*.

He was also respectful toward Beatrice's family in Rochester. Her parents and brothers always received Grade-A treatment. Leonard Bakrow, Beatrice's younger brother, said that Kaufman allowed him to buy into such shows as *Of Thee I Sing*, *The Doughgirls*, and *The Man Who Came to Dinner*.

While he liked the upstate relatives, he didn't like Rochester en masse. A local youth was being married in New York, and to that city came a hoard of folks from Bea's home town.

"All Rochester seems to be in New York this week," Beatrice remarked.

"Really?" said Kaufman. "What a wonderful time to visit Rochester."

Helen, his older sister, lived for a good part of her life in Florida. He saw her infrequently. Accordingly, he claimed to be extra fond of her.

When he was twenty-three and his younger sister Ruth was sixteen, George committed to paper an early example of Kaufman's light verse. It displays how close he felt toward her.

Two-forty-one one-hundred-first,
New York, *Sun*day, fifteenth of August.
Dear Ruth: It's hot. The pavements thirst,
But comes no rain nor wind nor raw gust.
But you, far from the beaten track.
Are cool; you eat, and loaf, and fatten.

But tell me: Aren't you coming back
    To old Manhattan?

As I remarked, you loaf and eat;
    You've got it pretty soft, confound you!
But I—I tramp the heated street
    And long to put my arms around you.
I know it's cool where you sojourn;
    I know Vermont is very pretty—
But still I ask you to return
    To New York City.

Would that you knew the wild desire
    That seems to have been mine for ages!
That you could sense the unquenched fire
    Inside of me that burns and rages!
So pack your things and come back soon;
    'Tis you that I must have—no other.
I'VE HAD NO FUDGE SINCE BACK IN JUNE!
                Your loving brother.

When they were older, he sent her an annual check for two hundred dollars on their mutual birthday. Though she criticized him and constantly challenged him, her enthusiasm and innocence attracted him.

Ruth had been up in Corning, New York, doing a commercial film for an advertising agency on the Pyrex account. On her return to Manhattan, Kaufman asked, "Well, kid, how was it?"

"Have you any idea what an expert glass blower earns?" Ruth asked him.

"Not the faintest."

"He gets over three hundred dollars a week," Ruth reported.

"That doesn't seem too much when you think about it," her brother answered. "You know, they only need to suck in once."

Collateral relatives were treated royally. "I remember when I

was in college, *Of Thee I Sing* was playing Boston," Bea's
younger cousin Ruth Adler reports. "I was at Smith, and I
remember writing to George asking if he could get me four
tickets. He sent them, and in those days I didn't realize what
house seats were. Two boys from Yale, another girl from
Smith, and myself went into the theatre, and there was George.
I mentioned the tickets and he said, 'No, you can't pay for
those.' Later, he came down into the theatre to see us in our
seats. It was the biggest thrill these people had ever had. George
was my most famous relative, the relative about whom I was the
proudest."

When his sister Ruth's twins, Bruce and Katie, arrived at
their seventeenth birthday, they received a joint telegram from
Uncle George: NOW THAT YOU ARE 34 . . . it read.

Bruce and his brother Allan were helped through college by
Kaufman's checks. Katie got started in a long career as a dancer
when her Uncle George gave her a job in *I'd Rather Be Right*.

It is the contention of many members of his family that
George drew heavily on them as characters in *You Can't Take
It With You*. George's father, Joe Kaufman, it is alleged, was
the prototype for Grandpa Vanderhof. Penelope is "a round
little woman in her early fifties, comfortable-looking, gentle,
homey. One would not suspect that under that placid exterior
there surges the Divine Urge—but it does, it does." Penelope,
members of the family believe, was Ruth. And Essie the bal-
lerina was of course Katie.

Distant relatives did not interest Kaufman in the slightest
until 1933. When Adolf Hitler took power in Germany, George
Kaufman recalled with bitter distaste the line Frank Munsey
had shouted in his direction: "What is that Jew doing in my
city room?"

Quietly, and without anyone knowing about it except his
lawyer of many years Howard Reinheimer, Kaufman began
getting his distant cousins out of Nazi Germany. He enabled

more than twenty relatives to migrate to the United States by paying for their transportation and other expenses. He had never seen or known them. And they would never see or know him. He wanted it that way. In fact, he insisted on it. No smiles, no tears, no effusive thanks.

Everything was done through Reinheimer. Kaufman, however, was the direct force who saved those people from the concentration camps. Contrary to Reinheimer's advice, Kaufman signed papers guaranteeing the financial security of those refugees for the remainder of their lives or for as long as they chose to stay in the United States.

The only provision was that none of them contact him. All communication was to go through his lawyer. It was, therefore, an understandably worried Howard Reinheimer who called George one day shortly after the war had begun. One of the Kaufman refugees had turned up in the lawyer's office. He was despondent, even suicidal. He could find no work, and he could not bear to live any longer on the allowance provided for him by his distant but mysterious relation. Either he got more money or he would destroy himself.

Without a pause, Kaufman told Reinheimer, "Give him more. Whatever he wants. Now!"

On his parents' fiftieth wedding anniversary, George invited two hundred elderly guests to the Savoy Plaza Hotel. He hired an orchestra that played tunes from the 1880's, and the guests, under his direction, danced the schottische and the lancers. He couldn't have worked harder on a Broadway production.

The climax of the evening came in a film that he shot at the Fort Lee Studios. In it George and his parents held a conference on his mother's future. They unanimously agreed that Mother Kaufman was to become a drama critic; the work was light and George's plays would get better reviews.

All in all it was an entertaining and extravagant evening, one that showed more tenderness than he was ever willing to admit he had.

But confront him publicly about his relatives, ask him how he liked them, and he would have said that he wouldn't have given them this much space.

14 *Friends and Enemies*

FOR A MAN WHO WAS SO ELUSIVE, SO FURTIVE, WHO PERMITTED
so little of himself to be seen above water, and ultimately, for a
man with so caustic a tongue, one might think it curious that
George Kaufman had not only enemies but friends as well.

His character was practically impeccable. If the insatiable
appetite of his adulterous nature is dismissed with a flick of the
modern morality, the remainder of his character comes out
shining. His integrity was unquestioned. His word to enter into
a project or his handshake to seal a bargain was all that was
needed. His sense of honor and justice belonged to a high court.
He was trustworthy to his acquaintances and loyal to his
friends. His honesty was never questioned, and the depths of
his generosity are still to be plumbed.

On the other hand, his personality was something about
which to conjecture. His moods took him from pettiness and
cowardliness to charm and warmth. He could dance like Ray
Bolger, sending his long skinny legs up to impossible heights, or
he could sulk in a corner and say nothing for the night. Was he

cruel, or was he kind? Did he want to skip the party, or play the liveried butler in a powdered wig? With Kaufman it was hard to tell.

He had no interest in serious poetry, painting, sculpture, music, ballet; he rarely set foot in a museum; he could not drive a car, swim, sail, skate, or ski.

He liked theatre, women, cards, and gossip, in that order.

Toward the end of his life a friend visited him. In an attempt to cheer up the unhappy Kaufman, the visitor mentioned that a mutual acquaintance, a man whose reputation was lily-white, who was, in fact, a living saint, recently had acquired a young woman as a mistress.

Kaufman's arm shot out and his index finger pointed at the front door.

"You get out of here," Kaufman roared. His friend realized he had made a mistake by bringing gossip of this nature to his host. He had no time to make amends, for George had not finished his sentence. "And don't you come back until you find out who she is."

As a gossip, he dealt primarily in the nonmalicious brand. Anything more serious than chit-chat brought on long moments of silence from Kaufman as he changed from one pair of glasses to another. Intimacy was not part of his makeup. He clung to privacy with the same miserliness with which he hoarded laughs in the theatre.

As an enemy with a poisoned tongue, he had no equal.

It is just possible that his only match was a very fine writer who was his early friend and later foe, Dorothy Parker. Petite, pretty, and deadly as an asp, Dorothy nee Rothschild Parker was a close friend of Bea and George's, an original member of the Algonquin Round Table, and the author of a pair of incomparable lines concerning girls who wear glasses and girls who attend promenades at Yale.

Jousting between the two became popular at the Round Table, where Woollcott one day, with false dignity, hurled at F.P.A. an imbecilic slur that anti-Semitic bigots have been screeching for years. "You goddamn Christ killer," Woollcott said. Everybody laughed, as Woollcott had intended. Mrs. Parker, who was Jewish only on her father's side and spent years pretending to forget it, said nothing. Kaufman, taking note of her silence, arose and in mock fury said, "I've had enough slurs on my race. I am now leaving this table, this dining room, and this hotel." Then he paused and timed his look at Dorothy Parker. "And I trust that Mrs. Parker will walk out with me—halfway."

That was the beginning. Some years later, Mrs. Parker had an opportunity to sum up Kaufman and Hart in a book review. So much kudos for so little talent, she said.

Unfortunately, the Sunday *Times* book section chose to quote that denigrating review on the weekend when Dorothy Parker and Lillian Hellman were house guests at the Kaufman farm.

Up early, Miss Hellman and Mrs. Parker seized the book section and hid it. Then they decided it would be best to lose themselves for the day among the meadows and along the paths of Doylestown, Pennsylvania. It was Miss Hellman's hope that by the time they returned all would be forgotten.

What they hadn't counted on was that Moss Hart, who also lived in Bucks County, received his own copy of the Sunday *Times*.

Sneaking back into the Kaufman house, the two ladies went upstairs, congratulated each other on how well they had carried off a most difficult situation, and then went down to thank their hostess before making their departure. George was at a bridge table in the living room playing cards. All seemed well.

They thanked Beatrice for a lovely weekend and were halfway across the floor to the door when George lowered his cards.

"Dottie?" he asked ominously. "Did you take the real estate section?"

Banter between the two kept up for years and, according to neutral observers, Mrs. Parker eventually emerged as second best.

The moment he learned of her first suicide attempt, Kaufman, with his ever present fear of death, stopped making remarks about her. But this did not keep Mrs. Parker from pouring a steady stream of slander over Kaufman.

The last recorded encounter between the two was on Madison Avenue near the Hotel Volney, where Mrs. Parker spent her declining years. Present was their mutual friend, the great leading man of Broadway and Hollywood, Fredric March.

Mrs. Parker, who had just been released from a hospital after yet another attempt on her own life, snarled and hissed a line at Kaufman. He, noting the bandages over her slashed wrists, was unable to resist the temptation.

"Dorothy," he murmured solicitously, "you've got to be careful. Next time you might hurt yourself."

They never spoke again.

Or, he could be your friend and still sting you.

Jerome Chodorov, a playwright and a favorite of Kaufman's, had an eating problem. Kaufman summed it up in one sentence at the dinner table.

"Chodorov thinks if he refuses it the first time and takes it the second time, he's dieting."

If he had little interest in food, he had none in drink. Helen Hayes is talking:

The first time I ever got tight in my life was with Aleck Woollcott and George Kaufman and a couple of other

285

people. They gave me one of those awful cocktails that're made with cream and creme de cacao and something else. It's a lethal mixture called the Alexander. Maybe Aleck invented it or maybe it was named after him because it was his favorite drink. Anyway, I was handed one, and it tasted like ice cream. I drank one down and took another and drank it down, and I was blind. I sat there, and can remember so vividly my distress, my agony, because I thought they're all going to know I'm tight if I can't say something to prove I'm not. So I was thinking, working up to saying something. I had a piano and I was moving to another apartment which was smaller. I didn't want that piano anymore, and this began to come into my drink-sodden mind. So I waited until there was a pause in the conversation and then I said, with a great intake of breath, "Anyone who wants my piano is willing to it." And this terrible silence followed, and George said, "That's very seldom of you, Helen."

It wasn't difficult to make an enemy of Kaufman. All one had to do was talk during the performance of a play, especially if he was part of the audience. Many a time he would turn around in his seat or lean forward and tap the shoulder of a between-the-lines talker.

The best record of such an action was when a group came into the theatre after the curtain had gone up. Ignoring the play, they continued to press their previous conversation in loud whispers. Kaufman burned.

"I wish you people would speak up," he snapped. "These actors are making so much noise, I can hardly hear what you're saying."

When *he* didn't care for a play, things were different. At an opening that bored him beyond endurance, he tapped the shoulder of the woman seated in front of him. "Madame," he whispered, "would you mind putting on your hat?"

During the intermission of another production he disliked, he heard Peggy Pulitzer coughing. "Peg," he flipped, "save that cough for the play."

Although he was at the mercy of cab drivers, he could never control his ill temper toward them. He was unforgivably merciless, and only once did he fail to get away with it.

At the very height of his career, he chose to take his mother and father to the ship on which they were sailing for a European holiday. It was one of those nights, cold, with the rain coming down as if through fire hoses hooked up to the sky.

Kaufman jumped into the cab along with his parents and their luggage, and began baiting the cab driver in the mid-eighties. "No, don't take Central Park West. It's too crowded at this time of night . . . Turn right . . . Not here! It's a one-way street . . . Here. This way . . . Not behind the truck . . . Take a left here . . . Here, I said! . . . No, this isn't your fault. It's mine. I should have told you exactly how to get down here when I got into the cab . . . Stop blowing that horn! . . . Must we put up with this fondness of yours for driving behind trucks? The ship leaves *tonight*. That's sometime this evening. In exactly two hours, if you have no objection . . . I know, I know. New York cab drivers are the smartest men in the world. That's why they're driving cabs and not running big companies." By the time they reached 57th Street and 10th Avenue, a long way from a cab stand and a longer way from the ship, the cabbie understandably jammed on his brakes and threw open the back door.

"Out!" he screamed. "I don't have to put up with this. Out of my cab!"

Protestations, bribes, even his mother's apologies did no

good. Kaufman and his parents were unceremoniously deposited on the sidewalk, and the cabbie roared away leaving them to wend their wet and weary way to the ship on foot.

Moss Hart, who was colonel-in-chief of the Kaufman guard, sent the galleys of his autobiography, *Act One*, to Kaufman one fine Friday afternoon. George devoured them. After all, Hart had written, "If it is possible for a book of this sort to have a hero, then that hero is George S. Kaufman." Very thoughtful, very complimentary, even very flattering, but to confront his former collaborator and discuss the book required an emotional outpouring that George S. Kaufman could not give or accept.

As a result, his favorite medium was brought into use. Sometime Saturday evening, George Kaufman sent the following telegram to Moss Hart:

GEORGE TYLER'S OFFICE WAS ON THE THIRD FLOOR NOT THE FOURTH BUT THAT IS MY ONLY COMPLAINT THE BOOK IS QUITE WONDERFUL AND THE SUMMER CAMP STUFF IS TERRIFIC I AM PROUD TO BE PART OF IT ALL THANKS AND LOVE

GEORGE

Selling millions of books, getting rave notices from literary critics all over the world, still that single wire meant more to Hart than anything. He and Kaufman never mentioned that telegram, but Hart told me many times over how he treasured it.

When *Act One* became a best seller, Kaufman was ready with comment.

"I'm very pleased for Moss that *Act One* is on the best seller list," he said. "I simply feel that it should be under fiction instead of non-fiction."

Another crestfallen fellow was Kaufman's former office boy who had arrived at the high station of chief drama reporter for the New York *Times*. It was in this seemingly sacred capacity that Sam Zolotow telephoned Kaufman regularly for news. Eventually, he made one call too many and received the following letter:

Dear Sam:

As you must know by now, I do not believe in announcing plays that may not ever reach production. I have worked on four or five things in recent years that never got anywhere—if I had told you about them, I would now feel like a fool, and you would have printed a lot of false items.

The playwriting business is not like putting up a building —in my case, a big hole is often dug and then nothing happens. . . .

He had a great affection for the young man he had hired years ago on the *Times* drama desk, Herman Mankiewicz.

In many quarters the film *Citizen Kane* is considered an American classic. It was written by Orson Welles and Herman Mankiewicz, and one of the scenes came from Herman's own personal experience. In the film, Joseph Cotten, playing a theatrical reviewer, comes back from an opera, writes a scathing review of the leading lady, who happens to be the publisher's wife, and falls asleep on his typewriter. Orson Welles, as the publisher, finds him in this condition and promptly fires him.

When he was a drama reporter for the New York *Times*, "Mank" had been sent to review *The School for Scandal*, starring Mrs. Samuel Insull, wife of a Chicago utilities baron. As Cotten did in the motion picture, Herman returned to the newspaper by way of a speakeasy and wrote a positively libelous review, not of the play but of Mrs. Insull, "for having the audacity to want to play Lady Teazle"—and then fell asleep on his typewriter.

As the story crossed the desk of the managing editor, Carr

Van Anda killed it and made inquiries about the reporter who wrote it. By then the drama editor was back in the city room of the *Times*. Kaufman was infuriated by the sight of his inebriated assistant. He ran a statement in a one-column box explaining that the review of *The School for Scandal* would be printed in the next issue.

After enough black coffee had been poured into Mankiewicz, Kaufman said, "I don't see that there's anything for you to do right now but send in your resignation."

"Okay," Mankiewicz said, "I'm fired."

"That's just what you are!" Kaufman told him.

The next morning, though, a cooled-off Kaufman telephoned Mankiewicz and asked, "Show up for work this afternoon, will you, Herman?"

It was, to say the very least, a story to carry around in a writer's head for a lifetime—and then, when the opportunity arose, as it did in *Citizen Kane*, to use to its fullest.

Clouded in the antiquated mists of the Twenties are the origins of a game recreated by Woollcott, Herbert Bayard Swope, and other innovators. First played in the thirteenth century in France, croquet—as devised by Woollcott, Swope, et al.—was as different from the game French children played as are children themselves different from adults.

The hoops and pegs were retained but the balls were larger and heavier, as were the mallets, their hand-turned heads frequently bound with English steel.

Emerging as an adult game at the Swope estate in Sands Point, New York, croquet was played with an intensity matched only by the tart tongues of the players. Insults and humor went side by side. Frank Adams, Harpo Marx, the Robert Sherwoods, the Averell Harrimans, Neysa McMein, the Raoul Fleischmanns, Edna Ferber, Howard Dietz, the Richard Rodgers, Marc

Connelly, Frank Sullivan, the Irving Berlins and, of course, the George Kaufmans were among the early players.

On weekends the game was played at the Swopes' place. On week days the croquet buffs actually received a permit from the City of New York to play their game in Central Park. Some played daily, in the 1920s, on the East Side below 72nd Street.

The only true winner of the game was the firm of Abercrombie & Fitch, which supplied mallets, balls, and wickets at prices just this side of keeping a string of polo ponies.

Importing the game to Bucks County was inevitable. In the early years, the stakes were high and the games were tense. After George and Leueen were married, he taught her to play, and then it became a game more for fun than high stakes. George would call up his Bucks County neighbors and say, "Stop work. Come on over. Leueen and I are ready for a little croquet."

Still, crouched over his mallet, wondering which strategy to employ, George remained true to the image Aleck Woollcott had conjured up of him: "a morning glory climbing a pole."

Richard Rodgers may be counted as a friendly enemy. He had reason.

In 1937 Kaufman and Moss Hart collaborated on the book for *I'd Rather Be Right*. Rodgers and Lorenz Hart wrote the music and lyrics. It is usual for the creator of a musical play to receive the same percentage of the weekly gross as the composer and lyricist. There are variations, of course, but nothing like the 8 percent Kaufman and Hart took to the 5 percent left to Rodgers and the other Hart.

Not only did this irritate Rodgers, but he soon became aware of Kaufman's singular distaste for music.

During the tryout of the musical in Baltimore, Rodgers and Hart were asked to replace a song. The new one stopped the show cold.

"This is our chance," Rodgers said out loud during a run-through. "Now we can have an encore and maybe somebody will remember a couple of bars."

Kaufman lost his temper but "only by proxy. He wouldn't come up to me and tell me so. He sent Moss Hart to do the dirty work," Rodgers said. "We had a great big argument on the street in front of Ford's Theatre in Baltimore. In the end, Kaufman won. He was bigger, richer, and older."

Kaufman knew how Rodgers felt, and as Rodgers grew increasingly successful it was Kaufman's turn to taste gall. By the time Rodgers and Hammerstein had *South Pacific* in Boston, Kaufman could stand it no more. The reviews were glorious and business was booming. During luncheon at Moss Hart's one Sunday, Kaufman threw down the paper in disgust.

"I see where the Shubert Theatre in Boston is locked up on Sunday," he said, "but people are so excited there about *South Pacific* they're pushing money under the lobby doors. They don't want anything; they just want to push money under the doors."

The Rodgers-Kaufman unpleasantness did not amount to much more. Although they never worked together again, they saw each other socially. Each went to the other's openings. Dorothy Rodgers thought George was very attractive (which he wasn't) and very good at parlor games (which he was), and Richard Rodgers conceded Kaufman was very good in the theatre and very bad on the croquet field.

But it never approached the bitterness of the Jed Harris-George Kaufman feud.

Not only had success come easily to Jed Harris; he had grown to expect it. But *Serena Blandish,* a play he produced in 1929, opened to extremely bad notices during its out-of-town tryout in Philadelphia.

It was the policy of the New York *Times* in those days to publish at least one of the reviews earned by a play during its pre-Broadway run. Because of his close association with Kaufman in the theatre, Harris felt he had every right to squelch any mention of bad notices in the *Times*. That, he believed, was the very least of his problems with *Serena Blandish*. With easy confidence he telephoned Kaufman from Philadelphia and requested a small favor: kill the *Blandish* story.

Could Harris have been connected with a different Kaufman on the *Times* drama desk? He wanted the jocular and winning Kaufman who had directed *The Front Page* for him a few months ago. Instead he got a cold intractable Kaufman who stood behind the rock of integrity and righteousness.

Kill the story in the Sunday paper, Harris repeated.

"I don't know if I can do that," Kaufman answered stubbornly.

He didn't do it, and the *Serena Blandish* story ran on Sunday.

Enraged, Harris telephoned Kaufman and had a terrific quarrel with him. Kaufman, as Harris recalls, didn't do much fighting. It was Harris who screamed and behaved badly.

"As I look back on it now, it seems ludicrous that I could have been so concerned with such a matter," Harris said.

Thereafter, he claimed, he and Kaufman only spoke of small matters.

For his part, Kaufman said he never spoke to Harris again. He was incensed that the producer would expect Kaufman the newspaperman to compromise himself for Kaufman the theatre man.

So bitter were his feelings toward Jed Harris that he got off one of his best lines of pure venom. It has since been attributed to several people in Hollywood and at least one American political figure and one member of New York society. There is no doubt, however, that the line originally was said by Kaufman in 1929. And what he said was, "When I die, I want to be cremated and have my ashes thrown in Jed Harris' face."

No great favorites of Kaufman were the military big brass. He distrusted all generals, be they General Motors, General Mills, General Foods, or General Staff. But it was a general officer of the U.S. Army who left the great repartee artist speechless.

In 1942 Kaufman was summoned by Army morale officers. They explained to him that they had a serious problem: they provided weekend entertainment for the draftees, but the boys stubbornly ignored it. Instead, they asked for passes and betook themselves to places where ladies of easy virtue could be found.

George listened sympathetically, then asked, "But why am I here? What do you want me to do?"

The top general replied blandly, "Why, give them something better."

Any hostess inviting George S. Kaufman to dinner had two options. Either she called the Kaufman home the day before and cleared the menu with George or Bea, or she served what she chose and ran the rather unhappy risk of having the finicky Kaufman stare at the table and refuse to eat anything.

At one point in the Kaufman-Ferber collaboration, tempers smoldered and matters came to an impasse. Miss Ferber, in a gallant attempt at reconciliation, invited the Kaufmans to a large Sunday evening dinner party.

Miss Ferber was trying to patch things up, true, but being as strong and as definite a personality as she was, she could never stoop to having her choice of foods determined by her guests.

On Sunday evening the Kaufmans and everyone else arrived. The large sit-down dinner began with a hot cheese hors d'oeuvre. Kaufman, who would not tolerate cheese even in its passive state, almost became ill at the sight of this warm, oozy substance whose odors filled his nostrils. Bea, knowing what was happening, but also knowing that Edna had chosen this night to make peace, ate her portion and George's as well.

Next was roast goose with a crisp skin, thick gravy, and all the trimmings. George started to leave the table, but Bea tugged him back into his seat and ate for both of them.

As he never touched a salad with roquefort dressing, he sat there until Bea reached over and consumed his as well as hers.

Coffee and dessert got by all right. Then Edna looked up and gestured that she was ready to leave the table. Bea was so relieved to have that dinner over, the dinner at which she had overeaten and overworried, that she stood up suddenly and started away from the table.

Unfortunately, during one of those moments of diplomacy, when she had reached over to take some of her husband's food, a buckle on her evening dress had caught the lace of the table cloth. As she left, the cloth, the silver, the china, the coffee, the mints—everything—went crashing onto the floor.

George looked at the broken china and then at his hostess.

"That's what I call pulling off a few good ones."

In the vanguard of Kaufman enemies were those unhappy souls who sued him for plagiarism: a dress manufacturer from the Bronx, a lawyer from Boston, an expatriate from Paris, an out-of-work newspaperman. The list is fairly long. The dramatic works include *Of Thee I Sing, You Can't Take It With You, The Man Who Came to Dinner, George Washington Slept Here*. There were others, but no one ever won. Either the case was dismissed or, if it went to trial, the court always found in favor of Kaufman.

While he was being sued for plagiarism on *The Man Who Came to Dinner*, he wrote Woollcott, "It seems we stole the character of Woollcott from a play called *Sticks and Stones*. It will probably turn out that you got it from there, too."

He and Edna did leave themselves open in *The Royal Family*. The play concerned itself with a theatrically prominent family, and as soon as it was written, Ethel Barrymore called Kaufman and asked if she might look through it. George sent her a copy. On reading it, she went directly to her lawyer, who studied the play carefully and informed Miss Barrymore that of the three —Ethel, Lionel, and John—only John had the possibility of a case, and not of plagiarism but of libel. John, however, was too busy to bother. Thereafter, Ethel only nodded coolly to Kaufman when the two met at parties.

Kaufman once had to answer to a New York Supreme Court judge and jury because of one of his flops. This ultimate step in aggravation came as a result of a law suit brought against him by one Isidore Polisuk, a Bronx dress manufacturer who in 1928 bought a play, *Hard Pan*, for one hundred dollars.

Early in 1931, he somehow convinced Sam H. Harris to produce it on Broadway. Harris got Kaufman and Laurence Stallings, co-author of *What Price Glory?*, to rewrite it.

The play opened in New Haven under the title of *El Dorado*. Under the same title, it closed in Newark.

Piqued that it wasn't brought into New York, furious at Kaufman for not having rewritten it more successfully, Polisuk, as was his legal right, sought redress in court.

Although he won the suit, he believed that his trial lawyer, Wolfgang Schwabacher, should have settled the case out of court. "A courtroom is no place for a playwright unless he's there to get a new plot," Kaufman told Howard Lindsay. Immediately after the trial he founded the Shakespeare Was Right Society. "The first thing we do, let's kill all the lawyers," Shakespeare had written in the second part of *Henry VI*.

The fact that he never lost these cases did not lessen Kaufman's abhorrence of legal eagles who allowed their clients to pursue hopeless causes.

His aversion to lawyers was closely followed by his abomination of doctors. A favorite story concerned his favorite doctor, Edward Greenspan, M.D.

Kaufman had undergone a complete physical examination, including a long and arduous series of tests that were to determine his overall condition. A week later he returned to learn their results. Sitting in the waiting room of Dr. Greenspan's office, his hypochondria reached a new high. Finally, the nurse beckoned and the door to the doctor's office was opened.

"Come in, George," the good doctor said. "Sit down."

Kaufman did as bidden.

"George, I don't know how to tell you this," the doctor began.

By then, Kaufman was sure of the worst.

"I really don't know what to say," the doctor said, as he shuffled the papers in front of him. They contained the complete Kaufman case history.

George always claimed that at that moment he was ready to faint.

"The only way to tell you," Dr. Greenspan said, "is to come right out and tell you. George, I'm going to get married."

Phyllis Cerf, one of those who remembered the story, believed it was Strike Number One against Dr. Greenspan.

And then there was the telegram he sent to the son of his old friend, Herbert Bayard Swope, when that young gentleman was making his debut as a Broadway producer: WELCOME TO THE WRONG SIDE OF THE TRACKS.

On the road with Jack Benny in a play that was having more than its share of trouble, the company decided one afternoon to stop work on the show and go bowling. Kaufman tagged along. One of the girls in the company was a great bowler. She'd made one strike after another. Kaufman watched her for a while and then whispered into Jack Benny's ear, "Maybe we can get her to fix the third act."

George arrived early at a dinner party. Alone in the living room sat his old friend Margaret Leech Pulitzer. "My God, Peg," Kaufman muttered, "I thought we were both dead!"

Kaufman thought of Joseph Wood Krutch as an enemy.

The Columbia University professor and dramatic critic of the *Nation* decided Kaufman did not know how to construct a plot and if he ever did attempt to build one it would be clumsy. He implied that "Mr. Kaufman, therefore, must borrow his plots."

Kaufman struck back politely in the *New Yorker* magazine in the issue of May 26, 1951.

If there is one subject I am completely fascinated by it's Samuel Johnson, and when I heard that Mr. Krutch was taking a sabbatical year in which to write a book about him, I didn't even wait for the publication date. I ordered the book at once. Little did I think at that time that whereas Mr. Krutch would be on that book for one year, I would be on it for seven, and only up to page nine at that.

In these seven years, *Samuel Johnson* has piled up the following history with me: it has made three round trips to Hollywood, staying twice at the Garden of Allah and once at the Beverly Hills Hotel, where the dust jacket was slightly spotted by a highball glass; it has gone twice to Florida and gotten quite a little sand on it, some of which I am still shaking out; and last summer it visited England and the French Riviera. On each occasion, I took it with me in the firm conviction that I was going to get somewhere with it, and I still feel that it is exactly my dish. I was fascinated by the very opening sentence and remember it as though it were only six years ago: "Samuel Johnson was a pessimist with an enormous zest for living." You must admit that is an intriguing sentence, one that will catch the reader and hold him. It has held me for seven years.

Also, I have an enormous respect for Mr. Joseph Wood Krutch, a scholar and a gentleman. The fact that I have carried his book halfway around the world is certain proof of that. I'll bet he hasn't got another reader who has shown such loyalty. I don't deserve any particular credit for this; *Samuel Johnson* just happens to be my kind of book. In Hollywood, someone wanted to borrow it once but I felt that I would get at it any minute, so I refused to lend it. In Florida, as I have already implied, I used to carry it with me to the beach. I remember that it got buried in the sand one day, and I was frantic until I found it again. I lost the dust jacket four or five years ago, but the book itself is in splendid condition. Why shouldn't it be? The place where I left off, on page nine, was absolutely enthralling; "The father was proud of his son—foolishly so, in that son's opinion—but he showed his pride in many clumsy ways which humiliated an intelligent child." Think of the heart-breaking stories that will illustrate the child's humiliation, the suffering of his sensitive soul! I can hardly wait for page ten. And I mean to read it, I promise you. I am taking it with me to California soon, and, if necessary, to Europe again in the summer. It is exactly my dish.

Kaufman really didn't dislike Krutch; he merely was irked by him. The people he hated were those who didn't earn their right in the theatre. Those who did earn their right he respected and cherished. Even composers.

He had no knowledge and very little understanding of song writing. "Let's take a walk," he'd say. "That's a song title. It's that easy. 'Sit down on a bench.' That's a song title, too. 'Time to go home.' Another song title. 'Let's have a cup of coffee.' A fourth song title. 'Pass me the cream, my dear.' What a ballad!" Kaufman's attitude toward music was that of a postman toward a heavy mailbag: odious but necessary.

He never really forgave himself for not recognizing the potential of Irving Berlin's song "Always."* Thirty-five years after Berlin agreed to withdraw it from *The Cocoanuts*, Kaufman wrote his whimsical apology in the *New Yorker* magazine.

A good many years ago, Irving Berlin and I went to Atlantic City together to work on a musical show for the Marx Brothers—all seventeen of them. We had adjoining rooms at the hotel, and along about the second week Irving woke me up at five o'clock one morning to sing me a song he had just finished. Now, Irving has a pure but hardly strong voice, and, since I am not very strong myself at five o'clock in the morning, I could not catch a word of it. Moving to the edge of the bed, he sat down and sang it again, and again I failed to get it. Just when it looked as though he would have to get in my bed before I could hear it, he managed, on the third try, to put it across. The song was a little number called "Always," and its easy-going rhythms were just up my street. I learned it quickly and as dawn broke we leaned out of the window and sang it to the Atlantic Ocean—its first performance in any hotel. It was destined to be sung millions of times after that, and invariably better.

The task done, we then talked about it. At that time I was woefully ignorant of music, and by dint of hard work over the years I have managed to keep myself in the same innocent state. To this day, I do not quite know the difference between Handel's "Largo" and—well—Largo's "Han-

* Because he gave the song to his wife, the former Ellin Mackay, as a wedding gift, Mr. Berlin claimed not to know how much money that great American standard made. People in show business say millions.

del." But I have always felt that I knew a little something about lyrics, and I was presumptuous enough then to question Irving's first line, "I'll be loving you always." "Always," was a long time for romance. There were almost daily stories to that effect in the newspapers—stories about middle-aged husbands who had bricked up their wives in the cellar wall and left for Toledo with the maid. I suggested, therefore, that the opening line might be a little more in accord with reality—something like "I'll be loving you Thursday." But Irving would have none of it.

Berlin himself liked the story of a friend who met Kaufman on the street one fall day. Kaufman was at work adapting Gilbert and Sullivan.

"How's it going, George?" Berlin's friend asked.

"Great!" Kaufman answered. "It's wonderful working with a dead composer."

As usual, there were two sides to Kaufman. Condemn composers he could and did with gusto, but when news of George Gershwin's death reached him, he wept and was inconsolable for days.

How did the Gershwins feel about Kaufman?

"We liked him tremendously," Ira Gershwin said. "Kaufman was certainly one of the most practical showmen alive. The Gershwins wouldn't argue with him. If he didn't like it, we'd write something new. I don't know of anybody who criticized him to his face."

Not true.

During *Guys and Dolls*, Frank Loesser, the composer and lyricist, had an exchange of words with Kaufman. Subject: reprises of songs in the second act.

Talk went on with voices growing higher and louder, when Kaufman suddenly stood up and quietly but menacingly said,

"I'll tell you what, Frank. I'll make you a deal. I'll let you reprise as many songs as you want in the second act if you let me reprise some of the jokes from the first act."

And that ended that for the moment.

George invited a young man to the Kaufman town house one evening after dinner. Shortly after the Kaufman guests left the table, all very elegant in their dinner clothes, the young man arrived, wearing a rumpled business suit.

After introductions were made, they began to play a game: someone was to go out of the room, the other players were to select an object, and then someone was to hold a plate or an ashtray and tap on it as the "finder" got closer to the object. The closer he got, the faster and louder the tapping was to become.

The young man with the rumpled suit was tapping. As Mrs. Franklin P. Adams got closer to the object, she recalled, he gave a helluva rap to a large bowl and smashed it into a thousand pieces. George turned away and rubbed an area behind his left ear with his index finger.

The bowl was an eight hundred dollar Lowestoft, and the young man, who was making his first appearance in New York's literary world, was William Saroyan.

Kaufman and Herman Mankiewicz wrote a play called *The Good Fellow*, which they were trying out in Atlantic City. Trying out a new play in Atlantic City at the same time was Ruth Gordon.

The Good Fellow was supposed to be a hilarious comedy. The audience did not find it so. They watched the play in absolute silence. One evening after the curtain, Kaufman met a distressed Miss Gordon in the lobby of their hotel.

"This is the most agonizing thing," Miss Gordon said. "This is a serious, tragic play I'm in, and the audience laughs."

"I've got the damnedest idea," Kaufman said. "It'll save both shows."

"What is it?" Miss Gordon asked.

"Let's switch audiences," he answered.

Harpo Marx, to whom he was devoted, took delight in rattling the easily embarrassed Kaufman. As a friend, Harpo was a practical joker of incredible proportions.

There was the day when Harpo, Bea, and George Kaufman were in a diner aboard a train going to Bucks County. A little old lady asked if she might take the fourth chair at their table. Bea said it was all right, but George, knowing how unpredictably mad Harpo was, squirmed. Harpo said nothing. He didn't even look at her.

The little old lady finished eating first and asked for her check. George was still concerned about Harpo. The waiter brought the lady's check on a saucer. George smiled with relief.

But Harpo, still not looking up from his plate, reached for the saucer, salted and peppered the lady's check, and ate it. Kaufman twisted in agony. And waited to even the score.

Following a triumphant performance in Russia, Harpo returned to New York and went to the Algonquin Hotel for dinner. Waiting for him were Woollcott, Broun, Benchley, and Dorothy Parker. Shortly after they sat down, Kaufman entered. He was carrying a newspaper clipping and had a fiendish look in his eyes. When his friends began to greet him, George put his finger to his lips and signaled for silence.

Sitting down, he pulled out his watch and placed it on the table beside the newspaper clipping. The headline read:

HARPO MARX SCORES BIG HIT IN MOSCOW
First American Popular Artist to Entertain Soviets
Receives Ten Minute Standing Ovation

303

Every time anyone started to speak, Kaufman held up his hand for silence. Otherwise, he sat still, his eyes fixed on his watch.

The waiter came. Woollcott told him they weren't ready to order. Time crept by. The waiter returned and was sent away again. The silence around the table was overpowering.

After a seemingly interminable while, Kaufman arose, put the watch in his pocket, and turned to Harpo.

"That was ten minutes, Marx. The Russians applauded you for ten minutes, eh?"

George snorted, picked up the clipping, and left the restaurant, laughter from the table following him out.

Jacqueline Susann, the novelist, started off as a big Kaufman fan but within twenty-four hours became a big Kaufman enemy. And he didn't know about either of her feelings toward him for years.

Miss Susann came to New York City to be an actress. In short order she became familiar with the Kaufman legend: success, success, success year in and year out. Her ambition, understandably, was to appear in a Kaufman play.

Her hopes in that direction took a decided leap forward when Kaufman's casting director Myra Streger stopped by Miss Susann's table in Sardi's and said, "You're perfect for a part in the new George Kaufman play. Don't change a hair. Be in the lounge of the Music Box at two-thirty tomorrow."

That night Jackie and her husband Irving Mansfield and Eddie Cantor celebrated. George Kaufman was going to "discover" her tomorrow and stardom was in sight at last.

The next afternoon she arrived at the Music Box Theatre.

"Don't move," Myra Streger said. "Stay right there. I'll bring him over to you."

Jackie watched as Kaufman made his way slowly through the waiting actors. He was courteous, polite, utterly charming.

"How do you do?" he said to one actor. "I'm sorry but I don't believe I remember what you did last . . . oh, of course. You were very good. Take a script and Myra will make a date for you to read tomorrow."

Jackie waited and waited as Kaufman spoke to actor after actor. Finally, Myra Streger stood in front of her.

"Mr. Kaufman," she said, "this is Jackie Susann. I have an idea she'd be absolutely right for the ingenue."

Kaufman glanced at her, raised his eyebrows, and pondered for a moment.

"I hardly think so," he said softly and walked away.

Devastated was the word for Jacqueline Susann. For years those four words, "I hardly think so," stayed with her. And then came the chance to even up matters with George Kaufman. Her husband was the producer of a television series on which Kaufman was a regular. Jackie went on one night and told the story not only to George but to an entire national television audience.

The glow of satisfaction lasted as long as it took Kaufman to change glasses and look at her.

"That's a very amusing story," he said, "but I'm sure it's completely apocryphal."

Once again Jackie Susann resented George Kaufman, because, as she tells it, in front of those live television cameras, she was unable to answer him. She didn't know what "apocryphal" meant.

That was long ago. Today, she knows *all* the words.

Kaufman, who spent fifty years in the legitimate theatre and never used an agent, would have nothing to do with Hollywood without one. And then, he only used the best. His first agent was Leland Hayward. His last was Irving Lazar. Hayward was a Princeton man who had gone wrong somewhere; eventually he straightened out and became a successful Broadway producer. Lazar was short, sharp, and nicknamed "Swifty." Both men were proud to represent George S. Kaufman. And both were proud of his personal friendship. "Every time I go to New York George invites me over for dinner," Lazar said.

"Every time Irving Lazar comes to New York from California," Kaufman told Nunnally Johnson, "he feels obligated to see me. And since he comes here twenty times a year, I see more of Lazar than most of my friends in New York."

Through his second wife Leueen MacGrath, Kaufman acquired a series of new friends, many of them carrying British passports. Almost exclusively they were writers and actors, including Emlyn Williams, Aldous Huxley, Sybil Thorndike, Edith Evans, Laurence Olivier, Vivian Leigh, Cathleen Nesbitt, Lilli Palmer, Peter Brooks, "Binky" Beaumont, and Rex Harrison. George enjoyed their company, and his home was always open to them.

He was more chiding than scolding when a group of advertisements began to appear in national magazines showing Mr. Harrison holding a cocktail. The copy beneath the picture sent George to his typewriter. A frequent contributor to Martin Levin's column, "The Phoenix Nest" in the *Saturday Review*, Kaufman got off the following salvo:

AN OPEN LETTER TO REX HARRISON
("A Martini is like a play. It can be terribly good or terribly poor."—Rex Harrison in current advertisements.)
Well, Rex, old boy, let's bat this thing around for a couple of minutes. I realize you were in a bit of a spot for an analogy—after all, there you are in show business, not the suspender business, so naturally you had to say that a martini was like a play, not a pair of suspenders. (I'd like to carry that suspender notion a bit further, if you have the time

. . . "both have lots of snap" . . . things like that. I don't suppose you ever could claim that a martini holds your pants up.)

Of course you might have come out and said that a martini is like your appendix, because you can't sit on either one of them. But some smart alex would have written in that he had his appendix taken out, dropped it into a martini, then sat on both of them at the same time. *Touche!*

So you played it safe and said that a martini was like a play. Now as I understand it, a martini has an olive in it. Is this true of a play? Of course, it could have Olive Deering in it, or Olive Wyndham, or Olive Reeves-Smith, but how often does that happen? It could even have Olivier in it, but let's not try to get funny. The dramatic critics—anyhow, the good ones—don't like jokes this season. This brings me to the fact that when you bring a martini to New York, the boys don't dream of criticizing it. They just drink it.

Or let's say you're opening a martini in Wilmington, just for a try-out. Do you call up Moss Hart and ask him to come down and take a swig at it, just to see what he thinks? I know Mr. Hart pretty well, and I don't think he wants to come down to Wilmington and sit up all night in a hotel bedroom—not over one martini, anyhow.

Incidentally, I notice from the photograph in the advertisement that your martini doesn't have an olive in it at all—it has a twist of lemon peel in it. This gives Mr. Hart an out on that trip to Wilmington—he suggests that you try twisting the lemon peel to the left instead of the right, and see how that works.

Mind you, I really don't blame you for saying that a martini is like a play, because you certainly know a lot about plays. You just don't know anything about martinis.

The enemies who finished him off in spades, as Kaufman himself said, were Feuer and Martin.

Short, pugnacious Cy Feuer was complemented by tall, deadly Ernest Martin. One blew hot, the other blew cold. Together they battled their way through an astounding number of musical hits. They took on everyone and won, and that included George S. Kaufman.

His last produced creative effort was a musical version of the film *Ninotchka*. His collaborator was his second wife Leueen.

Silk Stockings, as the production was called, was a long time in getting to Broadway. And when it did get on, it turned out to be one of those star-crossed efforts in which only trouble seemed to thrive. Kaufman had written better books, Cole Porter had written better music and lyrics, and Feuer and Martin had produced better shows.

Axiomatically, whenever a musical is in trouble the fault is the book's. According to Feuer and Martin, Kaufman was ill when the production tried out in Philadelphia, and while his wife did very good rewrites, much more was needed. Accordingly, the producers pressured Kaufman into calling Abe Burrows and asking him to take over the book. Feuer took over the direction. Mr. and Mrs. Kaufman returned to New York.

Back at home, in spite of the shabby treatment they received from Feuer and Martin, the Kaufmans, rested and fresh, felt they should go to Boston to see what they could do for the new version of *Silk Stockings*. But once there, to their chagrin, they were told they were not needed or even wanted. Kaufman rose to his full height.

"Are you asking me to leave?" he demanded.

Martin, who was at least as tall as Kaufman, had lived with the misapprehension that Kaufman stood over everybody else. When he stood up, he was surprised to suddenly realize he was as big as Kaufman. But surprise wasn't the strongest emotion he was feeling at that moment.

"Are you asking us to leave our own show, to leave Boston? Is that what you're doing?" Kaufman asked.

"Yes," Ernie Martin told him in a voice that was cold and had the sound of finality to it. "That's what we're doing. Literally."

And he and Cy Feuer left.

George and Leueen called the cast of *Silk Stockings* on stage and said a sweet but mournful good-by.

When he returned to New York, George Kaufman was guilty of The Wit's worst disease: repetition.

"When I die," he said, as he had once said of Jed Harris, "I want to be cremated and have my ashes thrown in Ernie Martin's face."

"I did hear that," Ernie Martin said, "and I always felt that that would be a satisfactory solution to the problem insofar as I was concerned."

George Kaufman's best friend was his first wife. He loved Leueen but he never forgot Bea. During all the time he was married to Leueen, one day each year belonged to Bea. On the anniversary of her death, George—this irreligious, irreverent man —always lit a candle, a yahrzeit candle, which burned for twenty-four hours in his bedroom. Loyalty and friendship are handmaidens. Bea had been his friend. He lit the light in her memory.

15 *The Performer*

Of all the characters George S. Kaufman created, he saved the best for himself. The curmudgeon was a role built to suit his timing, his delivery, his sense of humor, his shyness, and that modicum of innate irascibility.

The curmudgeon was a characterization that did not arrive full blown overnight. It developed in Kaufman gradually—as he himself developed it over the years. It was the public image of George S. Kaufman.

As a characterization, it was neither all funny nor all true. To cab drivers, doctors, pushy actors, and waiters there was a reality to it. To the public, which began to see him more and more as a performer, it was an act not to be missed.

Essentially, the character personified the very basis of most Kaufman plays: blast the pompous, scorn the mighty, but do it quickly and with laughter. Scowl, complain, grimace, deprecate, grumble, roar, fret, fume, sulk, castigate, deplore, deride, taunt— but do it all on a moral basis and with the kind of sting that the average little man would enjoy applying to the seat of the average big man. Chosen especially to aim that needle was the quiet wry American who sat around the cracker-barrel just waiting for someone to make an ass of himself, the old curmudgeon.

The old curmudgeon turned up at the age of forty-one. Moss Hart had written a play. Few of his friends liked it. More important, even fewer Broadway producers liked it. Sam Harris, however, saw something in it, and took it to George Kaufman. George Kaufman was not wild about it but he saw something there that interested him. As a result, Moss Hart rewrote the play, and then he and George Kaufman rewrote the play, and finally Sam Harris presented it.

There is every possibility that if George S. Kaufman had not chosen to play the part of Lawrence Vail, *Once in a Lifetime* might never have seen life. Lawrence Vail is the Broadway playwright who is inveigled into a Hollywood producer's office, and who, for the better part of the play, is kept waiting outside that office. Jaded, acid-tongued, Lawrence Vail's comments on the Hollywood of 1930 contributed in large part to making the play a hit.

The very idea of Kaufman actually performing on the stage of the Music Box Theatre pleased the critics. His performance was praised, and he himself had a marvelous time playing eight performances a week. He was enthralled with the idea of wearing makeup, captivated with the sound of an audience's laughter and applause, and enchanted beyond his wildest imagination as night after night people poured through the stage door into his dressing room to compliment him on his acting.

Although he was introverted and frightened of most people, the character of Lawrence Vail tickled his ego. This was exactly the sort of public pose he fancied. As a result he remained with *Once in a Lifetime* for many months.

"He was absolutely magnificent," said Jean Dixon, who played in the Hart-Kaufman comedy, "and nobody could replace him. We had actor after actor in that part and it wasn't the same—I don't know what it was . . ."

So the role of the curmudgeon was formed. It was furthered by another comedy by Kaufman and Hart, *The Man Who Came to Dinner*. The character Sheridan Whiteside was obviously a spoof of Alexander Woollcott. It was even dedicated to him by the authors, "For reasons that are nobody's business."

It was the last really big hit that Kaufman and Hart wrote together, and while Monty Woolley played it to rave notices at the Music Box, Kaufman and Hart and Alexander Woollcott himself waited impatiently for the summer stock rights to be released. All three of them played Sheridan Whiteside, the waspish curmudgeon, at different theatres during the same summer. Kaufman's Whiteside assumed a black spade-shaped beard that made him look like something between Sigmund Freud and a Jewish Abe Lincoln.

Groucho Marx endured the trip down to Bucks County to see him. "He was fine. He was very good," Groucho reported. "He didn't look like the part, but who knew what the part looked like? Everybody didn't know Woollcott. I wouldn't say he was Olivier, but I thought he gave a good performance."

For the next few years, Kaufman worked to polish the character of the curmudgeon. He would accept with feigned reticence an occasional guest shot on the radio quiz program "Information, Please." During World War II he was invited out to many of the Army bases surrounding New York to comment wryly on manners, morals, and similar situations. More than the sound of his own voice, he liked the sound of laughter following those crisp, staccato sentences. Outwardly, however, as in all Kaufman performances, both public and private, he gave the impression of being cool, aloof, unapproachable, and completely in control of every situation. Inwardly, he was absolutely terrified. "I've never gotten over stage fright," he told me, "no matter if it's in the theatre, a radio or television studio, or a dinner party here at the apartment."

In 1948 one of the most successful radio producers of the Columbia Broadcasting System came up with a sunburst of ideas. His first notion was to put together a program called "This Is Broadway," in which professional talent would perform before a panel of experts. After each performer had sung, told jokes, played an instrument, or whatever, that performer was to mention a problem that was currently bothering him. The panel of experts would attempt to solve it for him.

The second idea was to get Clifton Fadiman, the urbane literary critic and former moderator of "Information, Please," to moderate "This Is Broadway." As Mr. Fadiman was in New York and "Information, Please" was off the air, a simple matter of negotiation brought matters to a successful conclusion.

The third idea was to get a clever young man named Abe Burrows. Burrows was on the West Coast amusing folks by playing on other people's pianos songs he had written himself. An airplane ticket brought him to New York.

The fourth idea was to get Helen Hayes. This was done with ease. The producer simply told Miss Hayes that George S. Kaufman was going to appear on the program. On that basis, Miss Hayes accepted.

The fifth idea was to get Kaufman.

Creator and producer, the man who had all five ideas, was Irving Mansfield, who had been introduced to Kaufman once by Aleck Woollcott. Kaufman, playing the curmudgeon, never acknowledged the introduction. Mansfield was understandably bitter. "For about ten minutes," Mansfield said. "Then I was overawed by him because George Kaufman was a living legend in his time. And the fact that he walked in followed by Harold Ross and Alfred Lunt did nothing to dispel the Algonquin Round Table stories."

Still, in 1948, how to approach George Kaufman? His telephone was unlisted, his address was a closely guarded secret. Here was where Mansfield's wife, Jacqueline Susann, came in. She had a friend: the actress Joan Castle, an intimate of Kaufman's. In fact, she was dining with Kaufman that night and would mention the show to him.

Next morning, from Miss Castle to Miss Susann to Mr. Mansfield went Kaufman's private telephone number.

According to Mansfield the dialogue went this way:

KAUFMAN: (answering phone) Yes?

MANSFIELD: Mr. Kaufman, this is Irving Mansfield.

KAUFMAN: (after a long pause) Yes?

MANSFIELD: Miss Castle mentioned to me that she had talked to you and perhaps you would want to be part of a show.

KAUFMAN: (after an even longer pause) Oh, yes. She did mention it.

MANSFIELD: Well, I would like to meet you and talk with you.

KAUFMAN: (the longest pause of all) Is there much to talk about?

MANSFIELD: I'd like to tell you what the program consists of, and I also intend to discuss with you what salary there would be for you as a performer.

KAUFMAN: (quickly) Well, do you think I'll be able to make a contribution?

MANSFIELD: Mr. Kaufman, if a man like you can't make a contribution to this program, this program may just as well stay off the air.

KAUFMAN: (even quicker than before) When would you like to meet?

MANSFIELD: That's up to you, sir.

The "sir" was quite involuntary on Mansfield's part, but coupled with the words "salary" and "performer" it did the trick.

Kaufman arrived fifteen minutes early for his appointment at Mansfield's CBS office. Mansfield immediately launched into a panegyric of the radio show he intended to produce. Kaufman listened quietly. When Mansfield had finished, Kaufman asked, "When's the audition?"

Although Mansfield changed the title from "This Is Broadway" to "This Is Show Business," it made little difference. The audition was a success, the program went on the air, and in place of the busy Helen Hayes there was to be a different guest each week, preferably female.

Moderating was Fadiman. Laughing and smiling was Abe Burrows. The old curmudgeon sat quietly, and when the time was right, he would fire off a line timed and delivered to perfection. The program was sold commercially almost at once. The next year, it made the transition from radio to television with remarkable ease.

Within five or six weeks Kaufman confided to Mansfield, "It's a funny thing. I got out of a taxi the other day and some ridiculous taxi driver said, 'So long, Mr. Kaufman.' Can you imagine a taxi driver knowing my name?"

It was around that time that he started using makeup. At first, he'd allow only a little, but as the weeks went by, the makeup girl was permitted to apply more and more pancake. He gave up his large collection of silk foulards and chose to sport little bow ties. And he also began to wear blue shirts exclusively.

In those early days of television, white caused hyalation, a bouncing of light that could "burn" the cameras. Blue showed up as white on the early black and white screens, and it was the mark of those men who performed regularly on television to wear blue shirts. Mansfield went to Sulka's, bought Kaufman three blue shirts, and had them delivered to Kaufman's apartment. He never thanked Mansfield for them, but just as they were about to step on stage, he leaned over to his producer and with a little nod whispered, "And they fit!" From that day on, he wore blue shirts.

But most important of all was his hair. He would make a point to have a shampoo and treatment at Frances Fox's on the day of the show. That night just before going on stage, he would take a comb out of his inside pocket, and when he thought nobody was looking would comb his hair up and forward, thus presenting the image of a man with a huge shock of hair.

With his blue shirt, his bow tie, his hair standing on end, he would sit with his hand to his face, or wearing a scowl or a sneer, and wait for the right moment to pronounce the right line.

And a large portion of the American television viewing public waited with him. And for him. And identified with him. And quite clearly, although he never said or did anything publicly to show it, he loved it.

Why did this withdrawn, stiff, laconic, and often silent man turn into such an exhibitionistic person? Perhaps one explanation is that offered by a psychoanalyst, Dr. Philip Weissman, in his book *Creativity in the Theatre*: "Not only the actor but all creative artists have some need for as well as an ability to exhibit. These qualities are to be found in writers, composers, and painters who are certainly not considered to be performing artists . . . acting will attract those who have excessive inner needs for, and urgent insatiable gratification from, exhibiting themselves. Psychoanalytic investigation reveals that these are individuals who have failed to develop a normal sense of identity and body image during the early maturational phases of infancy."

In any case, George enormously enjoyed being a television star. When waiters or patrons of restaurants would recognize him or call him by name, he would turn to his companions, shrug slightly, and say, "That's television."

It wasn't always just a smile of recognition and a nod of the head. Listen to his production assistant, Annie Noyes:

You never were inclined to put your hands on George. He very much disliked any kind of personal contact.

George and Leueen and I were in Philadelphia with the tryout of a play. At that time George had been on a television series for some time and as a result, did not have the anonymity that he'd had before. And George—I quite agree with him—did not feel that people had the right to come up and speak to him simply because he happened to have been on television.

We were sitting in a booth at Lou Tendler's after the show, going over the notes of what was to be done the next day, when first we were horrified by a gentleman who came over to the table, grasped George's hand, and said, "Gee, George, I surely want to shake your hand!"

George's expression was, shall I say, only slightly more astonished than ours.

"I sure do like that program of yours. The only trouble is that it's at the wrong hour for us hick folks because we like to go to bed!"

George fixed a rather long look at him and declared, "I feel that is your problem and not mine."

At which the man left. Leueen and I took a deep breath and everything settled down for one moment, when a woman appeared at George's elbow. George had this sort of marvelous hair arrangement that one has to know about; I won't describe it. But she said, "Mr. Kaufman, I think you're the cutest man I ever saw and all my life I've been wanting to do this." And with that she ran her hands through his hair.

Leueen and I screamed simultaneously, and George—a

stunt I would love to master—literally levitated four feet into the air, with no knee action as far as I could make out.

He simply rose into the air and said, "Madam, kindly take your hands off me."

And she giggled and left.

Backstage at "This Is Show Business" Kaufman remained in character. He would allow himself to be made up, then would lie on a divan with a Kleenex tissue around his collar, observe everything, and say very little.

Jackie Susann became a frequent guest on the show. While they were waiting to go on stage one evening, Miss Susann, who by dint of constant reading had made herself something of a science fiction authority, was discussing the sun and the stars and the new literary form with erudite Clifton Fadiman, another science fiction buff.

As they spoke Kaufman stared into space. From time to time, he would change his stare from space to Miss Susann to Fadiman and then back to Miss Susann.

"He looked at me with a strange look all the time I was talking," Miss Susann admitted, "which, I have to say to my credit, did not throw me. I went on discussing my facts and figures as if he weren't Einstein lying there listening. When he got up finally, and stretched, and again looked at me as if I were from outer space, I said, 'George, I don't seem to have convinced you. Everything I'm saying is absolutely true, but you don't look as if you believe me.'"

"Oh, Jacqueline, I believe you," Kaufman said. "There's no reason why I shouldn't. After all, in 1929 I took advice about the stock market from the Marx Brothers so I see no reason why I shouldn't learn about science fiction from you."

Joey Adams, the comedian and author, was on "This Is Show Business" one week to plug a new book he had written. Ostensibly his question was, should he continue as a performer or, since his books were successful, should he turn to writing. Always a quick man with an ad lib, Mr. Adams departed from the arranged script.

"Maybe I *could* become a writer. As a matter of fact, George," Mr. Adams needled, turning away from Fadiman and fixing on Kaufman, "maybe we could start a team, Kaufman and Adams. No, make that Adams and Kaufman."

Kaufman not only feigned anger. He *was* angry.

But by then Mr. Adams was into five minutes of his own comedy act. When he concluded, there was applause. Fadiman started the conversation. Burrows was next. Then the woman who was that week's guest. At last, Mr. Adams got to Kaufman.

"Well, now, as to your question, Mr. Adams," Kaufman began, "whether or not you should be a writer. I read as much of your book as was possible for me to read, and I suggest that you don't have very much of a choice. I also suggest, after having seen your act, that I don't know but what you should open a candy store."

"Oh?" the injured performer asked. "You read my book, Mr. Kaufman? Who read it for you?"

Without a flicker, Kaufman shot back, "The same person who wrote it for you!"

"George wouldn't argue. He would scorn," Clifton Fadiman observed. "He denied the values in himself. It's as if he couldn't live with an ideal of himself in front of him, he had to tear down the ideal all the time. He was self-denigratory to an extraordinary degree. That was a very deep area of his character." Finally, "George kidded platitudes and hated cliches."

"George was inarticulate except when it came to wry or ironical comment," Fadiman's wife Annalee said. "With one exception, his ad libs were always on the spur of the moment. The exception was that George knew what the questions on the television programs were going to be, and he usually had some beginning reply that fitted this pose of mock indignation which he assumed."

Always worried that he would "dry up" on television, Kaufman would prepare two or three choice lines before each week's program. Even though he was the most brilliant ad lib artist on the networks, he still felt it necessary to write a quip or two on the cuff of his shirtsleeve before air time.

Unfortunately Kaufman had his off nights and his less-than-laughed-at lines, the worst of which was delivered the week before Christmas 1952.

The question put to the panel was, "What would you most like to get for Christmas?"

Kaufman said, "Let's make this one program on which no one sings 'Silent Night.'"

Before the program was off the air for the evening, the CBS switchboard was overtaxed with incoming calls of protest and indignation. Viewers bordered on the hysterical. That this long-nosed, evil-intentioned sourface should slander Christmas was too much.

Following the flood of telephone calls came the letters to the network and the sponsor.

Kaufman left the studio unaware that he had said anything controversial. His chief concern that night was his wife. Leueen was opening in a play with Rex Harrison and Lilli Palmer. *The Love of Four Colonels*, written by Peter Ustinov, was in Boston prior to its Broadway opening. So up to Boston went George.

Everything was all right with the play. It was Kaufman who was in trouble. This he learned at his suite at the Ritz. The newspapers were filled with his anti-Christmas line. Radio and television carried stories on it. When the press found out that Kaufman was in Boston, the phones began to ring at the Ritz.

Meanwhile back in New York, specifically at that rhythmically named Madison Avenue advertising agency, Batten, Barton, Durstine and Osborn, they were having a meeting. Ben Duffey, president of B.B.D.&O. Thayer "Tax" Cummings, vice president and account executive at B.B.D.&O. for Lucky Strike Tobacco. Hubbell Robinson, vice president in charge of programming for CBS. Irving Mansfield, producer of "This Is Show Business." Mahogany furniture. Hard eyes. Squared jaws. And lawyers. Lots of lawyers. And the word most in use was not "Kaufman" but "Cancellation."

It remained for Irving Mansfield to call Boston.

"Are you telling me I'm being fired?" Kaufman asked him.

Mansfield told him he was not fired but that B.B.D.&O. had every intention of dropping out as a sponsor of "This Is Show Business."

"Are you telling me I shouldn't have said what I said?" Kaufman persisted.

"I can't answer that, George," Mansfield replied. "The agency apparently sells a lot of cigarettes. They don't want you on the program." Mansfield also suggested that as Kaufman had originally asked for a two-week vacation from the program in order to be with his wife and her play, that he take the two weeks and stay in Boston.

Kaufman reacted as expected.

"I would like you to know that I want the real truth to be told to the newspapers of why I am no longer part of this program," he told his producer. "I won't have it any other way. A lie is a lie. The truth is always there. I don't want anything magnified. I want the truth. And rather than have you make a statement, I think I'll make it myself."

To face the press was another matter. Memories of the Hollywood diary popped up at once. The ringing telephones continued to go unanswered until Leueen picked one up. "What Mr. Kaufman really meant was that there be more of a true celebration of Christmas rather than the commercialization of it," she began telling reporters.

From Boston, the wire services' teletype machines began tapping in every city room in the country. Kaufman had been fired and for the wrong reasons. The New York switchboard of CBS lit up again. Telegrams and letters poured into the network. Editorials appeared in newspapers supporting Kaufman's sentiments. Four bishops came out in favor of him.

When George returned to New York on Monday, Jean the butler was waiting for him.

"Mr. Kaufman," Jean announced in his thick French accent, "Mr. Humble Robinson is on the telephone."

Kaufman smiled a little to himself and answered the phone.

"Hello, George?" the warm, syrupy voice of Hubbell Robinson asked.

This time Kaufman burst into a broad smile. He knew from the first two words he was back on the air.

Abe Burrows was eventually replaced by Sam Levinson, but Clifton Fadiman and the old curmudgeon remained firm.

Each summer when the program went off the air, Kaufman would tell Mansfield, "Well, it's time for me to say good-by to you because I've said everything that can be said on this program. You'll have to get somebody else."

But the next fall when they were ready to start up again, all Mansfield had to do was telephone Kaufman and he came back quickly enough. Mansfield's idea was solid programming, his casting was brilliant, the ratings were high. But television series have built-in expiration dates of their own, and the time came when "This Is Show Business" went off the air and stayed off.

Kaufman continued to wear the blue shirts, the bow ties, and the hair on end. Jack Paar, predecessor to Johnny Carson as host of NBC's "Tonight" show was the last to make use of Kaufman on television. In his book *My Saber Is Bent,* Paar entitles one chapter "Some Great Wits." His first choice is George S. Kaufman.

Paar writes graciously, "He was famous for his acid tongue, but his heart was gentle. And his mockery of the ridiculous was all-embracing enough to include a few jibes at himself. . . . When I first met him he passed along to me the advice his father gave him as a young man, 'Son, try everything in life but incest and folk-dancing.' "

His first appearances on the Paar show were pure Kaufman. He railed about a favorite subject, his lawyers.

"It sounds a little grand, I know, to say my lawyers in the plural," he began, "but I didn't start out that way. I started with one lawyer, but you know what happens. One moves in and pretty soon there are seven, all in the same office. They get together all day long and say to each other, 'What can we postpone next?' The only thing they don't postpone, of course, is their bill, which arrives regularly. You've heard about the man who got the bill from his lawyer which said, 'For crossing the street to speak to you and discovering it was not you . . . twelve dollars.' "

Paar was pleased with the performances and so was Kaufman. But Kaufman was not a well man. Once when Paar invited him to be on the show, George invited a lady friend to accompany him to the program and to dinner afterward. On the day scheduled he felt so ill that he cancelled out. To Paar, he made a phone call. To the lady friend, he sent the following telegram breaking their date: SORRY CANNOT MAKE IT TONIGHT. NOT UP TO PAAR.

The next time he was invited to appear on the Paar show, his physician advised against it. So did many of his friends. Kaufman listened to no one and showed up at NBC.

"He was so ill he could barely get up," Alexander King said.

King was on the Paar show that night and beseeched Kaufman to go home.

"No," Kaufman insisted. "First of all, they've announced my name."

"Don't be silly," King countered. "They've got six other people to go on."

"No, I'll make it."

When he got out on the stage he was carrying his cane, but even at that he could hardly walk. His timing, which to date had been faultless, wasn't off; it was gone. He was unable to remember what he wanted to say. When he recollected and started to say it, his speech was thick and slurred.

Alexander King watched. "Paar was deeply impressed with him and treated him with the greatest deference, because Paar is strictly a boy from the midwest who had heard about George Kaufman while he was still carrying a microphone in a canoe during the Mississippi flood. So now suddenly he had George Kaufman and Noel Coward and people like that, and he was enormously impressed. And he was very humble to these people. . . . Paar was in an absolute sweat that this man would die on the stage, which would be an important TV first, but one that he didn't necessarily want to be present at," King continued.

Referring to Kaufman, King said, "He got two real laughs. And when that first laugh came, he was like a new man. We tried to help him down the steps and he said, 'No, no, I'll make it fine.'

"And he did. Because he wanted the applause. You know, I once owned a Newfoundland dog, a retriever, and he was very old and had arthritis. But toward sunset, he'd walk into the water up to his rump and with his tongue hanging out would look into the horizon. He had once disported himself like a dolphin in these waters; now he was too sick, but still he liked to have his belly wet. Only the scum and the dead seaweed that washed up would touch him, and he could no longer retrieve anything; he could barely retrieve his breath. But that was Kaufman on the stage there with this mob of people out front. Tragic."

The old curmudgeon has grown very old indeed. He is bed-ridden. Tucked in for the night. His medicines are on the table beside him. So is his telephone. Everything is within his reach except his radio, which the nurse has turned on to a station playing some semiclassical music.

The nurse goes in to have a leisurely dinner and the radio goes on to Request Time. "It is Mr. So-and-So's birthday and Mrs. So-and-So has requested that we play 'Auf Wiedersehen.' Thank you, Mrs. So-and-So, happy birthday to you, Mr. So-and-So, and here is 'Auf Wiedersehen.'"

This goes on for an hour and George can't stand it any longer. And he can't reach the radio to turn it off. And the voice keeps saying, "If you have any requests, just call Murray Hill 6-6000 and we'll honor those requests."

So George picks up the telephone and dials MU 6-6000.

"George S. Kaufman?" the radio announcer asks incredulously.

"Yes, George S. Kaufman," he says.

"The famous playwright?" asks the announcer.

"Yes, the famous playwright."

"Do *you* have a request?" asks the announcer.

"Yes. I'd like five minutes of silence!"

And that, ladies and gentlemen, is the farewell performance of the old curmudgeon.

16   *I Knew a Boy Who . . .*

IMMEDIATELY AFTER THE DEATH OF GEORGE GERSHWIN, George Kaufman experienced a series of intense headaches.

Although she sympathized with his pain, his wife Beatrice said, "George, it is remarkable that you should have the same ailments as our friends, but what is even *more* remarkable is that you should have them in just the same order."

Of all of Kaufman's preoccupations—writing, card playing, philandering—his oldest and most persistent was hypochondria. Of all of Kaufman's fears—physical cowardice, financial ruin, failure as a writer, editor, director, or producer—the deepest and most recurrent was death.

The addiction to hypochondria and the fear of dying went well together from his earliest days to his last. The first seedlings were planted by his mother, who, from his childhood on had cautioned, "I know a boy who climbed a tree and he fell; his arm was in a cast for five months." "My cousin was in the buggy when the horse ran away." "I knew a boy who went swimming once, and he drowned . . ." But she cannot be held entirely re-

sponsible for the ultimate product. Other little boys have had
overprotective parents and have emerged less frightened than
George. In his case, he not only accepted the habit and its
final terror but as he matured he learned to enlarge it.

"He didn't get just a cough," Moss Hart's brother Bernie said,
"he was going to have TB."

His teeth, his eyes, his hair, especially his hair, were worried
over and looked after constantly. The fact that he was a healthy
young man had absolutely nothing to do with his concern that
he might *not* be a healthy young man.

His teeth began to go relatively early. No less than twice a
year he went to his dentist, plus a minimum of four annual
visits to his periodontist.

His eyes, which required glasses from boyhood, received constant care. As the glasses grew thicker with the years, he learned
to employ them as a weapon of offense or a means of defense.
Rather than smile or frown or snap out an answer, he would
peer over the rims of his spectacles. If challenged, he learned to
take off one set of glasses and put on another. This he would do
slowly and deliberately, utilizing enough time to get the right
words ready for the proper retort.

It was his hair, however, that absorbed his vanity most. Early
in their association Kaufman inquired of Jed Harris if he knew
of "a hair saver man."

Evidently, Harris did not, but Kaufman found what he was
looking for without Harris' help. And it wasn't a man hair saver,
either. Frances Fox was a woman who had introduced a
method of retaining hair for females. Among the first men to
seek her out was George S. Kaufman. From his early thirties
right through the long remainder of his life, he would show up
once a week for a shampoo and a treatment.

Frances Fox must have done something right, for although
age thinned his hair and turned it from jet black to gray to

white, Kaufman continued to retain a goodly amount of it, combing it, when no one was looking, in an upward direction from back to front, and living, it must be added, in sheer fear that his hair would go before he did. It did not.

In the *New Yorker* magazine profile, his colleague and friend Alexander Woollcott wrote of Kaufman, "he is frail and disposed to phthisis and has been known to swoon at the sight of a stethoscope. His notion of combatting this malady is to spend all of his time indoors, stoutly opposing any newfangled notions of opening the windows."

Woollcott both exaggerated and minimized. Kaufman liked to walk in the open air on Madison and Fifth Avenues. From time to time he also liked to talk aloud to himself as he walked. He was not only afraid of phthisis (a lung disease) but of every other illness be it physical or mental: heart trouble, cancer, tuberculosis, neuroses, psychoses, surgery of all sorts, fear of dust, of unclean silverware in restaurants and at home, of foreign places. (He once said, "I never want to go any place where I can't get back to Broadway and 44th Street by midnight.")

As with so many aspects of his life, he coated this one too with laughter, but the truth is he was always seeking out new methods and means of dealing with the anxiety over his wellbeing. His fear of germs on door knobs, he alleged, was allayed when he was in his late twenties through knowledge imparted to him by Howard Lindsay. It was Lindsay who taught him to insulate his hand by putting it in the pocket of his jacket before grasping the possible disease-ridden knob. Both men made light of it, but Kaufman followed that spurious medical advice throughout his life.

Lindsay was one year older than Kaufman. "I watch him very carefully," Kaufman said, "to see what I'm going to catch next year."

The wonder drugs that were introduced after World War II

seemed to have been developed particularly for Kaufman. How he had existed without them baffled him.

The words "virus," "ulcer," "pneumonia," "lesion," were not ones about which he made jokes. Such words caused illness, and illness caused death, and that was a word he never wanted to hear. If it *was* mentioned in his presence, he would change the subject, look anguished, or leave the room immediately.

His hypochondria was painful beyond anyone's knowledge. Afraid to shake hands, afraid to open doors, afraid of blindness, afraid of strokes, afraid of every known illness, Kaufman suffered continually and secretly. No amount of medical opinion could reassure him. It was only when *he* chose to overcome the hypochondria that it subsided temporarily.

The first time he and Natalie Schafer went out together was after a rehearsal in Washington, D.C. They picked a quiet, out-of-the-way restaurant. As the actress was dieting, she chose to skip the first course. Kaufman selected cream of tomato. "I have this terrible habit," Miss Schafer confessed. "I like to taste other people's food." When the cream of tomato soup arrived, it looked very good. "So I took my spoon, leaned over, and asked, 'Do you mind?' And I took a spoonful of George's tomato soup."

"Captain!" George called out. "Would you bring another tomato soup?"

"No, no, I don't want a tomato soup, really. I just wanted to taste it," Miss Schafer protested.

"Bring another tomato soup," Kaufman insisted.

"Now this was my first dinner with him," Miss Schafer recalled, "and I thought he'd gone mad. Anyway, when the second order arrived, he handed his bowl to the waiter and took the fresh one."

"I'm terribly sorry," he told her. "I'm rather peculiar about these things. We won't talk about it."

"Later," she said, "when we left the restaurant and went

for a drive, he kissed me. It was very much of a kiss, too. And I said, 'I can't understand your kissing me that way when you won't let me taste your soup.'"

"Well, Miss S.," he said, "your tasting my soup was one kind of risk. My kissing you was another. Let's concentrate on the second."

The risk, to Kaufman, was undeniably real. He lived with his fear of death day and night. Awake and asleep. All of his life, from earliest childhood, he had a recurring dream, a nightmare in which he was being strangled. His only escape was to awaken himself by shrieking. He would scream so loudly that people in the next room could hear him.

Kaufman clung in quiet panic to alarms and misgivings immeasurable to himself or the men and women he paid to rid him of them. And their number at no time was small. He was always under the care of oculists, optometrists, dentists, physicians, specialists of every kind, osteopaths, chiropractors, chiropodists; for no less than three years he employed the services of a man whom he actually introduced as "my nerve pointer."

And how he loathed them! He openly accused his physician of many years, Dr. Edward Greenspan, of being a tennis bum. No amount of argument could convince him that the doctor was one of the best internists in New York. Kaufman would simply recall that he had telephoned Dr. Greenspan at eleven o'clock one Sunday morning and had reported to the doctor's answering service that he, George S. Kaufman, was stricken with a most serious illness. A continuing series of calls to the answering service was made until, late that afternoon, sometime after 5 P.M., a sun-tanned and healthy Dr. Greenspan bounced into Kaufman's bedroom wearing a white cable-stitch tennis sweater.

Kaufman roared.

Greenspan explained that he had been playing a little tennis to keep himself in shape, the better to serve Kaufman.

330

"I pay my doctor to look after *my* health, not his," Kaufman said, ending the visit.

After that, the long relationship between doctor and patient went downhill.

The nursing profession didn't escape Kaufman's derision. He disliked nurses enough to make an archetype of Miss Bedpan in *The Man Who Came to Dinner*. And it didn't end there. In the May 1, 1954, issue of the *New Yorker* is a bit of light verse by George S. Kaufman.

LINES WRITTEN AFTER FOUR WEEKS IN A HOSPITAL
Nurses all—and I mean the breed—
Share one clamorous, blundering need:
Not to assist you in getting well,
Or hurry in when you ring the bell;
Not to banish the sense of gloom
That somehow penetrates your room;
Not, as a fellow might believe,
To soothe your brow or cool your feve;
Not to lessen with gentle hand,
The tightening pull of a stomach band;
Not to carry you in, complete
A single meal that is fit to eat;
Not to silence the bloody bore
Who's talking out in the corridor;
Not to massage the aching bone,
Or even to leave you just alone.
Their one ambition is quickly fed:
All they want is to make your bed.

Wriggle your toes or shake your head,
What do they do? They make your bed.
Requested orange juice instead,
First they want to make your bed.

331

Ask for a needle, a bit of thread,
Still they have to make your bed.
Tell 'em you'd like some whole-wheat bread,
What'll they do? They'll make your bed.
Years ago you were leeched and bled;
Nowadays they make your bed—
Fold the sheets and adjust the spread—
Make and make and make your bed.

Now all this trumpeting about illness was *before* he actually took sick. Yes, he'd *had* those colds and a few extracted teeth and his hairline *was* receding slightly, but from childhood until his late fifties, Kaufman was a remarkably healthy man in terms of physical fitness.

Fourteen months after his marriage to Leueen, hypochondria turned into reality when the first of many paralytic strokes occurred. Dr. Greenspan hospitalized him in New York City's Mount Sinai and after several anxious weeks Kaufman was discharged.

The Kaufman who emerged was similar to what the earlier Kaufman had been fearing for the better part of his life. Although he could distinguish light from dark, for all other purposes his left eye was blind. His left leg, somewhat less afflicted, was partially paralyzed. He, who had been so nimble on his feet, who had jumped so often from the darkened theatre onto a rehearsal stage, who had enjoyed long strolls up Madison or down Fifth, now walked slowly, inexpertly. Paralysis also affected his arm, the left, not the one with which he wrote. His typing, henceforth would be slower—only his right index finger would flash out to strike the keys of the typewriter.

He would accept sympathy from no one. Not his wife. Not his daughter. Nobody was allowed to mention his disabilities in his presence. As for himself, Kaufman once more resumed the art of writing plays and the profession of directing them as soon as he left the hospital.

If his physical appearance was somewhat altered, his psychological attitudes changed in more subtle ways. Prior to his stroke, he would tolerate no talk of death. Now, obliquely, he began to inquire about it.

The mystery story writer Dashiell Hammett was ill, extremely so. As he was unable to care for himself, his good friend Lillian Hellman had him moved into her town house in the East Eighties. There, she looked after him until his death. On hearing this, Kaufman took to telephoning Miss Hellman regularly. How did Dash feel? What was his attitude toward sickness? Toward the possibility of the end? Mildly surprised that Kaufman of all people should make such inquiries, Miss Hellman patiently answered each question each time it was asked. He was in his own way auditioning Dash Hammett's oncoming death with his own in five, ten, fifteen years.

This did not lessen his fear and complete resentment of death. He merely had reached a position from which he felt, despite his revulsion and terror, that he had to learn about the business of dying, and he attacked it in the same manner as he would direct or write a play. And research, no matter how objectionable, was necessary.

Toward the end of his days, the pattern of his life shifted to a lower gear. Kaufman traded his street shoes for needle-point slippers made for him exclusively by Mary Roberts Rinehart's granddaughter, Patricia Rinehart Breit Lassalle. His basic drive, however, did not change. Confined for the most part to his living quarters, he still made attempts to write. He invited old friends over—Marc Connelly, Ruth Goetz, S. N. Behrman—and many projects were started and rejected. As George himself said, "Not good enough."

With his wife Leueen MacGrath, he did succeed in finishing a full-length play. It was called *I Give It Six Months,* and George asked me to direct it. But it contained too many scenes and too many characters, and George lacked the energy to rewrite it. As a result, Miss MacGrath and I allowed it to slip into limbo.

Since he didn't have the attention span to devote to a full-length play reverted to some degree in his own writing. To the *New Yorker,* to the *Saturday Review,* to Sunday supplements of metropolitan newspapers, he sent short, entertaining pieces all showing how constrained his life had become. Memories of trips to Bucks County, chastising letters to ruthless drama critics, these and many more he sent out, and with them went the stamped, self-addressed envelope. Fifty years of writing, and he still lacked confidence. Once again he was waiting for the rejection slips.

In order to alleviate some of his pain, Kaufman turned to psychiatry for a third time. The first two attempts, urged on him by Beatrice and Moss Hart, had failed. The third try was after Beatrice's death. His desperation led him to Dr. Ruth C. Conkey. He remained a patient of hers for many years, albeit irregular and sometimes infrequent. The regularity and frequency would depend on the intensity of his anxieties. When they became great, he turned up daily; when they lessened, he disappeared from her office.

One afternoon, he turned to me and announced that he was not going back to his doctor because, "She's asking too damn many personal questions."

I was about to smile when I saw that Kaufman's face was stern and that there was no twinkle in his good right eye. So I let it pass, and George did not return to the couch again.

From then on, he faced his lifelong fears alone. Not having believed in God from the time he was able to make that decision in his own mind, Kaufman was much too honest and much too courageous to go scurrying back to an Infinite Being he knew did not exist, solely for the purpose of making an easy exit.

In his mid-sixties, Kaufman took on three prostate operations with excellent results. Within two years, however, his general condition began to deteriorate. In 1958, during the opening night performance of John Osborne's *The Entertainer*, Kaufman arose from his seat, started for the aisle, and then fainted across the lap of Mrs. Seymour Peck, wife of the editor of the arts section of the New York *Times*. Whispered rumors raced through the Royale Theatre to the effect that he was dead. Seymour Peck, Herman Shumlin, and Sam Zolotow carried him up the aisle and placed him on the floor at the rear of the theatre, where he lay until Ruth Goetz revived him with her smelling salts. She and Sam rode home with him in the taxi Herman Shumlin hailed. Once there, Kaufman recovered quickly and held court in his bedroom while a large portion of the opening night audience streaked up to 86th Street to learn how he was. By one o'clock in the morning, with all his friends relieved, with sandwiches and coffee served, he was well enough to telephone and regale listeners with stories of how he had broken up David Merrick's opening night.

A few months later, following another opening night, he became dizzy in the Oak Room of the Plaza Hotel. He spent the night in one of the rooms upstairs, and this time those close to him began to take matters more seriously. A council was held: his wife, his daughter, Moss and Kitty Hart, Max Gordon, and me.

Although Dr. Greenspan was a splendid physician, George's antagonism toward him had reached such proportions that a new man seemed necessary. Max Gordon agreed to ask Dr. Howard Rusk, who recommended his first associate, Dr. Menard Gertler, a specialist in cardiology and geriatrics.

A Canadian by birth, Gertler had quarterbacked the McGill

University football team. Although personally charming, as a physician he was a stern disciplinarian. George was delighted with him.

On August 13, 1959, Kaufman appeared at Gertler's office for his initial examination.

"Why the hell don't you get a more comfortable chair for me to sit on?" Kaufman demanded.

"Well, Mr. Kaufman," Gertler answered, "this is your first visit here. When you become a regular customer, I'll buy you your own chair."

Kaufman liked that. He also liked the firmness with which Gertler took him in hand.

"No smoking," Gertler ordered.

"Why not?" Kaufman asked.

He was given an immediate answer.

"Well, what about two or three cigarettes a day?"

The answer was a flat, unequivocal no, which did not bother Kaufman as Kaufman did not smoke anyway. But he had to find out what his adversary was like.

For his part, Gertler had no difficulty in learning what was wrong with his patient. What he couldn't see for himself, tests showed. What they didn't show, Kaufman told him.

"You know, Doctor," he said to Gertler early in his first visit, "I'm not a very brave man."

Gertler's evaluation of his new patient was that while he was rather weak and pathetic, both emotionally and physically, Kaufman was not nearly as sick a man as Kaufman thought he was. Lifetime habits are not easy to break and Kaufman's hypochondria was not ready to desert him yet.

Enough medication was prescribed, and that pleased George enormously, especially if some of it were administered by hypodermic needle. "If he had an injection," Gertler said, "he really thought he was getting something."

In addition to medication, indoor exercises were prescribed. A bicycle with an odometer was brought in and Kaufman was ordered to start doing two hundred revolutions three times a day. Eventually Gertler worked Kaufman up to fifteen hundred revolutions or three miles a day—or so he thought.

"I used to come to see him around five o'clock in the afternoon," Gertler said. "One day I sneaked in around four, and there was Howard Teichmann sitting on the bicycle, pumping away the three miles I thought George was doing!"

He played other games, too. One Sunday evening Gertler received a call.

"I need you immediately," Kaufman said into the telephone, and then hung up.

Gertler lived diagonally across and slightly down the street from Kaufman. Without putting on a necktie, he grabbed his medical bag, ran across Park Avenue, and told the elevator man to take him up to Kaufman's penthouse; it was an emergency.

The elevator man did as ordered. When he opened the door to Kaufman's apartment, Gertler saw Kaufman standing in the foyer with a stopwatch in his hand.

"Mr. Kaufman, I thought you were ill," Gertler said.

"I am, but I wanted to see how long it would take you to get here if I were *really* ill."

After that, the incidents grew far less amusing. The doorman of the Kaufman apartment building telephoned to say that Mr. Kaufman had summoned the elevator, ridden downstairs, and was sitting in the lobby observing the tenants and their guests enter and leave. What was particularly unusual was that Mr. Kaufman was wearing his pajamas and robe. Another time, he left the apartment building and walked south on Park Avenue wearing only his loosely tied dressing gown.

Edna Ferber came to visit him one afternoon. He received her in his bedroom and dozed most of the time. After trying her best to keep up a one-way conversation, Miss Ferber finally got up and started out of the apartment. As she reached the elevator, the voice of a strong, young George Kaufman boomed out.

"Edna!" he called. "Edna, come back here."

She hurried to the bedroom. Kaufman was sitting straight up in bed. He sounded wonderfully alert.

"Edna," he asked, "are you going to the funeral?"

"What funeral?" she replied.

"Yours. You're dead, Edna, dead!" And he threw himself back onto his pillows.

Horrified, Miss Ferber fled. She never saw him again.

The last play George Kaufman worked on was a comedy that he and I had done a first draft of in 1954. *In the Money* had been announced for production but postponed because Kaufman suddenly thought of a wonderful melodrama that he wanted the two of us to write for his wife. The melodrama turned out to be something a long way from wonderful, but *In the Money* was a comedy in the classic Kaufman style.

To give him something to satiate his appetite for work, I brought *In the Money* out of a file in 1960, and together we began polishing it. It was the story of a highly unsuccessful insurance salesman who has a loving wife and two spiteful sisters. One is married to a very rich doctor on Park Avenue, the other is married to an immensely wealthy lawyer on Fifth Avenue. Both treat their brother worse than the garbage collector until he comes into a fortune. Then they fawn upon his every word. When poor investments reduce him to poverty, they refuse to speak to him. At the end, the unsuccessful insurance salesman finds himself "in the money" again.

This plot was a recurring fantasy of Kaufman's. The noted psychoanalyst Dr. Henry Lowenfeld, who specialized in treating writers, said that "early traumatic experiences are preconditions to artistic creativity."

We were well on the way to finishing our work when I arrived at Kaufman's bedroom early one afternoon. He told me that he had been unable to sleep the night before and that he had gotten up and rewritten two of the scenes. There on his desk, he pointed, were the rewrites. What did I think of them? I sat down and looked at a thick stack of lined yellow foolscap. Each line was covered not with words but with a completely illegible scrawl, not a single word, not a letter, just page after page of scrawling. I folded them carefully and asked if I could read them again at home.

What was occurring in the Kaufman case was medically predictable. The arteriosclerosis from which he was suffering was beginning to allow smaller and smaller quantities of blood to reach his brain. He would, as a result, hallucinate from time to time. Occasionally, small vessels in the brain itself would break, causing a series of tiny strokes.

By late winter of 1961, his condition had deteriorated to the point where a male nurse was assigned to the case twenty-four hours a day. One night, early in the spring, George arose from his bed while the male nurse was watching television in the living room. In the bathroom, he fainted and fell against a hot radiator. When he returned to consciousness, one arm was firmly wedged between the radiator and the wall. No amount of calling could override the sound made by the television set. Two hours later, the male nurse returned to find Kaufman with his arm still wedged between the wall and the radiator. The patient was deep in shock and suffered first- and second-degree burns. Although the burns were not as severe as they appeared initially, the emotional trauma was so great that he became permanently bedridden.

"Isn't this what people in mental hospitals do, soil themselves?" Kaufman would ask his doctor. "Isn't this the stage that's a pre-death stage? Tell me!"

When he wasn't rambling or asleep he spoke admiringly of an actress who kept a bottle of sleeping pills on a table beside her

bed; of how she had promised herself that if she became ultimately ill, she would not allow the indignity of suffering to persist. He said he envied the kind of courage that would allow one
to gulp a handful of pills and end it. He knew he did not have it.

How penetrating the fear of death must have been during
those weeks is wide open to speculation. But then, late one afternoon, with Leueen holding his hand in hers and stroking it
slowly and gently, he opened his eyes and looked at his daughter
Anne.

"I'm not afraid anymore," he said in a clear, quiet voice. "I
love Leueen so much that I'm not afraid anymore."

Tears were running down Leueen's face, and tears were running down Anne's face, too, and according to the diary I kept, I
raced from the room. After a while I fixed Leueen a glass, half
milk, half brandy—the very least she deserved for having dis-
pelled that greatest of all fears from his last few weeks.

On a sunny Friday morning, June 2, 1961, after he had eaten
breakfast, always his favorite meal, George S. Kaufman sighed
two deep sighs, and he was gone.

It was easier than he had always thought.

S.R.O.

THE DAY AFTER THE CATASTROPHIC OPENING OF *The Solid Gold Cadillac* in Washington, D.C., I met George S. Kaufman beside the Palm Court of the Plaza Hotel in New York. The time was early October 1953. He looked as though he didn't belong in the Plaza Hotel. His suit was rumpled, the wrinkles in his face seemed deeper, both his hair and his spirit were flat.

Since arriving in New York City, he had spoken with Max Gordon, our producer, who had told him that he, for one, was not ready to give up on the play. So Kaufman and I discussed the trouble we were in. But not for long. He had to go to Frances Fox's for a hair treatment; he was appearing that night on "This Is Show Business." He told me to go home and think about the play. He would, he promised, call me after the hair treatment.

He did. I told him my thoughts. He said, good, keep working, and be sure to catch him on television. I didn't bother with television that evening. I began cutting the script.

Apparently, what was wrong was Mrs. Hull's age versus the age of her leading man, Loring Smith. I had not worked with

Josephine Hull for ten years. Kaufman had not worked with her for fifteen years. She was now a dear but very old little lady. For those fascinated by numbers, Josephine Hull was graduated from Radcliffe College with the class of 1898.

Loring Smith played golf every day, dyed his hair blond, and looked and was in fact years younger. In our play, he was to propose marriage to her in one scene, and come out of a judge's chambers with her on his arm as his bride in the next scene.

Freud, who had done so much for boys going to bed with their mothers, did nothing to boost the relationships between boys and their grandmothers. Each time Loring Smith proposed marriage to Mrs. Hull, the audience gasped. Each time she accepted him, they were repelled.

What I cut out that afternoon and evening was what Kaufman had called "the author's love story." After his television show, we met at his apartment, and he looked over a script that was minus Loring Smith proposing to and marrying Mrs. Hull. Both of us believed the play could stand up without it.

It was after midnight, a late hour for Mr. Gordon, when an elated George Kaufman reached him on the telephone in Washington.

"Max," he said, "Sir Howard Teichmann, who will be Lord Howard Teichmann if these cuts hold up, has come up with an idea. We're working on it now. We'll leave for Washington tomorrow morning." A look of anticipation was on his face.

Not for long. In our judgment the President of the United States should have declared Washington a disaster area. There our actors' egos were damaged almost beyond repair. Josephine Hull wept. "She has the body of an old coal barge and the face of an ugly English pug," one of the Washington critics had written. Dirty pool! There was very little she could do about her body at this stage of her life, she sobbed, and the same went for her face. If he had criticized her acting, it would have been one thing, but to criticize an old lady's physical qualities was something else.

The other actors felt as badly. So did the treasurer, the house manager, and the producer. Nobody came to the theatre. We couldn't wait to get out of town.

It was all so depressing for Kaufman that he could not stand it alone any longer. His wife was in London; he called Leueen and asked her to join him when she could. She must have caught the next flight because there she was in Philadelphia.

The Quaker City promised no more than the Nation's Capital. During the technical run-through on the day of our opening there, the sound equipment went to pieces. Every time Fred Allen's voice was to come through on the loudspeakers from the tape recorder, we heard, "Dr. Brown, call your wife, please. Dr. Schwartz, call obstetrics. Dr. Brent, call surgery."

Whatever was wrong was easily fixed, the experts told us. It was simply a matter of being on the same wave length as a physician's answering service. By five-thirty in the afternoon, we were told we were lucky we were in Philadelphia. Philadelphia, it was explained, is just across the river from Camden, New Jersey, and Camden is the home of R.C.A. and R.C.A. manufactured our sound equipment and the experts there were really experts.

Kaufman's patience was being tried.

"Get the experts from Camden and postpone the opening till tomorrow night," he said, not very pleasantly either.

Assured by the Camden engineers that we could open as planned, we followed Kaufman's advice.

At eleven-thirty that night Kaufman left the theatre in what might politely be termed "a snit." The Camden engineers were still getting calls for the local doctors.

I left at two-thirty A.M.

The stage manager left at five.

343

We returned to the theatre at eleven the next morning, and the experts from Camden had sent to New York for the real experts.

The reviews were good in Philadelphia, but actors, being part-time philosophers, told each other that Philadelphia was not New York. Kaufman was silent. He rehearsed the actors, ate alone with his wife, and spoke to no one.

During the last performance in Philadelphia, we walked outside into the stage alley of the Chestnut Street Theatre. It was a warm evening and the stage door had been left open. As we stood there, an unusually loud sound floated out to us. Wave after wave of enthusiastic laughter seemed to be coming from our stage door. We listened. The audience was actually laughing in the right places.

Suddenly, George Kaufman, in a fit of high spirits such as I had never seen, held his cane steady, took his hand away, kicked his good right leg high over the cane, and caught it before it touched the ground.

"If you ever tell any son-of-a-bitch I did that, I'll never talk to you as long as I live!" he said.

About that cane.

In Times Square there is a statue of George M. Cohan. It faces south toward the Old Times Tower, now the Allied Chemical Tower. The likeness of George M. Cohan stands there covered with pigeon droppings. In his right hand is a cane.

Evidently, the most precious material gift Jerry Cohan could leave at his death to his son George was a cane with an ivory head and a gold band. Now, George M. Cohan and his partner Sam H. Harris were not only friends, they had married sisters. When Cohan died he left his father's cane to his brother-in-law. An extra gold band had been added. Engraved in the gold was the legend, "From George to Sam."

When Sam Harris died, he left the cane to George Kaufman. Engraved into a second band was, "From Sam to George."

And after all those years, there George Kaufman stood in the stage alley in Philadelphia kicking his leg over old Jerry Cohan's legacy to his son George M. Things couldn't be as bad as I thought they were.

We played three previews in New York. Monday night was only fair. Tuesday was a little worse. Wednesday calamity struck. Mrs. Hull walked on stage and spoke her first line.

"Oh! Well, I'm sorry—it's nothing really." She smiled. She was greeted with mild applause.

"Then you don't wish the chair to recognize you?" Geoffrey Lumb, a fine character actor, replied.

"Certainly." Mrs. Hull beamed. "Because whoever picked the time for this meeting . . . well, it wasn't a very good time for you, was it?"

Understand this. Between her first speech and her last speech there were supposed to be twenty-two minutes of characterization and plot. She had "gone up in her lines"; she had forgotten every single thing between the first line of her dialogue and the curtain to end the scene!

The stage manager had no alternative but to give the cue to close the curtains on Scene I and set up for Scene II. The audience got out of the Belasco Theatre that night well before ten-thirty. They were bewildered, dissatisfied, puzzled; *who* was that little woman? *How* did she get a job with that giant corporation? *Where* did she come from? *Why* had they all come to the Belasco Theatre that night?

Kaufman was backstage long before I was. He wouldn't talk to me. When I started to ask questions, he just shook his head and walked away.

Injured animals, hurt people, Leueen could sense pain at forty feet. Which was the exact distance I was standing from the stage door. Kaufman was framed in that stage door and Leueen

345

was talking urgently into his ear. He raised his cane and beckoned once. I went over to him.

"Get your wife," he said. "We may as well have a last supper."

George Kaufman stood in the empty darkness of the orchestra floor of the Belasco Theatre forty minutes before opening night. The house curtain was up, and Max Gordon was talking to him quietly. He was convincing him that this play could still be a success. What's more, he almost had him convinced, when out of the wings, stage right, hobbled Josephine Hull in her dressing gown. She was a pathetically frail figure. Without her makeup and without her hairpiece, which she'd forgotten to wear, she looked even smaller than she was in fact. (Standing up straight, Josephine Hull was a good four foot ten.) She stood there peering into the darkness from the empty stage. Then she turned and made her way slowly into the wings.

Words failed even the remarkable Max Gordon. The three of us walked slowly to the rear of the theatre. Mr. Gordon belched, Mr. Kaufman sniffed, and I felt as though I was going to be sick.

"You're all right," Mr. Kaufman told me. "You're young. Now, you start walking here," he indicated a spot at the back of the theatre, "and you walk to there. Then turn around and come back. I can't walk anymore but you can. From the minute the curtain goes up until it comes down, walk." With that he left the theatre.

The curtain went up. I started to pace the rear of the Belasco Theatre. It was Thursday, November 5, 1953. The voice of Fred Allen, recorded on tape, came over clearly and beautifully nasal. I kept walking.

The four ugly corporation directors, Geoffrey Lumb, Wendell K. Phillips, Reynolds Evans, and Henry Jones began the play. Josephine Hull made her entrance. The audience applauded her with what amounted to thoughtfulness. I stopped dead in my tracks. She spoke her first line. She spoke her second line. That blessed lady didn't forget a single word that night. She made that play go as it had never gone before. I was making one of my countless turns, walking in the rear of the house, when a hand caught hold of my arm. George Kaufman hadn't been able to stay away after all.

"How's it going?" he shouted.

I waited for a laugh to subside.

"It's never gone this well. Never."

Two more big laughs broke. His fingers tightened on my arm. Josephine Hull was delivering her last line.

"Oh, no! That's how I got *my* start! The meeting is adjourned! The meeting is adjourned!"

The curtain fell. It rose. I didn't see it come down again because George Kaufman was urging me out of the theatre, down the stage alley, and into the stage door. The audience was still cheering as the closing curtain came in.

Almost immediately the stage was filled by the actors' friends and relatives. I was no longer supporting George Kaufman. He was pulling me by the arm, working his way through the crowd toward Mr. Gordon.

"Max," he said, "this young man tells me it never went so well. Does he know what he's talking about?"

"Does he know what he's talking about," Mr. Gordon told him. I felt Kaufman's fingers let go of my arm, and he disappeared.

Four feet from the stage right wall of the Belasco Theatre were the company electric boards. Tied into them were dozens of thick black cables that sent current to the spot lights. There, seated on a low, three-legged stool between the wall and the cables, sat George Kaufman. My wife found him. He was crying.

347

"This is a hard business," he said through his tears. "It never gets easier. Never."

There was a party at Sardi's, but we went back to the Kaufmans'. Time seemed to be hanging like an old banjo in a pawnbroker's window. Kaufman sat in his armchair and looked into the fire. We were waiting for the critics' notices. An opening night audience can cheer itself hoarse, the cast can take curtain calls by the dozen, the ovations can shake the chandeliers. But let the critics say no, and everything turns into nothing.

The telephone rang. It was Nat Dorfman, the press agent.

Kaufman got up and with great dignity marched as well as he could manage into his bedroom. Leueen held out the living room telephone for me.

"Are you ready?" Dorfman asked.

Mr. Kaufman told him we were.

"Well," Dorfman announced, after what he considered to be a dramatic pause, "it's a hulluva hit."

The strained and now suddenly exhilarating evening was over. Kaufman stood at the front door with his arm around Leueen. He raised his right index finger in that familiar salute. Then he looked at me.

"Tomorrow," he said. "One o'clock. Sharp."

As we lived in the neighborhood, my wife and I walked home. It was a great night for walking even if the air did feel as if snow might be on the way.

Over Manhattan Island, the weather for November 6 came up raw and cold, with a generous helping of fog from the Hudson River. By ten o'clock in the morning, the fog was joined by a seemingly endless rain. By eleven, the rain was mixed with sleet.

From the brass grille of the box office of the Belasco right through the ornate rococo lobby, and spilling out onto the sidewalk was a thick line of persons wishing to buy tickets. Fortunately for those on the outside, the marquee stretched the length of the theatre, protecting them from the precipitation.

I couldn't believe it. I watched them for a while and then blissfully walked to Max Gordon's office. The afternoon papers gave us notices to equal the morning papers.

When Mr. Gordon and I went outside, it was snowing hard and turning cold. We walked past the Belasco. The Shuberts had put on two more treasurers. They had also hung a sign above the box office window. "S.R.O.," it read, "For Tonight's Performance—Standing Room Only." The line was now out from under the marquee and clear down to Sixth Avenue. Unprotected by any architectural cover, the line kept growing in size so that it turned northward on Sixth and approached 45th Street. They were people, standing patiently, some with umbrellas, some without them, and they were waiting in that snow to buy tickets to that play. Max Gordon laughed the jolliest laugh I have ever heard this side of Santa Claus. I got into a cab and went to Kaufman's.

The clock on the mantel chimed one. The butler nodded his head to the left. Mr. Kaufman was seated in the living room before the fire. I got onto the chocolate-colored sofa, but that day, for the first time in fourteen months, I leaned back on it.

"When they stand in a snowstorm in November to buy tickets for an evening in April, you know you've got a hit," he said. He seemed genuinely pleased. "Very gratifying—for both of us."

That was my cue.

"Mr. Kaufman," I began, "I know you don't like to be thanked, but . . ."

He got to his feet as quickly as he could. He grabbed his cane and he was pointing it at me across the coffee table.

"Mr. Kaufman," I said, trying again, but the tip of the cane came close to my nose.

349

"Do me a favor, will you?" he asked.

"Anything," I muttered.

And then, as if I hadn't had enough rewards in the last few hours, he peered over the rims of his glasses and said, "From now on, call me George."

Acknowledgments

All the published plays, anthologies, books, the magazine and newspaper articles couldn't really tell enough about George. There is
no substitute for direct conversation with the men and women who
shared his life. At the beginning of this book, I wrote that inter-
viewing one person about George S. Kaufman led me to seek out
five more. Scores of Kaufman's friends and intimates were kind
enough to allow me to bring my tape recorder into their homes,
offices, dressing rooms. Almost all of them spoke freely about George;
a few spoke with some hesitation, others with little reservation. A
handful insisted the tape recorder be turned off but allowed me to
make notes of what they had to say. Still others spoke on the
telephone or committed their thoughts to paper, which they were
kind enough to mail to me. The vast bulk of those interviewed
spoke directly onto magnetic tape.

In all, the material I've collected on Kaufman fills two four-
drawer steel files. The tapes themselves occupy a two-drawer file.
All of this, plus assorted Kaufmania will soon be deposited in the
Mass Communications Center of the State Historical Society at the
University of Wisconsin in Madison. I must confess that I will part
with it reluctantly. Most of it has been such a part of me for the
last ten years that it will be rather like saying a final farewell to

old and dear friends. Pulitzer Prize playwrights, Pulitzer Prize novelists, a Pulitzer Prize historian who happens to be Mrs. Pulitzer herself, drama critics, literary critics, publishers of great national newspapers, governors of states, actors, producers, directors, box office personnel, doctors, lawyers, and, it must be confessed, a rather large number of women who, for obvious reasons, did not wish their names to be used but who spoke with candor and frankness, comprise the primary source of information on George Kaufman. I saw some in elegant apartments on Fifth Avenue in New York, others in lavish estates in Beverly Hills. I met them in bars in Manhattan, Boston, Philadelphia, on the "strip" in Los Angeles and in the desert in Palm Springs. For their patience, their devotion, or even their antagonism toward George Kaufman, and their willingness to communicate it honestly to me, I am most grateful to:

Esther Adams
Larry Adler
Ruth Adler
Mary Astor
Brooks Atkinson
Lauren Bacall
Stephanie Bachelor
Leonard Bakrow
Jack Benny
Irving Berlin
Karl Bernstein
Charles Brackett
John Mason Brown
Abe Burrows
John Byram
Louis Calta
Kitty Carlisle
William Carson
Joan Castle
Bennett Cerf
Phyllis Cerf
Nola Chilton
Edward Chodorov
Jerome Chodorov

Dr. Ruth C. Conkey
Marc Connelly
Russel Crouse
Alfred de Liagre
Howard Dietz
Rebecca Drucker
Jean Dixon Ely
Morris Ernst
Annalee Fadiman
Clifton Fadiman
Abe Feder
Edna Ferber
Cy Feuer
Joseph Fields
Raoul Fleischmann
Lynn Fontanne
Gene Fowler, Jr.
Janet Fox
William Frank
Vinton Freedley
Dr. Allan Friedlich
Bruce Friedlich
Ruth Friedlich
Louis Funke

John Gassner
Ira Gershwin
Lee Gershwin
John Gerstad
Dr. Menard Gertler
Ben Gimbel
Ruth Goetz
Nathan Goldstein
Frances Goldwyn
Samuel Goldwyn
Max Gordon
Ruth Gordon
Charles Goren
Morton Gottlieb
Jane Grant
Abel Green
Nancy Green
Dr. Edward Greenspan
Dorothy Hammerstein
Jed Harris
Bernard Hart
Helen Hayes
Leland Hayward
Albert Hirschfeld
Dr. Leonard Hirschfeld
Joy Hodges
Lois Jacoby
George Jessel
Nunnally Johnson
Garson Kanin
Walter Kerr
Alexander King
Arthur Kober
Fred Kohlmar
Hon. Goodwin Knight
Arthur Krock
Irving Lazar
Charles Lederer
Carolyn Leigh

June Levant
Oscar Levant
Martin Levin
Selene Levin
Al Lewis
Helen Lieberman
William Liebling
Howard Lindsay
Lynn Loesser
Sue Davidson Lowe
Claire Luce
Alfred Lunt
Leonard Lyons
Sylvia Lyons
Leueen MacGrath
Irving Mansfield
Don Mankiewicz
Sarah Mankiewicz
Fredric March
Lester Markel
Ernest Martin
Groucho Marx
Harpo Marx
Carol Matthau
Walter Matthau
David Merrick
George Middleton
Jo Mielziner
Walter Monfried
Jack Morris
Hobe Morrison
Irving Morrison
Anne Noyes
Elliot Nugent
Donald Oenslager
Harold Ogust
Joseph Olney
George Oppenheimer
David Pardall

Acknowledgments

Seymour Peck
Susan Peck
Dorothy Pratt
Richard Pratt
Eleanor Prentiss
Margaret Pulitzer
Helen Reid
Howard Reinheimer
Hubbell Robinson
Dorothy Rodgers
Richard Rodgers
Harry Ruby
Morrie Ryskind
Adele Sardi
Vincent Sardi, Sr.
Natalie Schafer
Anne Schneider
Irving Schneider
Arthur Schwartz
Irene Selznick
Madeline Sherwood
Herman Shumlin

Marian Spitzer
John Steinbeck
Dorothy Stickney
Saint Subber
Jacqueline Susann
Gloria Swanson
Herbert Swope, Jr.
Margaret Hayes Swope
Margaret Powell Swope
Julius Tasca
Howard Taubman
Harlan Thompson
Richard Watts
Arnold Weissburger
Onna White
Thornton Wilder
Annie Laurie Williams
Earl Wilson
Walter Winchell
Kate Witkin
Audrey Wood
Sam Zolotow

To the three ladies who transcribed the aforementioned interviews, Claire Wallace Breitner, Valerie Neild Mitchell, and Lori Inman Sturm, I offer my thanks. My special thanks go to Mrs. Sturm who typed and retyped this manuscript.

Bibliography

When he was alive, the plays written by George S. Kaufman were all handsomely bound in light blue calfskin leather, the titles were stamped in gold, and they occupied an entire shelf of the long bookcase to the left of the fireplace in the Kaufman living room. Today, copies of those plays are on shelves of libraries all over the country, perhaps a large part of the world. The articles he wrote as well as the articles written about him are also in many of those libraries. Books and critical comment concerning Kaufman and germane to his work, personality, and times abound. A selected and well sifted list of those books used in the preparation of this biography follows.

Adams, Franklin P., *The Diary of Our Own Samuel Pepys*, 2 vols., Simon & Schuster, New York, 1935.
———, editor, *F.P.A. Book of Quotations*, Funk & Wagnalls, New York, 1952.
Adams, Samuel Hopkins, *A. Woollcott, His Life & His World*, Reynal & Hitchcock, New York, 1945.
———, *The American Heritage History of the 20's & 30's*, American Heritage Publishing Co., New York, 1970.
Astor, Mary, *My Story: An Autobiography*, Doubleday, Garden City, N.Y., 1959.

355

Bibliography

Atherton, Gertrude Franklin, *Black Oxen*, Boni & Liveright, New York, 1923.

Atkinson, Brooks, *Broadway Scrapbook*, Theatre Arts, New York, 1947.

Benet, William Rose, editor, *The Reader's Encyclopedia*, Crowell Co., New York, 1948.

Blum, Daniel, *A Pictorial History of the American Theatre, 1900–1950*, Greenberg, New York, 1950.

———, editor, *Theatre World: Season 1947–48*, Stuyvesant Press, New York, 1948.

———, editor, *Theatre World: 1949–1950*, Greenberg, New York, 1950.

Brown, John Mason, *Dramatis Personae*, Viking, New York, 1963.

———, *The Worlds of Robert E. Sherwood*, Harper & Row, New York, 1962.

Burnett, Whit, editor, *This Is My Best*, Dial Press, New York, 1942.

Carson, William G. B., *Dear Josephine*, University of Oklahoma Press, Norman, 1963.

Case, Frank, *Tales of a Wayward Inn*, Fredrick A. Stokes, New York, 1938.

Cerf, Bennett, *Try and Stop Me*, Simon & Schuster, New York, 1944.

Cerf, Bennett and Van H. Cartmell, editors, *Sixteen Famous American Plays*, Garden City Publishing Co., Garden City, N.Y., 1941.

———, editors, *Thirty Famous One-Act Plays*, "If Men Played Cards as Women Do" by George S. Kaufman, Modern Library, New York, 1949.

Chapman, John, "The Gloomy Dean of Broadway," *Saturday Evening Post*, January 1, 1938.

———, editor, *Theatre '54*, Random House, New York, 1954.

Chase, Ilka, *Past Imperfect*, Doubleday, Doran, Garden City, N.Y., 1942.

Churchill, Allen, *The Literary Decade*, Prentice-Hall, Englewood Cliffs, New Jersey, 1971.

Cole, Toby and Helen Krich Chinoy, editors, *Directing the Play*, Bobbs-Merrill, Indianapolis, 1953.

Connelly, Marc, *Voices Off Stage*, Holt, Rinehart & Winston, New York, 1968.

Cooper, Morton, "Kaufman Was Comedy," *Diners Club Magazine*, December, 1966.

Dayton, Katharine and George S. Kaufman, *First Lady*, Random House, New York, 1935.

Drennan, Robert E., editor, *The Algonquin Wits*, Citadel, New York, 1968.

Eisenstaedt, Alfred, *Witness to Our Time*, Viking, New York, 1966.

Fadiman, Clifton, *American Treasury*, Harper, New York, 1955.

Ferber, Edna, *A Kind of Magic*, Doubleday, Garden City, N.Y., 1963.

———, *A Peculiar Treasure*, Doubleday, Garden City, N.Y., 1960.

Foster, Lee, editor, *The New York Times Encyclopedic Almanac*, New York Times, New York, 1971.

Gassner, John, *Dramatic Soundings*, Crown, New York, 1968.

———, editor, *Best Plays of the Modern American Theatre*, Crown, New York, 1947.

———, *Producing the Play*, Dryden, New York, 1953.

———, *Twenty Best Plays of the Modern American Theatre*, Crown, New York, 1943.

———, *Twenty-five Best Plays of the Modern American Theatre*, "Beggar on Horseback," by George S. Kaufman and Marc Connelly, Crown, New York, 1949.

Geisinger, Marion, *Plays, Players & Playwrights*, Hart Publishing Company, New York, 1971.

Gershwin, Ira, *Lyrics on Several Occasions*, Alfred A. Knopf, New York, 1959.

Goldman, William, *The Season*, Harcourt, Brace & World, New York, 1969.

Gordon, Ruth, *Myself Among Others*, Atheneum, New York, 1971.

Gordon, Max, "My Most Unforgettable Character," *Reader's Digest*, March, 1967.

——— (with Lewis Funke), *Max Gordon Presents*, Bernard Geis, New York, 1963.

Goren, Charles H., *Better Bridge for Better Players*, Doubleday, Doran and Company, Garden City, N.Y., 1942.

Gottlieb, Polly Rose, *The Nine Lives of Billy Rose*, Crown, New York, 1968.

Graham, Sheilah, *The Garden of Allah*, Crown, New York, 1970.

Grant, Jane, *Ross, The New Yorker and Me*, Reynal, in association with William Morrow, New York, 1968.

Green, Abel and Joe Laurie, Jr., *Show Biz*, Henry Holt, New York, 1951.

Gruen, John, "The Season's Hottest Playwright," *New York World Journal Tribune Magazine*, November 13, 1966.

Hall, James B. and Barry Ulanov, *Modern Culture and the Arts*, McGraw-Hill, New York, 1967.

Harriman, Margaret Case, *The Vicious Circle*, Rinehart & Co., New York, 1951.

Harris, Jed, *Watchman, What of the Night?*, Doubleday, Garden City, N.Y., 1963.

Hart, Moss, *Act One*, Random House, New York, 1959.

Hartnoll, Phyllis, editor, *The Oxford Companion to the Theatre*, 3rd ed., Oxford University Press, London, 1967.

Hirschfeld, Al, *Show Business Is No Business*, Simon & Schuster, New York, 1951.

————, *The World of Hirschfeld*, Harry N. Abrams, New York, 1971.

Jablonski, Edward and Lawrence D. Stewart, *The Gershwin Years*, Doubleday, Garden City, N.Y., 1958.

Jones, Ernest, M.D., *The Life and Work of Sigmund Freud*, vol. 2, Basic Books, New York, 1955.

Kaplan, Justin, *Mr. Clemens and Mark Twain*, Simon & Schuster, New York, 1966.

Kaufman, Beatrice, "Says Beatrice Kaufman," *PM*, September 23, 1941.

Kaufman, Beatrice and Joseph Hennessey, editors, *The Letters of Alexander Woollcott*, Viking Press, New York, 1944.

Kaufman, George S., "Annoy Kaufman, Inc.," *New Yorker*, December 21, 1957.

————, *The Butter and Egg Man*, Samuel French, New York, 1957.

————, "Department of Amplification, Holicong, Pa.," *New Yorker*, June 20, 1946.

————, "Does Newark Have to Be Where It Is?," *New Yorker*, September 19, 1953.

————, "Lines Written After Four Weeks in a Hospital," *New Yorker*, May 1, 1954.

————, "Memoir," *New Yorker*, June 11, 1960.

————, "Musical Comedy—or Musical Serious?," *New York Times Magazine*, November 3, 1957.

————, "My Book and I," *New Yorker*, May 26, 1951.

————, "New York: A Prayer," *New Yorker*, September 3, 1955.

————, "School for Waiters," *New Yorker*, August 2, 1947.

————, *The Still Alarm*, Samuel French, New York, 1930.

————, "When Your Honey's on the Telephone," *New Yorker*, February 22, 1958.

Kaufman, George S. and Marc Connelly, *The Deep Tangled Wildwood*, 1923; not published—available in typescript, New York Public Library.

————, *Dulcy*, Putnam's, New York, 1921.

————, *Merton of the Movies*, Samuel French, New York, 1925.

————, *To the Ladies*, Samuel French, New York, 1923.

Kaufman, George S. and Edna Ferber, *Dinner at Eight*, Samuel French, New York, 1935.

————, *Minick*, Doubleday, Garden City, N.Y., 1924.

————, *The Royal Family*, Doubleday, Doran, Garden City, N.Y., 1928.

————, *Stage Door*, Doubleday, Doran, Garden City, N.Y., 1936.

Kaufman, George S. and Moss Hart, *I'd Rather Be Right*, Random House, New York, 1937 (Music and lyrics by R. Rodgers and L. Hart).

————, *Merrily We Roll Along*, Random House, New York, 1934.

————, *Six Plays*, Modern Library, New York, 1958.

Kaufman, George S. and Leueen MacGrath, *Amicable Parting*, Dramatists Play Service, New York, 1957.

————, *Fancy Meeting You Again*, Dramatists Play Service, New York, 1951.

————, *The Small Hours*, Dramatists Play Service, New York, 1951.

Kaufman, George S. and Herman Mankiewicz, *The Good Fellow*, Samuel French, New York, 1931.

Kaufman, George S. and Morrie Ryskind, *Let 'Em Eat Cake*, A. A. Knopf, New York, 1933.

———— (music and lyrics by George and Ira Gershwin), *Of Thee I Sing*, Knopf, New York, 1933.

Keats, John, *You Might as Well Live*, Simon & Schuster, New York, 1970.

Kerr, Jean, *Please Don't Eat the Daisies*, Doubleday, Garden City, N.Y., 1957.

Kerr, Walter, "In One Era, Out Another," *New York Times*, October 9, 1966.

Knef, Hildegarde, *The Gift Horse*, David Cameron Palastanga, translator, McGraw-Hill, New York, 1971.

Kouwenhoven, John, *The Columbia Historical Portrait of New York*, Doubleday, Garden City, N.Y., 1953.

Kramer, Dale, *Ross and The New Yorker*, Doubleday, Garden City, N.Y., 1951.

Kris, Ernst, M.D., *Psychoanalytic Exploration in Art*, International University Press, New York, 1952.

Kunitz, Stanley Joseph, *Living Authors Book of Biography*, H. W. Wilson Co., New York, 1931.

Kunitz, Stanley L., *Twentieth Century Authors*, H. W. Wilson Co., New York, 1955.

Lardner, Ring, "Dante and—," *New Yorker*, July 7, 1928.

Lardner, Ring and George S. Kaufman, *June Moon*, Samuel French, New York, 1958.

Levant, Oscar, *Memoirs of an Amnesiac*, Putnam's, New York, 1965.

Levin, Martin, *The Phoenix Nest*, Doubleday, New York, 1960.

Mantle, Burns and John Gassner, editors, *A Treasury of The Theatre*, Simon & Schuster, New York, 1935.

Bibliography

Marquand, John P., *Thirty Years*, Little Brown, Boston, 1926.

Marquand, John P. and George S. Kaufman, *The Late George Apley*, Dramatists Play Service, New York, 1946.

Marx, Arthur, *Life with Groucho*, Simon & Schuster, New York, 1954.

Marx, Harpo (with Rowland Barber), *Harpo Speaks!*, Bernard Geis, New York, 1961.

Middleton, George, *The Dramatists Guild*, Authors League of America, New York, 1959.

———, *These Things Are Mine*, Macmillan, New York, 1947.

Mielziner, Jo, *Designing for the Theatre*, Atheneum, New York, 1965.

Millett, Fred B., *Contemporary American Authors*, Harcourt, Brace, New York, 1944.

Muray, Nickolas and Paul Gallico, *The Revealing Eye*, Atheneum, New York, 1967.

Nathan, George Jean, *The Intimate Notebooks*, Knopf, New York, 1932.

Nugent, Elliott, *Events Leading Up to the Comedy*, Trident, New York, 1965.

Oppenheimer, George, "Kaufman: The Perfect Playwright," *Newsday*, July 25, 1964.

———, *The Passionate Playgoer*, Viking, New York, 1958.

Paar, Jack, *My Saber Is Bent*, Simon & Schuster, New York, 1961.

"Past Master," *Time*, November 20, 1939.

Phillips, Cabell, *From the Crash to the Blitz 1929–1939*, Macmillan, Toronto, 1969.

Play, James H. and Daniel Crempel, *The Theatrical Image*, McGraw-Hill, New York, 1967.

Prideaux, Tom, "Happy Encore for Kaufman Classics," *Life*, October 1966.

Rogers, Agnes and Frederick Lewis Allen, *I Remember Distinctly*, Harper, New York, 1947.

Taylor, Deems, Marcelene Peterson, and Bryant Hale, *A Pictorial History of the Movies*, Simon & Schuster, New York, 1943.

Teichmann, Howard, "By George S. Kaufman and . . . ," *New York Times Magazine*, November 13, 1966.

Teichmann, Howard and George S. Kaufman, *The Solid Gold Cadillac*, Random House, New York, 1954.

Thomas, Bob, *Thalberg*, Doubleday, Garden City, N.Y., 1969.

Thurber, James, *Credos & Curios*, Harper & Row, New York, 1962.

———, "The Man Who Was Comedy," *Theatre Arts*, August 1961.

Toohey, John L., *A History of the Pulitzer*, Citadel, New York, 1967.

Toohey, John Peter, "Kaufman and Hart Devise Another," *New York Herald Tribune*, July 31, 1938.

Bibliography

————, "Thurber Hails George S. Kaufman (And Wishes Someone Would Do a Biog)," *Variety*, August 16, 1961.

Veiller, Bayard, *The Fun I've Had*, Reynal & Hitchcock, New York, 1941.

Watson, E. Bradlee and Benfield Pressey, editors, *Contemporary American Plays*, Scribner's, New York, 1931.

Weissmann, Philip, *Creativity in the Theatre*, Basic Books, New York, 1965.

Whiting, Frank M., *An Introduction to the Theatre*, 3rd ed., Harper & Row, New York, 1969.

Woollcott, Alexander, "That Benign Demon George S. Kaufman," *New York Times*, December 3, 1933.

————, "The Deep Tangled Kaufman," *New Yorker*, May 18, 1927.

Woollcott, Alexander and George S. Kaufman, *The Dark Tower*, Random House, New York, 1934.

Zimmerman, Paul D. and Burt Goldblatt, *The Marx Brothers at the Movies*, Putnam's, New York, 1968.

Zolotow, Maurice, *Stagestruck: The Romance of Alfred Lunt and Lynn Fontanne*, Harcourt, Brace & World, New York, 1964.

Index

Index

Index

365

Index

366

Index

Index

Howard Teichmann

Howard Teichmann was born in Chicago, and raised and educated in Illinois and Wisconsin. An avid interest in the theatre led him to New York, where he became Orson Welles's stage manager. From there, under John Houseman's editing, he wrote Welles's radio program, "The Mercury Theatre of the Air" for two seasons. During World War II he was the Senior Editor of the Office of War Information, Overseas Branch. Later he was attached to the staff of Lt. Gen. Brehon Somervell as the general's Expert Consultant in radio. When television came in he did the award-winning series for The American National Theatre and Academy, and won a series of prizes for writing the first television "special," narrated by Edward R. Murrow. At the same time he was writing that program, he began his collaboration with George S. Kaufman. Together they wrote four plays, one of which was produced. On his own, Mr. Teichmann has had four other plays presented on Broadway. For the last ten years he has been an executive with the Shubert Theatres. In 1946 he joined the teaching staff of Barnard College, Columbia University, and still teaches there as a professor in the Department of English.